the art of not having it all

the art of not having it all

~

TRUE STORIES OF
MEN, SEX, AND
OTHER DISASTERS

Melissa Kite

THOMAS DUNNE BOOKS
St. Martin's Press
New York

THOMAS DUNNE BOOKS.

An imprint of St. Martin's Press.

THE ART OF NOT HAVING IT ALL. Copyright © 2012 by Melissa Kite. All rights reserved. Printed in the United States of America. For information, address St. Martin's Press, 175 Fifth Avenue, New York, N.Y. 10010.

www.thomasdunnebooks.com

www.stmartins.com

Designed by Ellen Cipriano

LIBRARY OF CONGRESS CATALOGING-IN-PUBLICATION DATA

Kite, Melissa.
    [Real life]
    The art of not having it all: true stories of men, sex, and other disasters / Melissa Kite.— first U.S. edition.
        p. cm.
    First published in Great Britain under the title *Real Life* by Constable & Robinson in 2012.
    ISBN 978-1-250-05514-9 (hardcover)
    ISBN 978-1-4668-5823-7 (e-book)
    1. Kite, Melissa—Humor. 2. Single women—Great Britain—Humor. I. Title.
    PN6231.S5485K57 2015
    828'.9202—dc23

                                                          2014032366

St. Martin's Press books may be purchased for educational, business, or promotional use. For information on bulk purchases, please contact the Macmillan corporate and Premium Sales Department at 1-800-221-7945, extension 5442, or write to specialmarkets@macmillan.com.

First published in Great Britain under the title *Real Life* by Constable & Robinson in 2012.

First U.S. Edition: January 2015

10 9 8 7 6 5 4 3 2 1

To "The Builder"

the art of not
having it all

The Art of
Not Having It All

When I started writing a column called "Real Life" in the *Spectator* magazine five years ago, I had no idea there was anyone else out there remotely like me. Nearly every other woman I knew seemed to be heroically juggling work and family life in a way that was so inspiring it was only a matter of time before someone made a film starring a *Sex and the City* actress about each and every one of them. And while it looked tricky, running an investment bank from the kitchen table while stopping a toddler from crawling across the floor to eat from the dog's bowl, my friends seemed to be really enjoying this having-it-all business. I, meanwhile, was having none of it. Once I'd put all the energy I had into my career there was literally nothing left over to achieve anything else. It was all I could do to work out how to park the car and not get a ticket. Or put the trash cans out without getting a warning letter from the authorities. I felt like I was the only woman in the world who was struggling to keep one ball in the air, and dropping that most of the time.

It felt as though, in the fluttering mass of yellow Post-it notes on my fridge, there was one that read "Don't forget to get married and have kids," which had got covered in shopping lists, dry-cleaner receipts, and bulky waste collection schedules. Even Bridget Jones remembered to get married by the time she was thirty-four. What sort of fool was I?

I felt like a total freak. And I'm not convinced I wasn't right. OK, so a few of you wrote in to say you sympathized with me out of what I assumed was pity. But most of you just wrote to say, "Dear Ms. Kite, How come you are constitutionally incapable of crossing the street without having a catastrophe of some sort, usually to do with a man? Have you thought about taking out some sort of public liability insurance?"

Some of you made up stories to make it seem like you identified with me, and although I found it touching at the time, I'm not sure it helped in the long run. For example, I once wrote a column about my agoraphobic tropical fish getting stuck in the ornamental log of its tank. People wrote to me in droves to say how much they identified with my panic-stricken journey to the hardware store to buy a handsaw that could slice through polyester resin.

Some even claimed that they, too, had called an ex-fiancé and affected a temporary, fake reconciliation, during which they casually dropped into the conversation the words "By the way, the angel fish is stuck in the log," so they could get him to saw while they held the thing underwater.

I appreciate it, I really do. But I have a sneaking suspicion you might be lying to make me feel better. Either that or there really are legions of single women out there struggling like me. In which case, shouldn't someone be taking us seriously? Shouldn't the government be coming up with some sort of half-baked policy aimed at countering our alienation from society?

When it comes to some of life's more mainstream frustrations, I am prepared to believe you have suffered as I have. Unfair motoring fines, parking tickets, pay-by-phone meters, refuse rules stipulating the precise latitude and longitude coordinates at which I must place my trash bin . . . I cannot claim to be the only one who has been driven to the point of suicide by these things. Nor can I claim to have the monopoly on minor strokes caused by negotiating automated telephone systems with recorded options that require you to input your blood type before you can pay your gas bill.

We all know how that feels, because somehow, at some unspecified point in the past few years, we went from being one of the world's great democracies to being a tin-pot dictatorship where citizens who fail to press the star key on their keypad twice are now treated more harshly than axe murderers. On these issues, I share your pain.

I can't promise to do anything about it, however. I did once promise to do something about it in a rather foolish column where I got a bit ahead of myself and pledged to fight a parking ticket all the way to the European Court of Human Rights on behalf of taxpayers everywhere. Unfortunately, the authorities then threatened to double the fine, so I paid up. Sorry, and all that.

To be totally honest with you from the beginning, this book is not about how to find love, or how to be a woman, or how to juggle work and family life, or anything useful like that. As I said, I can't tell you how to have it all, or even most of it. I think I had a bit of it once, but I'm pretty sure I've never had anywhere near all of it, and I'm positive I've never had all of it together at any one time. I am aware, however, that a book should offer its readers some important information that might enrich their lives, so at some point in these pages I will include my Italian mother's recipe for spaghetti bolognese. I will also be giving you my ten handy hints for getting yourself home from a foreign vacation when your super-high-powered City of London stockbroker boyfriend has gone mad, and there will be a chapter with broader emergency travel advice, which can be used to evacuate yourself to safety when you've fallen out with your girlfriends in, for example, Saint-Tropez.

At no extra cost, I will throw in my definitive take on the oft asked but seldom answered question, "How much KFC is it safe for a miserable person to eat in one week? And do the leftover bits *ever* go bad if you refrigerate them? Because they really don't seem to, do they?" Those cold takeout chicken legs just seem to get better and better. I'm not saying where these gems of enlightenment will occur, exactly, so you'll just have to keep reading. There will be beauty tips, too. Friends often ask me, "How do you manage to look so young?" And I say to them, "Mess up your love life, forget to have children, put a huge wall around your emotions and you, too, can look this good at forty!" It's true. I am living proof that there is no antiaging cream or diet regime on the market that will give you the edge the way not growing up and taking on normal responsibilities will.

Unlike those smug juggler women who have it all, I can tell you how to be economical and make a little bit of it go a long way, which might be useful if you're thinking of giving up the having-it-all business to become obsessed with doing one thing at a time like me. There's no glory in being mono-preoccupied (that's a technical term I've just invented because no one else thinks up fancy words to describe single people, unless you count "selfish cow," which is just one of the many prejudices we encounter). People will not lionize you the way they will if you wedge a toddler on your hip while dumping bad stock. Contrary to what Beyoncé

would have you believe, if you shout out, "All the single ladies!" and whoop in the street, you will be greeted by the sound of tumbleweed, which your e-book should play now, unless it's malfunctioning. If you're reading this book in an old-format analog 3-D paper manual page-turning version—and good for you—you'll just have to make do with imagining what wind whistling around a graveyard sounds like, which is a little more labor intensive, but then you're used to that if you're turning pages.

Lastly, I would like to say in my defense that being single, lonely, and at the cutting edge of the "having a bit of it" generation is not a bad way of life, all told. At heart, I'm still the carefree seven-year-old in this picture. I'm balancing cheese puffs in my eyes to get a cheap laugh. I still do that, by the way.

1

The Wedding
Cancellation Planner

....

In which I ditch a perfectly nice man at the altar and embark on an inclement voyage to a mythical place called "inner fulfillment."

....

Despite being inundated with plaudits for doing it, I simply cannot recommend calling off a wedding. It sounds exciting and dynamic, as if it might have a lot to do with being true to oneself, but it isn't really. It's a daft thing to do. If you have managed to get a man to agree to marry you in the traditional way—frog-marching him down mainstreet to a jeweler's after warning him that your mother won't take much more of this—go through with it, I say. Because ten years later, when you're approaching forty and no one else even vaguely serviceable has come along, you will regret calling off that wedding more than you would think it possible to regret anything. You will cry yourself to sleep at night thinking it would have been better to have married a man you frog-marched to a jeweler than to be in bed alone with a cat sleeping on your head.

Having said that, everyone loves a called-off wedding. When I called off my wedding everyone was incredibly excited about it. "Oh you're so brave," people would exclaim rapturously. It was as if I was calling off my wedding on behalf of bored, married people everywhere. "I could never have done it," they would say wistfully. "Yes," I remember thinking, "you could never have done it because you are too sensible. Only I do stupid, impulsive things like calling off a wedding."

"Well, if it's not right, it's not right . . ." Yes, but I have no idea if it's not right. Or not not right. I couldn't tell you one way or another, even if you extraordinarily rendered me to Guantánamo and had me thoroughly waterboarded. I know nothing of any substance about whether or not I should get married to this man, who is incredibly nice to me and whom I like a lot, but then I like a lot of people a lot. It doesn't mean I want to marry them all. Marriage, when I was staring down the barrel of it, seemed to me to be essentially about the following: (a) writing a check for £1,160 for a dress I didn't much like, (b) changing my name to a name I didn't like at all, (c) staging a logistically nightmarish party I was sure I would actively dislike, and (d) moving to a starter home. I'm still not certain what a starter home is, but it scares the bejesus out of me.

What I cannot understand is why more women don't get cold feet about all this. I can't be the only girl who's had a panic about the small print of the holy estate. Is there some sort of conspiracy to cover up the number of doubters? Has someone bribed them to stay silent for seven years, when inevitably they then divorce and get out of it anyway? Or am I blazing a trail by owning up to being extremely cross about the whole thing *before* I do it? (This would be just my luck. I always end up trailblazing by accident.)

The worst thing about getting married is the name-changing

business. I lie awake at night worrying about who originally came up with the idea of the woman taking the man's name. My own pet theory is as follows: scientists have established that we're all descended from the same great mother ape.* Clearly, at some point, one of the female descendants of this great mother ape decided to give up her name. I cannot countenance the possibility that the great mother ape herself gave up her name. That would be too big a betrayal to bear. Possibly a lesser female ape called Oo-Oo got together with an ape called Ah-Ah and felt so loved up she started answering to his name. Another possible scenario is that Ah-Ah, in the first ever fit of chauvinistic pique, beat his chest particularly vehemently one day and insisted that Oo-Oo answer to his name from now on because his self-esteem had taken a bit of a knock in a fight with another male ape and he needed to make himself feel better.

In either case, some woman must have been called something original to herself at some point in the history of the universe. And then when Mrs. Oo-Oo sold out, the whole individual identity of women thing was lost forever. When you think about it like this, it seems unlikely that any woman on earth has a name that's actually hers. Doesn't that get your goat? Doesn't that make you think this marriage business might be profoundly wrong?

Although I'm the only person I know who has called off a wedding, I feel sure that there will be more of this in the future when everyone realizes I am right, as they surely will. As such, for the budding entrepreneurs among you, there must be an important emerging market in smartphone wedding cancelation apps and wedding cancelation greeting cards. For example: "Sorry to

---

* Dear Creationists, I'm really sorry about this but it's true. Also, Father Christmas doesn't come down all the chimneys himself. He has elves helping him.

hear you've called off your wedding, hope you have fun, wherever you're heading."

Confession: it wasn't the first wedding I had called off. Strictly speaking, I had previous. Fifteen years earlier I spurned the engagement entreaties of a nice Scottish boy called David, whom I had met on a campsite in France when I was fourteen.

I don't think you should dismiss this prospect out of hand on account of my youth. Looking back, I reckon David could well have been The One. He was tall, dark, handsome, clever, and kind. I have never managed to combine these qualities in a boyfriend since. On which basis, I reckon my first boyfriend could well have been the apex of my romantic life. All conventional wit and wisdom point to romance being a journey that gets better and better, until you meet the love of your life when you are around twenty-eight—or a supposedly hair-raising thirty-four if you're Bridget Jones—but in my experience it starts off well enough then gets progressively worse until, aged forty, you are on your knees, swearing to whatever god will listen that you will never, ever do it again. In this respect, love is a bit like chronic alcoholism.

With hindsight, if I had known that I would only meet one suitable man in my entire life I would have accepted David's proposal. But, of course, I didn't. I thought I had a lifetime of fantastic encounters with the opposite sex in front of me.

When David proposed I told him where to go, then I forgot about him immediately and became obsessed with an obnoxious young buck at the tennis club called Glen, who was famous for two things: he was the best-looking boy in town and he only had nine fingers. The story was that he had staged an accident at his father's timber yard so he could claim compensation. It all went awry when he only managed to cut off half his little finger, resulting in a paltry £2,000 payout, which, for the trouble involved, really wasn't worth it. Among other things, he had to learn to play tennis with his left hand. He was still a hit with the ladies, though. He had a "flat top" hairdo, as made famous by brat-pack film stars of the time such as Matt Dillon. If you had such a hairdo in the eighties you could get away with almost anything, including having a stump for a little finger and the IQ of a boiled potato.

This much I do know: I'm emotionally illiterate. For most of my life I have not been able to distinguish between a genuine romance and a load of old hooey. Give me a Glen and a David to choose from and I'll go for nine-and-a-half-fingered Glen every time.

My friend Henrietta, who is into crystals and tarot readings, once told me this is because I am a self-sabotager and my moon is in Taurus. My friend Sally, who's into shopping and smoking Marlboro Lights, says it's because I'm a total idiot. I'm inclined to agree with Sally.

A few years after his proposal, David rang me out of the blue to tell me he was getting married. It only occurs to me now that he made that phone call as a last attempt to wave me down as I hurtled along the superhighway of romantic failure, giving me one last chance to take the turnoff marked "Happiness." But I just kept journeying intrepidly onward, to a higher destination marked "Freedom, fulfillment, independence, and integrity."

I can safely say, I am at that noble destination now. And so, with the benefit of hindsight and experience, I would say this to all independent-minded teenage girls with a richly diverse, challenging, and fulfilling life ahead of them, who are weighing a premature proposal from an eager young buck: girls, I beg of you, never, ever, turn down an early proposal. Get yourself hitched as young as possible, and then think about being richly diverse and challenging. You can't do it the other way round. Once you become richly diverse and challenging you will be about as attractive to men as a badger in a burka.

It wasn't all bad news for me, though. Fast-forward nearly twenty years and I did manage to get myself engaged to a really nice guy called . . . let's call him Jim, for legal reasons. We had been going out for five years, and one day I told him he had better buy me a ring because my mother was getting cross. How this was better than me just proposing myself I don't know.

I'm baffled by why it's so frowned on for women to propose. I once read an article on the right-wing website Conservative Home, in which a leading Tory implored women not to be foolish and propose to their menfolk. His thesis was that if a woman proposed to a man, he would resent her forever for emasculating him and taking something integral to his manhood away from him.

I don't think this can be right as it assumes that men actually like proposing. But men don't like proposing any more than they like emptying the dishwasher. No normal guy wants to propose, any more than he wants to wipe the toilet seat, put the lid back on the toothpaste, or swill the washing-up suds out of the sink. As such, the choices are these: sit around all our lives waiting for them to spontaneously do it and like it (high risk, hardly ever pays off); force them to do it and hate it by getting ourselves pregnant or threatening to leave them for another man (almost always successful, though not high on the romance quotient); or do it ourselves (as yet totally untried and untested. I bet you any money if we did, a lot of men would be bloody relieved).

The worst thing about canceling a wedding is not the vicarious excitement on the faces of your nearest and dearest, but the marketing chaos that ensues.

These wedding-business people do not give up lightly. "Hello, Ms. Kite," they say when they ring. "You asked for some information a few weeks ago about our vintage car-hire service and we wondered if you had made your selection yet?"

"Wedding's off."

"Would you like us to send you more details?"

"No thanks. I don't need a wedding car. I'm not having a wedding."

"Was it the color that was wrong?"

"Nope. It's just that I'm not getting married."

"Can I send you a brochure of our classic American vehicles? I'm sure there will be something in there that will meet your requirements."

You see, everyone who has ever got married has used the line "the wedding's off" to stop the hundreds of companies they've contacted for estimates from hassling them. So the companies just don't believe it. Consequently, I spent the months following my wedding cancelation, planning *not* having a wedding. Planning *not* having a wedding was in every way as complicated as planning having a wedding, if not more. The phone would ring and a chirpy female voice would say, "Hello, it's Tina from That's Entertainment here. You rang to ask about booking the eighties tribute band?"

"Wedding's off," I would say grumpily.

"Yes, well, we just wondered whether you might be able to make a small deposit to secure the booking because Abba Kadabra are getting quite busy now."

"Really, I'm not getting married anymore. I don't need Abba Kadabra, or Yankee Goes to Bollywood, for that matter."

"If it's a problem with the estimate we would be happy to negotiate . . ."

"There's no problem with the estimate. I'm just not getting married, that's all."

"Or maybe you'd like to hear some other sample tapes?"

"Look, I could book them, but they would have to come to my house and play in the kitchen because there is no wedding and I think spending £900 is a bit much for an evening's entertainment for one person. I would really rather watch a DVD box set of *Boardwalk Empire* if it's all the same to you."

A few minutes later the phone would ring again.

"Hello, it's Mystique Gowns of Ripley here. We've noticed you canceled your dress order last week and we were wondering when you wanted to come in and choose another one?"

"I'm not getting married anymore."

"So, did you want to come in tomorrow? About three p.m.?"

"No, I want to come in never, because my life's in ruins. I'm about to put my head in the oven."

"Actually we've got a fitting at three thirty, so two would be better."

"Right, my head's now in the oven. I've got to put the phone down so I can switch on the gas. Goddammit this oven's electric . . ."

And so on. The retail sector simply does not do off-the-peg wedding cancelations. It's bespoke or nothing. You have to engage in the process every step of the way, and you can't take your eye off the ball for a minute.

If you ever do cancel your wedding, I suggest you retain the services of a wedding-cancelation planner or else it will take over your entire life.

I had to work for two weeks canceling the dresses, and two months talking down the bridesmaids. One of them said, "Oh but I loved that navy blue dress. Do you mean I can't have it now?"

I had to buy the outfit to pay her off, like a divorce settlement. But I drew the line at the velvet jacket. "You can have the dress," I said eventually, "but the jacket's definitely out." She was only involved in the preparations for three months. She went to two fittings. She was entitled to something, but she wasn't getting the bolero.

As for the fiancé, he took a check for the few bits of furniture in the apartment that he had part paid for over the years and the computer he left in the spare room. But he refused to negotiate in any way about the fish tank . . .

஌

"What do you mean you can't redecorate?" said my friend Sally as we sat in her kitchen eating one of her legendary salads.

"I can't redecorate. I've got a huge fish tank in my house."

"Well, get rid of it," she said, serving me another heap of lamb's lettuce, taleggio, and asparagus.

"Why do they call it lamb's lettuce? Is it because lambs like eating it? Or because it looks a bit like a lamb, or a bit of a lamb? And if so, which bit of the lamb?"

"I don't know. Why have you got a fish tank in your house?"

"I can't get rid of it. It was Jim's. He left it when he moved out. He said he couldn't be expected to take a fish tank to the tiny flat he was going to have to move to now that I had thrown him out and ruined his life and turned my back on him."

Sally put her head on one side and raised her eyebrows as if to say, He's got a point. "How big is this fish tank?" A side helping of lentils, beetroot, and feta was making its way onto my heaving plate.

"It's huge. It's like a professional aquarium, like the ones you see in hotel lobbies. It takes up the entire length of one wall. I don't even know how to clean it out. I think I'm probably meant to call a specialist company to come and do it."

"How many fish are in there?"

"Two," I said through mouthfuls of cheese and leaves. "Have you put pomegranate seeds in this? It's wrong, but somehow good."

"Two?"

"Yes, two. We started off with more but the rest of them died. Now there's just these two clown fish, golden and black things, like the ones in *Finding Nemo*."

Sally gave me one of her looks. It was the look of a successfully married person, someone who had been living in domestic harmony with her childhood sweetheart for thirty years. She and her husband Bobby had three teenage children and a big, rambling townhouse in Belgravia. Bobby was the nicest man in the world and one of Britain's leading classical actors. She was the daughter of one of the world's most revered film directors, which made her showbiz royalty. Together they were the most well-connected couple on the planet. Their children were funny and charming. Kitchen suppers around their table were a joy. There were always lots of people, their friends, their children, friends of the children—youth, laughter, life.

While I sat in my sad little kitchen in Balham, alone with my Waitrose ready-meal-for-one, and wrote columns about the fact that my clown fish was clinically obese, Sally ran a salon for fabulous people and wrote articles about beauty treatments for *Tatler* and *Vanity Fair*. Anyone could appear around her supper table, from Cheryl Cole to the Aga Khan. An impromptu dinner party arranged at the last minute would typically feature Elton John, Joan Collins, the Chancellor of the Exchequer, and Paddy Doherty from *My Big Fat Gypsy Wedding*. Her guest lists were as wondrously eclectic and unexpected as the ingredients in her signature salads. And, against all odds, seemed to mix together just as well.

With children old enough to be doing their own thing while she was still only in her late forties, she looked forward to a glamorous period of empty nesting spent flinging together stars from the worlds of film, theater, music, and trash TV in ways they had never been flung together before.

She also put a lot of displaced nurturing energy into playing the role of protective big sister to my dysfunctional single girl about town.

On nights when the children were all out and she didn't have a supper party featuring Kerry Katona and David Cameron, Bobby would go upstairs to the TV room with his dinner on a tray and leave Sally and me around the breakfast bar in the high-raftered kitchen, as we were now, a huge bowl of salad in front of us and a Le Creuset pan of risotto on the range.

"I still don't understand why you can't get rid of the fish tank," she said, grimacing. "Gift it to a school or something." Sally didn't give things, she gifted them. Gifting was like giving, only more classy.

"Because they're Jim's fish and they symbolize something. I want to fulfill my responsibilities to them. I feel guilty. I've ruined his life. I need to do right by his fish."

Sally shook her head. "They're just fish."

But that was where she was wrong. At first I thought the same, but then I started watching them.

There was clearly a love affair between the big one and the

little one, which I took to be male and female respectively. This love affair had blossomed gradually and had been all the more poignant because the male was clearly battling chronic agoraphobia to be near her. He was a troubled soul and an overeater. This worried me because I'd had a fish with an eating disorder before—the one who'd grown so big and moved so little he'd had to be mechanically extracted from his log after getting stuck in it. This one had pretty much lived in the log for three years, with his nose sticking out the end snaffling food. It was awful, just like one of those obese people who have to be lifted out of the window of their bedroom with a crane. The rescue operation took three hours, and he didn't make it, so before this happened again I decided to shoo the fat fish out of his log and find a bigger log he couldn't get stuck in. After days spent scouring the streets of London, it turned out there was an industry standard size for fish logs and that was that. I had to settle on a revolting-looking pirate ship. At first the fat fish looked at the pirate ship in horror. He hid in a corner as far away from it as he could get. He moped all day. He refused to eat. He lay flat on the pebbles pretending to be dead. When I looked in on him before bed, he was floating aimlessly as if life had lost all meaning. His partner was swimming in and out of the ship as if to assure him it was all right, but to no avail.

Then, the next morning, a miracle happened. I went into the study to read my e-mails, peered into the tank, and a picture of aquatic domestic bliss greeted me: the two clown fish were lying on their sides in the pirate ship, one on top of the other, tails swishing, snoozing happily. A warm glow flooded my heart.

After a while he came out for longer periods and then he started to lose a tiny bit of weight. He was no longer eating all day and seemed to have found a reason to pull himself together. After being a loner in his log for years, he had found the strength to reach out. It was the power of love, I explained to Sally.

"Well," she said. "I don't know about fish falling in love, but I do know that you need a man. You can't go on like this. How about Richard?"

Oh no, not Richard. Sally had lectured me long and hard about Richard and every time I broke up with someone, Richard was brandished like a wooden spoon. Richard was a rich minor-aristo type, nice enough, wildly uninteresting, and, if you caught him between short stints with blond actresses, endlessly available.

Bobby appeared with his empty plate. "Darling," he said, looking at me intensely, "you mustn't let Sizzle fix you up with ghastly Richard. He really is the most dreadful oaf. I won't allow it."

"But he's perfect for her. He loves horses," said Sally, sparking up a Marlboro Light and exhaling philosophically.

"Fuck horses, Sizzle. He's a crashing bore. And have you seen the size of him lately? Really, darling, he's perfectly hideous. Not nearly good enough for you, angel. Not even beginning to be good enough."

As usual I had to explain to dear Bobby that I was in no position to worry about whether or not the crashing bore Richard was good enough for me. The harsh realities of late thirties dating meant that I had more chance of being run over by a bus than finding a man at my age, a statistic I was fond of quoting, as if knowing the odds made them better. I knew absolutely no single men, unless you counted the handsome but rather strange neighbor a few doors down from me who walked his cats, Bismarck and Napoleon, and on the face of it he had to be, on some level, gay.

"I'm getting on, you know," I said to Bobby. "Beggars can't be choosers. And if he likes horses that may just be the clincher at this stage in the game."

"But darling, look at you. You're gorgeous. You're clever, beautiful, fantastically funny, and witty and charming . . ."

Silently, a small part of me was thinking, "You've got a point, you know, I'm not half bad." Out loud I said, "But I need to find a man."

Sally nodded. "It's a fucking crisis, Bobby. She needs a husband. Richard's single again. I'm going to invite him over for dinner."

"But I thought he was with that blond actress, what's her name, not Emilia Fox, the other one. Skinny as hell and mad as a March hare. Wasn't she driving him crazy?"

"They've split up," said Sally. "He won't be on the market for long. He's inherited the estate in Oxfordshire now. We need to move fast."

"Sienna Miller. No, not Sienna Miller, the other one. Oh, Sizzle, what's her name? Blond girl, skinny . . . Christ, I can't think . . . Scarlett Johansson. No, not her, that other one . . ."

Bobby spooned another heap of salad on to his plate, cut a doorstep of Daylesford *pain rustique* the size of the *Oxford English Dictionary*, and disappeared back upstairs muttering the names of blond actresses.

◌◌

The next week, I got my orders by text message to turn up at Sally and Bobby's for a kitchen supper with Richard: "dinner thursday night at mine, us, you, and few others 8pm wear something bright do NOT wear black."

I love black, but Sally always forbids it. She says only red makes men notice you because men are hopeless at noticing anything more subtle than the blindingly obvious. I don't know why women stop at wearing bright colors. If wearing red doesn't work you should simply go around with a huge sign saying, "Look at me, I'm single and not fussy!"

A friend of mine who was having a spot of bother on the dating front once printed T-shirts bearing the slogan "Why not ask me to dinner?" She ran me off two, but I haven't had the nerve to wear them. By the time I'm desperate enough to put them on, I shall probably be so old and unattractive that the T-shirts would be more apt if they said, "Why not ask me to bingo?"

But I did as I was told because I didn't want to cross Sally. I turned up early for dinner wearing a bright-red dress and a pair of vertiginous Louboutins and, as we waited for the rest of the guests to arrive, I chain-smoked my way through feelings of impending doom until I stank so much of smoke I could barely stand to be near myself.

I needn't have panicked. When the doorbell rang and he walked in I was blown away. He was tall and dark, with a chiseled jaw and black piercing eyes. He had really, really good hair. Expensive hair. And a Cary Grant dimple in his chin.

He looked like Tom Ford's better-looking brother. He was smolderingly, devastatingly, nerve-shatteringly handsome. He was impeccably dressed, too, in just the right amount of Ralph Lauren. He was so good-looking he made Jon Hamm from *Mad Men* look ugly.

As he strode across the floor to greet me, the earth moved, the heavens opened, and a chorus of angels began singing the greatest hits of Andrea Bocelli, but that may have been because Sally had just switched on the iPod dock.

He smiled the smile of a movie star in an old black-and-white movie; he gave me a look that said he already loved me because we were meant to be. He grabbed my hand with one of his big, handsome tanned hands. And when he pulled me close to mwah-mwah me, he inhaled deeply and declared, "Mmm, cheap cigs and Chanel. Very Catherine Deneuve." Hallelujah! He got me! Oh, the ecstasy.

Then Sally pulled me into the kitchen and said, "What are you doing? That's Simon Harper. The food writer. He's gay."

I've had this before. Because I always fall for the really handsome ones, a lot of them turn out to be gay. But I'm not convinced (bear with me on this, it's not a homophobic statement, I assure you). "We'll see about that," I said to myself.

Sally had done a pitiless seating plan in which I was sandwiched between her and Richard, who was moping about the canapés like an agoraphobic clown fish—the similarities were uncanny—so that there was no escape from what I was meant to be doing and so that she could kick me under the table every time I didn't say the right thing.

I managed to get out of it and wheedle myself a seat next to Simon.

We talked all night—no one could get a word in either of our directions. We only had eyes for each other. We even played kneesies under the table. Gay or not, he couldn't take his eyes off me. He wanted to know everything about me.

He was an award-winning food writer and nutritionist with a clinic in Knightsbridge and a long list of celebrity clients. We spent hours discussing food allergies and the newfangled diets of the rich and famous. I couldn't remember when I'd been so happy with a man. We exchanged business cards and arranged to meet for breakfast at the Wolseley soon.

"You spent the whole night talking to Simon," Sally chided me as we did the washing up afterward.

"He's heaven."

"He's gay."

"He's so clever."

"He's gay."

"And funny . . ."

"And gay."

"And sexy and glamorous."

"And gay."

"He'd make lovely babies."

"He's gay."

"He's so clever. Did I mention that? He's practically a doctor."

"He's gay."

"I'm sorry, are you trying to make a point?"

"Yes. And the point I'm trying to make is, he's gay."

"Stop pigeonholing him. Your definition of gay is so nineties. Gay men can fancy women now."

"What are you talking about?"

"Gay men fall for straight women all the time nowadays. It's true. My gay friend Marcus told me about it. He's got this woman called Honoria he's totally in love with. Says he could quite happily marry her and spend the rest of his life with her. And he hangs out in the men's room at Liverpool Street station on Saturday night, so don't tell me he's not a proper gay because he is. He's a proper gay who has fallen hopelessly in love with a woman. He loves her so much he says he would even be prepared to go without having sex with men in public lavatories and picking up men on the Underground. It happens."

"It so *doesn't* happen," said Sally, lighting a Marlboro and opening up a copy of *Now* magazine.

"Simon and I are perfect for each other. He's just split up with his boyfriend. He's lonely. I'm lonely. What's not to like?"

"You're insane . . . Ohmygod, Madonna's got cellulite. Look."

"And besides, with Simon I wouldn't have to do any of that wifey stuff. He would probably let me go on living in Balham. She hasn't got cellulite; it's just bad lighting."

"Well I should imagine so. I don't suppose he would mind where you lived."

"Exactly. And he could have the children on weekends so I can ride my horse. It's perfect."

"I suppose you could have a child with him. People do do that. It's not the light."

"Oh yes, one of those designer IVF babies with a handsome, gay father. I'm going to ring him tomorrow and ask him. Or do you think it's a bit soon after one dinner? It's definitely the light, and the camera angle."

"What about Richard?"

"He reminded me of my clown fish."

"That's a start, isn't it? Maybe you could tempt him out of his log. I'll help you saw it in half. He's probably wedged solid in it. It's *not* the light. Look, there's a patch. Oh hang on, maybe it is the light. Damn. What are you wearing to the do next weekend?"

"I don't know. I haven't thought about it yet."

"Well, think about it, baby. You need to start pushing the boat out if you're going to find a man at your age."

◌◌

One of the really great things about being a nobody who writes a column is that you get invited to a lot of highfalutin' parties that no one would dream of inviting you to otherwise. The slightly less good thing is that no one apart from the person who has invited you knows who the hell you are.

You get out of your South London minicab, a battered Toyota driven by a traumatized Afghani who has just fallen off the back of a truck on the Eurostar, which you ask to park up a little ways from the entrance, then hobble on your heels toward the barriers keeping back the crowds, where banks of paparazzi look you up and down as, to everyone's astonishment, you produce your invite and scuttle alone, unloved and unphotographed, up the blasted red carpet. The banks of restive fans behind the barriers, eager for a glimpse of Kimye or Brangelina, suddenly go silent; you can hear a pin drop. They stare at you in steely silence. "Who does she think she is?" they are thinking. "She's nobody *and* she hasn't got a date!"

For this reason, and because we always seem to get the same invites, I always go to film premieres and awards ceremonies with Sally and Bobby. Being accompanied by someone famous makes going to places full of famous people a whole lot more bearable.

Bobby was a genuine celebrity, not a fake modern one but an old-fashioned star. He had been in movies directed by David Attenborough and had known people like Cary Grant.

We would arrive together and, apart from a frisson of "Who the hell is the one in the middle?" things usually passed off without incident.

Inside, I would stick close to my glamorous friends. Bobby would quickly find a director to talk to about the old times working with Dear Larry or Sir Alec, while Sally would start power-mingling with the glitziest celebs. This was a wonder to behold. She would spot Tom Hanks across a crowded room and she'd be off. I would follow in her tailwind, then stand behind her as she chatted, slurping from my glass sheepishly until she turned

round and asked me, "Do you know Tom?" To which I would
mumble, "No, hello." And he would look slightly confused and
nod politely. They would then quickly go back to talking to each
other and ignoring me and I would go back to slurping. And so
on until Tom got pulled away and/or Sally spotted someone else,
at which point we'd be off, scything through cocktail dresses
like a rig speeding through a sea of catamarans.

"Do you know Kylie?"

"No, hello."

"Do you know Charlize?"

"No, hello."

"Do you know Brad and Ange?"

Gulp. Spill drink. Tread on Ange's dress.

The amount of enormously impressive people I've said "no,
hello" to and who have then nodded vaguely in my general direction is a figure I would quote to my grandchildren—if I get my
act together one day and have any.

When friends ask me if I've met any famous people lately I say
I've nearly met loads. I couldn't tell you anything other than how
short and thin they were in real life because I didn't get past the
"no hello nod" phase with any of them.

On this occasion, I was accompanying Sally and Bobby to the
opening of a new restaurant by one of those improbably famous
chefs who do weird things with offal.

As we got out of our cab a little way from the entrance, a photographer from *Vanity Fair* spotted Bobby and chased after him
along the street. "Bobby! Can I get a photo of you with your lovely
wife?"

"Of course, my dear boy," said Bobby, pulling Sally close. The
photographer checked the light and made a huge fuss of getting
exactly the right shot, taking frame after frame. Then Bobby

grabbed me and pulled me into the shot, proclaiming, "And now you must get a photo of me with both of these ravishing goddesses."

The photographer shrugged irritably, held his camera in the air, pointed it vaguely in our general direction, and clicked randomly without even looking into the viewfinder.

"That was literally the most humiliating thing that has ever happened to me," I said, debating inwardly whether to burst into tears.

"Don't be ridiculous," said Sally vehemently. "The time you mistook Martin Scorsese for Woody Allen at the *GQ* Men of the Year awards was much more embarrassing."

☙

We had only just got inside the foyer of the hotel where the restaurant was when I caught sight of him. I recognized the perfect, close-cut back of his head, and the world went into slow motion as he turned and smiled.

Simon, in a tux. Simon, looking sexier than life itself. Simon, looking so good it was impossible to focus on him for longer than two seconds at a time because it hurt your eyes. Simon, with a young boy in shiny, tight trousers and a stupid haircut.

He came straight over to introduce me.

"This is Ricky Moon. *The* Ricky Moon, from reality TV show *Bow Belles*, about life in East London. He's the one who always wears clothes he can't afford by Dolce & Gabbana and spends three hours every morning doing his hair. He lives in a high-rise." Simon said this as if it were the crowning glory in the whole affair.

"I haven't seen it." I looked Ricky up and down and curled my lip.

"Well, you're seeing me now! I'm even better in the flesh!" said the revolting specimen.

"He's going to be in the next series of *Celebrity Big Brother*," said Simon, proudly putting an arm around his skinny little shoulders. "He's even got his own catchphrase. Go on, say it . . ."

"Fuck you!"

"I beg your pardon?"

"That's his catchphrase."

"Charming."

༄

Later, when I spotted Simon on his own, I pulled him aside.

"What are you doing? He looks like his mother's knitted him."

"Au contraire, ma petite ray de misere, he's the love of my life. I met him at the Sweat Club after I left Sally and Bobby's. Let go of my sleeve, you're pulling it out of shape. I've got to get back to him. I've left him talking to the Chancellor of the Exchequer. He's probably solved the world debt crisis by now. He's such a clever boy."

Grudgingly, I let go. The look on his face was enough. He really was in love. I felt murderously jealous. I couldn't go to my table. I could feel tears prickling my eyes. Any minute now my eyeliner would be making its way down my cheeks, scouring little winding rivers into my bronzer.

I dived into the loo, where I sat on the plush imitation Louis XIV-style loo furniture and wailed. It wasn't long before a considerate A-lister in Versace was trying to console me. "What on earth is the matter?"

"He's . . . he's with someone else . . ."

"The bastard. Well, you look gorgeous tonight. I should think that will show him. Who are you wearing? Mouret?"

"Marks & Spencer."

"Oh, well, it's very nice. You'd never know. Who is she?"

"He."

"Dear me, that is tricky. But it happens to the best of us nowadays. Who is *he*?" I recognized her a bit. I think she was either Keira Knightley or Rachel Weisz. Then again, she could have been Natalie Portman.

"Ricky Moon," I said, sniveling. "They met at the Sweat Club. The Sweat Club! He doesn't sweat . . ."

Keira Weisz-Portman shrieked. "Ricky Moon! Fuck you! Oh, he's dreamy. I'd give up now if I were you."

I burst into tears again. It wasn't just the Simon situation. It was the whole me messing things up and embarrassing myself thing. Horrible memories of the Scorsese incident at the *GQ* awards came flooding back. A dark corner, a small, bespectacled figure in silhouette that looked like he might be my favorite film director. "You're a legend. I adore all your movies. They changed my life. It's such a thrill to finally meet you, Mr. Allen, sir." Oh, the horror. I could get a column out of these things, and it would make the readers laugh, but one day I would just like My Big Fat Single Life not to be so hilarious for a change.

2

The Perfect Mr. Fixit

In which I get to grips with the realities of single life, namely plumbing emergencies.

I actually have a lot of sympathy for the Liberal Democrat MP and equalities minister, Lynne Featherstone,* who despite being a minister of the crown in charge of many important affairs of state was reduced to calling out the fire brigade one night when her boiler made a strange noise.

In an emergency, what's a girl to do? Apart from wanting whatever it is that has broken fixed, you want male reassurance. That's the most important part. No matter how capable she is in her public or work life, when she gets home a woman wants a man

---

* I do not agree with her about "body fascism," however. Ms. Featherstone contends that women should eschew thin to look a bit more like Christina Hendricks. I'm five foot three and naturally 112 pounds (sorry, but I am). To achieve tits and ass like Hendricks I would have to eat my way to extreme obesity, then have a cosmetic surgeon chisel away the excess in a series of grueling, possibly life-threatening procedures at a cost of tens of thousands of pounds. How body fascist is that?

to tell her it's all going to be OK. Even if it isn't. That's not the point. Even if there's water pouring from the ceiling and there's no hope, what she wants is a man to tell her that he is going to take care of it. Even if he's going to make it worse, which, let's face it, he usually does.

A woman alone must wrestle with a thousand petty torments. The loose nuts and bolts of everyday existence seem to smell desperation and pop out of every creaking unsafe crevice the minute you are without a man.

Before you know it, you are living in mortal terror of the cable connection failing, or the TV remote coming up with a new and unusually cruel way of thwarting you from accessing a channel called AV1, which seems to be the magical source of all things, and without which nothing televisual can be achieved and your life will be ruined forever.

A woman alone has to call out the cable repairmen and pay them £60 every time she can't work the remote. Then there's the issue of how to get the logs out of your car, which the gamekeeper at the stable yard where you keep your horses has put there in a huge sack, thinking he is doing you a favor.

It would be a favor, if you had a man at the other end to take them out again, but when you get back to London all you have is a sack of logs wedged in the passenger footwell, and the only way to get them out is to carry each one into the house individually, or go to a local bar that night and pick up a man who isn't too drunk and tell him that before he gets anything he has to carry that sack of logs into your garden. Then, when he's done, you tell him there's another sack in the front garden, just round there behind that bush, and when he goes back outside to get it you can shut him out. What? What's wrong with that?

It's the same with gherkins. I have to ask the people in

Sainsbury's or Waitrose to open my gherkin jars at the checkout, and that is not something I would wish on my worst enemy. Asking someone at the Sainsbury's checkout to open your gherkins is as good as climbing on to the counter and screaming into a megaphone, "I have not had sex for a long time." But it has to be done.

Personally, I don't just want someone to open my gherkins. I want someone male to open my gherkins. A woman at customer services opened a jar of gherkins for me once. She refused to call a male colleague and bashed the thing on the lid until the seal gave way just to prove she could do it. It wasn't the same and the gherkins didn't taste right as a result.

But for a woman alone, nothing compares to the tyranny of plumbing. This is because boilers are not machines. They are sentient beings with malicious personal agendas. They wait patiently until it gets really cold, then start dripping and spluttering and making pathetic choking noises that sound ever so slightly like, "Help! I'm dying!" until you are forced to call Tony the plumber.

There are many fascinating things about Tony the plumber, but by far the most fascinating is that he always charges exactly the same amount of money—£326:20—no matter what you ask him to do. This is terrific value if you want to have a new bathroom put in, but not so good if you just want a radiator with a stuck knob turned down. To call Tony you've got to be damned sure that what you are dealing with is £326:20's worth of trouble.

When you call Tony out to a boiler, you had also better be ready with the buckets and towels. He always starts by being optimistic: "Not much wrong here, just needs a quick service . . ." You think, "Oh, God, no! Please let it be more than that." "I've changed my mind," you say, "I've decided I want to let it drip. I quite like the drip." One day, not long ago, Tony was enthusiastically pulling the boiler to pieces before I could stop him at an estimated cost, if it just needed a quick service, of about £5 a minute. Luckily, however, once he started rummaging he found a whole section that needed replacing. Things were looking up. Then a screw revealed itself to be corroded and took hours to coax out. I sighed with relief as Tony did battle with his pliers.

After he had finished mangling the boiler to the tune of £326:20, Tony settled down to drink tea and debate Keynesian economics. Tony is the world's most intellectual plumber. He may not be the best plumber, but he is certainly the most well-read. He was educated at Ruskin College, Oxford, and spent many years in the unions fomenting disputes and meeting some of the great extremists of the Labor movement. He was instrumental in formulating many groundbreaking ideas about advancing the power of the workers to hold back economic progress and is even now still traumatized by Tony Blair ending the Labor Party's historic support for them owning the means of production. This doesn't excuse Tony the plumber's propensity to ruin heating systems, but it does set it in some kind of context.

"The world's a terrible place, my dear," he said, philosophically slurping his tea with three sugars. "Blair and Brown, they ruined Britain . . . And that Ed Miliband, what a plonker . . ."

Like most staunch left-wingers, Tony loathes all Labor MPs and deeply admires the Conservatives. Cameron can do no wrong in his eyes. But he has a particular passion for Margaret Thatcher— "Say what you like about her, she was a strong leader. You knew where you were . . ."

Despite opposing everything she stood for, he longed for someone like her to emerge from the current ranks of the mediocre and lead the country out of the wilderness to a place of extreme right-wing prosperity and libertarianism that he could then take issue with vehemently.

It was only after he'd emptied my head of everything I thought about politics that he would start on my love life.

"Why haven't you got a man then?" he asked, leaning back in his chair and narrowing his eyes. "What happened to that nice guy, Jim?"

I always find this a difficult question to answer. Normally I would say, "How long have you got?" but this is never a good thing to say to a plumber drinking tea in your kitchen, because a plumber drinking tea in your kitchen has an almost infinite amount of time. It has never been measured accurately, but NASA scientists have estimated that a plumber drinking someone else's tea has something like fifty million light-years to spare.

"More tea?" I said, getting up to boil the kettle and not waiting for the answer, because asking Tony if he wants more tea is like asking Posh Spice if she wants more Birkin bags. "I will do," said Tony, "and put some sugar in it this time, my dear, none of this one-spoon business."

As the kettle boiled I told Tony the story of Jim the jilted fiancé and how I was more convinced than ever that I would never find love, if only because I didn't deserve to after leaving a nice, kind man practically standing at the altar.

Unlike everyone else I had told, who had either reacted by panicking or getting hysterically happy about it, Tony took it all in his stride.

"My dear," said Tony, pushing his mug at me for a refill. "It was obviously for the best. It's going to take a very strong man to be your husband. You're not an easy woman." Well, obviously. "You need someone who isn't threatened, who's going to stand up to you, who's going to . . ."

On and on he went, listing the exact qualities I was looking for until I wasn't at all sure if he wasn't making me an offer, nor that I wanted to refuse it.

Tony is a big, bearded man in his sixties with swarthy, weather-beaten skin. He looks slightly like he should be serving behind the counter of a tavern in a television adaption of a Charles Dickens novel. But I have a thing for odd-job men. It's the rescuer complex writ large—very large, with buttock cleavage. Because I long for a man to look after me but cannot make it happen romantically, I end up fixating on plumbers and cable repairmen and anyone who can make things that don't work start working while being even notionally masculine in the process.

Before I found Tony, and entered into a sort of monogamous relationship whereby he "fixed" pretty much everything that went wrong in my house, there were dozens of them, I'm ashamed to say.

There was a very butch young Australian guy who was on the end of an expensive telephone number and who would arrive wearing baggy trousers, a tight white T-shirt, and a huge tool belt round his waist, ominously stuffed with bundles of banknotes. Evidently, desperate women had tucked cash into his belt as he fixed their washing machines. Or he had placed the wads of £10 and £20 notes there for effect. Either way, he was a right odd-job lothario. I can't even remember his name—I think it might have been Bruce—but I don't think he minded that.

After divesting himself of his T-shirt, he would work silently, not making the slightest conversation, apart from grunting every now and then when I asked him if he could fix it. He never drank tea, or entered into the slightest pretense that this was anything other than a loveless arrangement for money. Our relationship, to use the term loosely, ended after he charged me £350 to plumb in a new washing machine that subsequently leaked so badly I had to take up the floor. When I chased him for compensation he liquidated the company and said he had no assets. Like hell. He was well known to the trade bodies, who said he wound up his business countless times a year to avoid his desperate creditors.

I wonder now whether Bruce wouldn't have been better off just providing a straightforward male-escort service. Administering his female clients with a good seeing to would have been much less messy than what he did to their washing machines.

Yes, thank goodness for Tony . . . and his ability to "fix" everything. I use the term "fix" advisedly because, as I've said, he doesn't always fix things. Sometimes he just rearranges what's wrong with them. Often he makes what's wrong with them worse, then goes off for weeks at a time "to get a part." Nevertheless, he had become so much a part of my life that at some stage I'd given him a set of keys to my house, after which he came and went as he pleased, not fixing leaking radiators when I wasn't even there and popping bills for £326:20 on the kitchen table.

On this occasion, Tony told me that there was something wrong with my boiler that he couldn't put right that evening, but he would come back the following day with a part he had to get from the hardware store. Then he drank another three cups of tea and told me a lot of stuff I didn't really want to know about the internal politics of the Transport and General Workers Union in the 1980s. Then he heaved himself up to go.

He looked back at me and said, "Yes, I've often wondered if I should marry again . . ."

For a second, I allowed myself to wonder whether it wouldn't be so bad if I ended up entering into some sort of romantic arrangement with Tony. I thought about it long and hard, and by the time he came back the next day I was really warming to the idea. I was sure he looked a bit slimmer as he galumphed down my hallway in his baggy tracksuit bottoms and builder's boots. And wasn't his weather-beaten complexion and unruly beard actually quite rugged, if you half shut your eyes and squinted?

He hadn't been able to get the part from the local store, he said. He'd had to go to a builder's yard a long way away, and it had been a good deal more expensive than he'd thought.

"Fine," I said, smiling sweetly. "Tea?"

Ask a silly question. I made it with ten sugars—surely the way to a plumber's heart—and watched him as he took the boiler to pieces again. As usual, he gave me a little talk on the wonders of the modern central heating system while he worked. "You see this bit? That's all clogged up with limescale, my dear. Needs a good clear-out. I can do that for you, no worries. You see that? That's your transpansion conflagulator . . ."

And then it happened. One minute Tony was a man in majestic command of a boiler, the next minute he was drowning in an explosion of water, a wall of water that seemed to have no end. It crashed on top of him like a huge tidal wave, and he just stood there taking the full force of the tsunami in his face.

For a long time I couldn't think what to do, then I managed to find a bucket and to position it at an angle to catch the force of the flood as it exploded out. The bucket filled in about ten seconds and then the water crashed on to the floor again. And then, just when I thought I was looking at installing an entirely new kitchen, it stopped.

Tony stood there drenched to the skin, spitting water out of his mouth through his beard. "That's it," he gasped, "the boiler's empty. It'll be OK now." Another large splash of water then exploded into his face, before all went quiet. It turned out he hadn't released the pressure before he opened up a whatsit. He wanted

to explain the whole thing, but it was pointless. I couldn't understand. The upshot was that all the electrics were messed up, so
now he had to go back to the store to buy a new whatchamacallit.

He was very sympathetic, and insisted he would cover the full
cost himself, but it was no good. The magic was gone. Whatever
Tony and I had once had was over. His allure as the man who
would fix everything—eventually, if quite badly—was destroyed
forever.

I didn't mind him making the occasional mess or taking
weeks to get round to ordering in a new transpansion conflagulator drucket, but this was on a whole other scale.

When you've seen someone take a wall of water in the face
after neglecting to release a vital safety valve, you cannot, no
matter how hard you try, re-envisage them as a potential rescuer.
After Tony had fitted the new electrics to the boiler I asked him
for my key back. I was bereft, but I was moving on.

∽

Fortunately for me, a new knight in dirty overalls was waiting
just around the corner. A few weeks later, I came out of my front
door to find a huge man on a ladder in my pathway.

"Can I help you?" I said, in a voice that I thought communi-
cated more than adequately how inconvenient I considered it to
find a stranger up a ladder leaning on the front wall of my house.

"No. Is fine," he called down cheerily, "I jas doing sam weeeerk
nexdoor."

I'm always amazed at how happy my neighbors are to come
on to my property without asking. They're always at it. "Do you
mind if I put some grass cuttings in your garden sack?" they say
as they potter into my front garden with their Flymo bucket.

I want to scream, "NO! Move away from my garden sack! My garden sack is specially licensed by Lambeth Council and has been registered for, and purchased, at great expense and trouble, including a long phone conversation with a call center during which I negotiated many circular automated options and a very sarcastic recorded message before arguing at length with someone who had no grasp of the English language and kept saying, 'Is it for yourself?' instead of, 'Is it for you?' which makes me angrier and sadder than almost anything else. In fact, it makes me sick to my stomach. So NO! You may not put some grass cuttings in my garden sack! Get your own!"

But of course I don't shout, "NO!" I say, "Oh fine. Yes, by all means, please do," and then I go away and seethe for weeks, and hate them horribly and worry about how they probably put grass cuttings with little bits of silver paper in my garden sack, which will result in me getting fined for putting nonrecyclables in there. Then I spend ages worrying about how I will confront them when I get the fine. The fact that there are no bits of silver paper in their grass cuttings will be immaterial by the time I've worried myself into an early grave about it.

On this occasion, I had to explicitly order the builder to come down from his ladder and then explain to him the common law of trespass, which was operating in Great Britain and Northern Ireland the last time I checked.

"Ah, very sorry," he said, with a thick accent. He really was huge. When he came off the last rung of the ladder I thought he was still halfway up it. He was colossal—six foot six at least—with broad shoulders and a massive head covered in an unruly mop of thick black hair. He had very deep-set eyes and one of those humongous jaws you see on Eastern European villains in Bond movies. He was handsome, in an Eastern European Bond villain sort of way. He smiled as if he wanted to be friends. But he also looked like he might throw me in a tank full of piranhas at any moment.

He explained that he was doing a big job for my next-door neighbors, sanding down, filling, and painting all their window frames and sills.

I get house envy very easily. I have absolutely no rendering instincts of my own, but as soon as a neighbor gets something done to the outside of their building, I am driven by blind panic to do the same (unless it's solar panels. I couldn't give a stuff about those).

My neighbor's sills and frames were indeed looking very white and smooth, and when I looked at mine the difference was unbearable.

Without even thinking about the cost I said, "I need you to make my house look the same. When can you start?"

His name was Stefano and he was from Albania. He gave me his number and said he would start next week.

When he had finished painting the outside of the house, Stefano took a good look inside. He stood staring at my kitchen ceiling for a long time. "Who paint this?" he said, shaking his head.

I told him it was me. He sighed heavily and mimicked the action of a stupid person with a brush as he said, "You miss, miss, miss."

"Tell me about it," I said. "Story of my life."

Stefano gave me a good price for doing the inside of the house as well, so after one week we embarked on something more long-term.

Stefano was not like Tony. He had no respect for me as an independent woman in my own right. He treated me like chattel, and when I offered him tea he said, "You make tea all right?"

The inference was that he had seen my painting skills and had concluded from them that I was incapable of absolutely everything.

"I make tea. I don't know if it's all right."

"In that case I don't have," he said, grimacing. "You got boyfriend?"

Oh dear. It was a bit early for that. I was hoping he would do the whole "Why are you single?" thing later. At least wait until he had done the damp patch by the washing machine. Still, at least he wasn't drinking tea. "How long have you got?" I said.

"I got time," he said, rather too convincingly.

When I had explained my relationship with Jim to Stefano he seemed happier to continue the job. He was delighted to hear about the called-off wedding—getting to work on the plaster with gusto afterward. Odd-job men are like this. They want a piece of your soul before they fill the cracks in your plaster. "Quid pro quo, Clarice," they say as they stir their bucket of Polyfilla. Stefano fixed me with a stare. He spoke very low. "Do you still hear the screaming of the jilted fiancé? Late at night, can you hear him screaming about you canceling his morning suit?"

Fine, he didn't say that. After he had finished painting the kitchen I commissioned him to build me some shelves. I couldn't help it. A part of me was growing fond of this big chauvinistic pig of a man, who strode into my house with his trousers hanging down just far enough to show an inch of very broad bottom cleavage.

I also had a dream, a dream of somewhere to line up plates at head height. It was a dream I had nurtured for many years, holding it close to my heart. "Can you put up a set of shelves above the sink, wide enough to stack plates like in Nigella's fake kitchen?" I asked Stefano, trembling with anticipation.

"Nigella? Who is Nigella?"

"Never mind. Can you put me in a set of wide shelves?"

"Of course. Is easy," he said, laughing as he watched me swoon.

I gave myself a stern talking to at this point. "Am I thinking up odd jobs to keep Stefano in my life?" I asked. I ran it past Sally, who was adamant that I should not feel the slightest bit guilty and should keep him in my life for as long as possible. "God how wonderful," she said, taking a deep drag on a Marlboro. "You *have* to marry him. You'll have gorgeous olive-skinned babies with bewitching black eyes. I'll babysit. Not all the time. Just on Tuesdays. I hardly ever have anything to do Tuesdays. Albanian's probably a really good second language for a child to have. Also"— she stubbed out her cigarette and started logging on to Twitter— "do you think he'd lay a floor for me?"

෧෨

Because he wanted to get the shelves just right, Stefano said he would take me to Ikea. We crawled around the south circular in his SUV, chugging and choking because he wouldn't, for some reason, drive in any other gear than fourth. Even when he was pulling away from traffic lights. I tried to interest him in first and second, but to no avail.

On the way to Croydon we discussed corruption in Albania. Stefano told me that he'd had to slip a dodgy official a handsome bribe in order to get his passport to come to Britain. It was terrible, he explained. You had to give them cash inside the passport application if you had any chance of getting it through without having to wait for months and months.

He stared painfully out of the window as if to say, "You

people have no idea how privileged you are, and what the rest of the world puts up with."

I didn't like to disavow him of his pain, but I couldn't resist it. "Yes," I said, "a similar system operates here. You have to pay the officials at the Passport Office £ 100 if you want a passport quickly."

"No!" gasped Stefano.

"Yes," I said. "Sometimes, even if you pay them the £ 100, you have to queue up at the office for days. And they make you have a picture done in a booth, which costs £ 5 a go, and if even a bit of your hair is over your ears they send you back and make you do it again."

"No!" gasped Stefano.

"Yes," I said. "That's Britain for you."

If my Albanian builder was already a bit disillusioned with the establishment before we got to Croydon, things were hardly going to improve when we got inside the entrance hall of Ikea.

The first incongruity—there were many to choose from— that he alighted on was the "Prayer and Contemplation Room" to the left of the main entrance.

"Why they have that here?" he said, wandering inside it.

"No, you can't go in there."

"Why? Maybe I want pray and contemplation."

"No, you don't. Believe me."

Stefano is a Muslim. I know this because he has a leather-bound Koran in his car. He must pull over and do a quick pray sometimes when he's driving, so maybe it wasn't so strange for him to want to nip into the Ikea multi-faith contemplation room.

Nevertheless, I felt it was incumbent upon me to move the enterprise forward, otherwise we would be there all night, and I really couldn't stand that. I already had the Ikea shakes and we'd only been there five minutes. (It is well known that if you spend longer than an hour in Ikea you come out in hives.)

The next problem was the arrows pointing us round the showroom floor in a clockwise direction. "Why can't we go through here," Stefano kept saying, darting off against the flow and through a passage that wasn't marked up with arrows and was clearly off piste.

"That may be what you do in Albania, but it's not what we do here," I said rather imperiously. "We need to do what we're told or it will end badly. Believe me. You can't argue with the system. You're in Croydon now."

In the end, I had to choose the shelves myself because Stefano became hypnotized with wonderment. He was picking up cushions and fake books from the staged living room areas and admiring clocks that didn't work. If we stayed much longer he was going to get stuck into a plastic apple.

༖

On the way back from Ikea Stefano said, "You want eat something?" We were driving past Domino's pizza in Thornton Heath at the time and I worried that he might have been intimating that we should eat there.

It was very nice of him to ask, of course, and I was starving, so I didn't entirely poo-poo the idea. I just suggested that maybe it would be nice if we waited until we got back to Balham and then tried somewhere like Pizza Express. "Pizza Ex-er-spress," he said, as if he'd just got off the boat.

"Come on, you've been here a while now, you must know what Pizza Express is?" I said.

"Is like Domino's?"

"Yes, just like Domino's," I lied.

When we got there he looked crestfallen. I now realized he had obviously been wanting to buy me dinner, but on his budget that meant not in a place with tables.

When we got inside he looked at the menu suspiciously. "Is good pizza?" he said, narrowing his eyes.

"It's brilliant pizza," I said. "I recommend the four cheeses, Romana base, with tuna melted in."

He stared at his menu, frowning. "You won't find it on the menu. I invented it." I hadn't got round to coming up with a name for it and entering it into the customer pizza competition yet. I was thinking of calling it La Desperada.

"What is this?" he said, pointing at the first pizza on the menu. And then the second. And the third.

Happily the waiter came before I had to explain. Stefano thought it was a good idea to ask the waiter for detailed information about all twenty-five pizzas on the menu before finally turning to me and saying, "I'll have the one you said."

Over our four-cheese-and-tuna pizzas we discussed where exactly the Nigella shelf would go, and when we had exhausted that issue we sat in silence. Then he told me about his car insurance. It was very expensive. He told me he went on comparethemarket .com because the ad was very funny. And he laughed a lot and kept repeating the catchphrase, "Compare the meerkat! Ha ha ha! What is meerkat?" Enough, I thought. I cannot be going on with this. This Albanian builder and I are never going to be viable. The cultural differences are too great. I don't mind him being a Muslim and carrying a Koran around on the dashboard, but thinking the comparethemarket.com advert is funny is too much. I paid the bill and we went back to my house, where he insisted on fitting the shelf, despite the fact that it was getting dark.

He heaved the flat pack out of his car and started unloading the shelf from its box.

As he worked I started to feel guilty about hurrying him out of the restaurant without dessert and had the insane idea of showing him one of my columns to be friendly. I only show my columns to people who don't know what I do when I'm trying to (a) impress them into fancying me or (b) frighten them out of fancying me.

"This is what I do," I said, holding up a magazine page with my photo on the top.

He stared at it incredulously for a few seconds and then he burst out laughing. Something told me he was not laughing at the wit and ingenuity of my prose. He grabbed the magazine and squinted over it for a bit, then exclaimed, "No! . . . No!" He laughed some more and then said, "Why you write this?"

"To make money," I said. "And because some people enjoy reading it."

"Really?" he said, sitting down, as if the shock was entirely too much for him. As he sat staring at it he smiled and laughed and rocked back and forth until I wanted to smack him.

"Some people enjoy what I write," I said proudly. "I am a leading journalist."

But Stefano was laughing so hard he couldn't speak. He was doing that silent laughing when you can't make sounds because you're laughing so much.

"It's not funny," I said, outraged. "People really do respect my opinion. Why is that so hard to believe?"

"You *write* . . . and people *read* . . ." said Stefano, pointing to the magazine and wiping tears from his eyes, his face deep red from hysteria.

I was pleased when he got back to his shelf. He unpacked all the bits, still exclaiming, "Aaaah!" while shaking his head and muttering to himself about me in the magazine. He started bashing the shelf parts together, and in due course discovered that the usual amount of screws were missing: three. Just enough to make the decision on whether to go ahead and assemble it anyway a bit of a lottery. He declared this a national outrage.

He wasn't laughing now. He was shouting, "Shit, man!" a lot and throwing bits of shelving unit around the kitchen. I told him this was par for the course in Britain, but he was so cross I thought he wasn't going to stop shouting about the injustice of it until I called the United Nations.

After a while he calmed down and found a way of making it hang together with only half the nuts and bolts and then he made me put a pencil mark on the wall where I wanted it. He did something with a spirit level and positioned his drill against the wall.

One minute he was drilling—and having a chance at being my new odd-job hero—and the next minute it was all over.

The wall of water hit him straight in the face, just like it did Tony. It was a hundred times more shocking than the boiler incident, though, because this water just exploded out of the wall.

Stefano did the same thing as Tony, which is to say he stood with the jet in his face, spitting and trying to open his eyes while moving his head from side to side as the water crashed around him.

"Oh dear. There goes another one," I thought.

I had no idea where the water was coming from, but I am never surprised when my home starts leaking from previously undisclosed orifices. I'm sure that whoever installed the original plumbing in turn-of-the-century London garden flats got off on the fact that one day a thirtysomething single woman living on her own would be desperately incapable of coping with it.

Stefano was screaming now. Something about turning off the water at the source. I didn't know how to break it to him that I didn't know where that was. "Stopcock!" he kept screaming. How could I tell him that five years ago some builders I commissioned to build a false ceiling so I could have spotlighting had built the false ceiling over the stopcock, which the sadist who built the house had put at the very top of the wall?

I decided there was only one thing for it. I had to get Tony.

The prospect of asking the last man to cover my kitchen floor in water to stop the current man covering my kitchen floor in water was not one I considered lightly, but it was 10 p.m. and I was never going to get a call-out plumber before my entire flat flooded, while Tony lived right across the street.

It took ages for someone to answer the door and when she did I could hardly see her through a haze of smoke. The lady behind the smoke looked South American and she enthusiastically welcomed me into the living room, where I found Tony splayed out on the sofa smoking something I could only conclude was not a shop-bought cigarette.

He looked at me through bloodshot eyes as I gabbled on about the floodgates of hell opening in my kitchen. He was a bit shaky, as if the whole thing was making him paranoid, but he said he was coming, so I ran back across the street to tell Stefano the good news. I found him with his finger lodged in the hole, close to tears.

I went back into the street, but there was no sign of Tony. I waited and waited. And then the door was flung open and Tony strode out wearing a particularly large pair of builder's boots. He marched straight up to a flap in the pavement and shut off the entire street's water supply, then he marched straight past me into the house.

"Stand aside," he ordered Stefano.

If I had any doubts about a stoned pensioner being able to handle a plumbing emergency, they didn't linger for long. Despite being three sheets to the wind, Tony was spectacular. He snapped out of his spliffed-up state almost immediately and took command of the situation with a swagger. He was like the Clint Eastwood of plumbing.

Stefano was very put out, and kept shouting about how he couldn't have hit a pipe that far up.

"You've hit a pipe all right," said Tony. "You've got to really know how they build these places to know where the pipes go. It takes years of experience."

"But it's up a wall!" said Stefano, squeaking like a boy.

"Nah," said Tony gruffly, chewing gum, "you can't think like that. In these places . . ." he paused for dramatic effect ". . . the pipes could be anywhere."

Stefano sat down at the kitchen table, a broken man. Tony looked at me and smiled. He couldn't resist it. "Well, my dear, you are lucky, aren't you?"

"Lucky?" I said.

"Yes. Lucky to have me." He looked at Stefano like a wronged husband would look at a man he'd found his missus in bed with, a man who had turned out to be a scoundrel and who had left her in a mess. Now he was picking up the pieces.

"Right," he said, turning to the interloper. "Get your drill and drill out that whole area there. I want a really big hole so I can get in and solder the pipe."

I had to be taken out of the kitchen while the drilling happened, and when it was done they brought me back in.

A short while earlier I had been minutes away from putting the finishing touch on my kitchen: my dream Nigella shelf to

stack plates on at head height. Now I was looking at a gaping
hole in the wall, the size of a crater.

Tony made a huge deal out of soldering the pipe. He kept saying it wasn't working and he was going to have to start again. He
made a lot of sparks and drama with his soldering torch, but I
wasn't convinced. He was making me pay for cheating on him
with Stefano. Stefano was in a blind funk by this stage and kept
shouting out over the noise of the soldering, "Will it be OK?" to
which Tony shouted, "Stop panicking, my boy, you have to stay
calm in this business. Good job I'm here, eh?"

When he had finished, he gave Stefano a pep talk. "If you're
going to drill another hole to put that shelf up, my boy, you need
to find out where those pipes are going."

Through the bit of the wall that had been knocked out we
could see the damn things snaking up and across and down in a
pattern that looked like the London Underground map. There
was no way we could know where they went.

Stefano grabbed his drill. "I'm going in."

Tony grabbed him by the shoulders. "You're mad. You'd be
mad to . . . You'll never make it . . ."

But Stefano was like a man possessed. He positioned his drill
on the wall, a look of pure grit on his face. "Stand back," he said,
the beads of sweat glistening on his brow, "I'm going to finish this."

❦

My search for the perfect macho male fixer could only get better,
surely. I told all my girlfriends about my desire to meet a nice,
straightforward practical man who could do jobs around the
house, and as if by magic, my friend Sonia acquired a fireman. I

couldn't quite get my head around it, but she was always collecting waifs and strays and this one had come to her from a friend who had kicked the fireman out of her spare room, where he had been lodging following a messy divorce, because she was having to sell her house and downsize.

Sonia was a blond bombshell of a divorcée who had once been married to a chirpy chat show host. She lived very happily with him for many years in a beautiful house in the country until she woke up one morning and opened her freshly delivered celebrity gossip magazine to find a picture of him leaving an equally beautiful house nearby with another woman he had also been living with for goodness knows how long. Divorce proceedings ensued and at the end of it all, Sonia invested in an enormous castle of a house as big as both her ex-husband's houses put together. You could lose people in it, even big burly ones. Sonia, who had become understandably blasé about absolutely everything after discovering her husband had been leading a double life, put the fireman in her guest wing and thought no more about it.

I was at her house one day having coffee when the handsome fireman, his unfeasibly large pecs bulging under a tight T-shirt, strode into the kitchen. Sonia didn't even acknowledge him, let alone introduce me. He looked me up and down and winked, got himself a drink, and walked back out.

"Er, hello?" I said. "Who was that?"

"Oh that's just Danny."

"Danny? Danny?" I was practically hyperventilating.

"He's the fireman who's moved in. I thought I told you."

"You didn't tell me. What the heck?" She looked at me. I pointed to myself ostentatiously. A look of realization slowly spread across her face.

"Oh my God! Yes!"

The next time I went to Sonia's for coffee, she disappeared strategically when Danny came in and left us to it.

It was quickly obvious that Danny was more than I had hoped for. He was not just strong, silent, and good at fixing things; he was a genuine action man. He had been in the army and had toured Northern Ireland, Iraq, and Afghanistan.

I don't know why I feel compelled to tell men I've only just met about the broken bits in my house, but I assume it's something to do with the rescuer complex.

After just one and a half minutes of talking to Danny I had told him my TV remote control didn't work. Just like that. Introductions, how do you do, where's Sonia gone, getting changed, she'll be down in a minute, my TV remote is stuck on mute.

He took it completely in his stride, offering, "I'll come round and fix it if you like."

"Really?" I said, like a praying mantis sharpening its knife and fork. "When?"

"I'm in your neck of the woods on my shift tomorrow. Me and the boys will drop round in between jobs."

"You mean you're going to come round in your fire engine, with a full crew, to fix my TV remote?"

"Yeah."

"Isn't there a law against that? Won't I be prosecuted for wasting fire service time?"

"No. We'll come between jobs."

"What if there's a fire somewhere at the same time as you're fixing my remote? In any case you can't park outside my house; it's residents only."

"We'll be in a fire engine. We can park where we like."

"Seriously. Lambeth Council will ticket you. They ticketed a bus in a bus stop once. I saw it with my own eyes."

But he was determined. He said he would be round at some point during his shift tomorrow. And he was going to bring a full team of firemen in a fire engine. And that was that.

I felt like God was saying, "Is that enough rescuing for you, you silly madam? Are you satisfied now that people are going to die so you can get a man to fix your remote? Call the cable guy, you cheapskate." (God is very communicative at times like these, I find.)

The next day my conscience pricked me so much I texted Danny to say I didn't think I could allow him to come round to my house in a fire engine to fix my remote. But it was too late. With a great hissing of hydraulic brakes a fire engine pulled up outside, and then five firemen were standing on my doorstep. I had never seen so many sets of pecs straining at the seams of so many tight T-shirts. As they piled into my hallway, the heady smell of testosterone made me want to faint.

To be honest, it wasn't that sexy. My flat is quite small and the firemen were so huge they barely fitted in. Once they were all standing in the hallway we had to shuffle round each other to get into the living room. From the outside, it must have looked a lot like the scene in *Life of Brian* when an entire Roman battalion marches into the tiny stone house where Brian is hiding, not very convincingly, behind a curtain, and a few seconds later marches back out declaring that they have found a suspicious-looking spoon.

The firemen filed in and stood in my living room staring at the television and prodding the remote.

Horrifically, my handsome but slightly strange single neighbor who walks his cats up and down the street every day chose that moment to knock on the door and ask if I was OK. "I saw the fire engine, and the firemen coming in. Lots of firemen . . ."

"Yes, yes, everything's fine," I said, trying to block his view. "I've just got a small emergency with an electrical appliance."

"Oh dear, is something on fire?" he said, straining to see behind me.

"Yes, very much so," I lied. "Bang on fire. Flames everywhere."

I squared this with myself by reasoning that as my pants were metaphorically on fire it wasn't too far from the truth.

Handsome single guy was still straining to see past me and looked like he might be a problem, but thankfully at that moment one of his cats made a squawking noise. He spun round. "Bismarck?" he called, as he went back out into the street to look for it.

When I squeezed back inside the living room full of firemen, Danny was prodding the remote. Then he passed it on, shaking his head. This prompts the question: how many trained firefighters does it take to get a Sony Bravia remote control off mute? I don't know the definitive answer, but I had five and they couldn't do it.

In the end, I decided I had to get them out of my house before another public-spirited person walked by, looked in the window, and noticed that a full fire crew were in my living room trying to fix my TV. So I asked Danny out to dinner. It wasn't until I said, "Let's go for pizza after your shift finishes," that he agreed to leave and take his fire crew with him.

I guess he calculated that as I was now asking him out properly there was no need to impress me by waving his hose, so to speak.

⁊⁊

He turned up at Pizza Express a few hours later in civilian clothes, an outfit which also involved a tight T-shirt stretched taut across his pecs. I tried to recommend the four-cheese-and-tuna Desperada special, but he wasn't convinced.

The conversation stalled way before the point where I had struggled with Stefano. "So, you must have some amazing stories of things that have happened to you as a fireman?" I said, throwing him a nice, easy underarm ball.

"Not really," he said, slurping from his bottle of Peroni.

"Come on. Surely you must have been involved in some exciting things? I mean, what's it like to fight a fire?"

I swear he actually said this: "It's hot."

"Yes, well obviously, but I mean you guys, you must come close to death all the time."

"Not really. It's about following procedure."

In the end I had to spell it out. "Look, tell me the best story you've got about your time as a fireman. Something unusual or exciting that happened to you when you were putting out burning buildings and pulling people out of flames."

There was a long pause as he stared gloomily at his bottle of beer, then something like a light came on in his eyes and he said, "There was this funny thing once . . ."

"Yes," I said, "go on."

"Well, me and a mate were sent to this house where an old woman had had a fall. We found her collapsed in the loo, she'd been in there for days. Her husband was bedridden so he couldn't get to her. Things like that really make you think, you know . . ."

I thought, "This house had better catch fire so they end up throwing the old couple out of the window on to a strategically placed mattress or I'm walking out of here before the pizza arrives."

"Anyway, he was just lying in bed with this strange look on his face."

Danny also had a strange look on his face. He stared further and further into the middle distance until I had to remind him that I was still there, waiting for the end of the story, although I had my doubts about whether I wanted to hear it.

"Yes?" I said.

"This old man just smiled a huge grin, and then he said,"— here Danny paused for effect—" 'That's the most peace I've had in fifty years.' "

I sat staring at him for a while, as if I was still waiting for the end to the story, the good bit that would impress me.

"You see," he explained, as if I was remedial, "the old man had been henpecked by his wife all his life, and when she fell over in the loo he was delighted because it meant he actually got a bit of peace for a few days."

"Yes," I said, "what a moving story."

We stared into our plates for a bit until it struck me that as we were never going to hit it off on an intellectual level, I might as well get straight to the point and proposition him. He was, at least, a very fit physical specimen. He might not be everything I wanted in the field of entertainment, but hell, I had cable didn't I, even if it was on silent mode. I didn't need a man to entertain me. What I needed a man for at this stage in the game, let's not beat about the bush, was procreation. Pure and simple. All the rest I could provide for myself.

This is the harsh reality of single life approaching forty. You cease to want a man for any genuine romantic reason and become focused entirely on the utilitarian business of extracting a male human being's DNA. It was horrible, but I couldn't do anything about it. It was almost as if it had happened automatically, as if a primeval switch had been thrown in my head. There was a dreadful symmetry to it. I was now treating men the way men had treated me my whole life. I only wanted them for their body.

"So," I said, "you're divorced, Sonia says."

Danny stared balefully at me, as though I had just kicked him in the guts. Then he embarked on the story of his marriage, which involved countless acts of cruelty on the part of his ex-wife, who'd never really loved him, and went on until the waitress took our plates away. After that he told me the story of his only relationship since the marriage ended, with a woman who had subjected him to countless acts of cruelty and had never really loved him.

Then he said, "I did everything she wanted. I even had the snip."

"What now?" I nearly spat my San Pellegrino out across the table.

"Yeah. She said it would be romantic, seeing as we both have kids, if I had a vasectomy."

The sound of screeching gears inside my head was so loud I'm sure the other diners could hear it. I wanted to shout at the waitress for the bill, but I thought I'd better stay a few minutes longer, or however long it was decent to remain in my seat before running for the door.

"I'm not sure I can see how that could be romantic," I said.

"Well, because it was like us making this statement to each other that we were never going to want to be with anyone else and that this was forever."

I had never heard this one before. Say it with flowers, yes. Say it with a vasectomy? Not so much.

"I wouldn't call it romantic," I said.

A small part of me wanted to stay and have dessert with Danny just to demonstrate that I wasn't going to abandon him like damaged goods. Then I looked at him and he had this gloopy expression on his face and I just felt angry. Here was a man who gave every physical impression of being a real man, and yet he had meekly offered himself up to be gelded in the name of sentimentality. Would Dirty Harry have had a vasectomy as a nice gesture? Like hell he would have.

Where have all the real men gone? Where?

෨෨

As if the gelded fireman wasn't disappointment enough, the TV was still stuck on mute. I really couldn't work out how to make my new remote control do what I wanted. It was beyond me. No matter what I pressed I couldn't get the sound to come on. I wished I had never bought a new flat-screen television. I knew there would be a sting in the tail.

I hadn't even been able to work out how to plug the darn thing in and had rung the cable call center where a cheerful Scottish lady had said, "Just put the cable in the back."

"Just put the cable in the back" is the century's least helpful sentence.

How do I just put the cable in the back? "You get the cable coming out of the receiver box and you put it in the back of the TV." Hilarious.

In reality, you stare at the end of the cable, which has a silver plug thing on it and bits of gold wire spewing out, and you know that the operation described blithely by the woman on the phone actually requires some sort of qualified electrician chicanery involving unscrewing the silver plug thing and a manipulation of the gold wires with a pair of pliers. But when you tell the lady this she says, "Just put the cable in the back." She will never admit that pliers are needed. Never, never, never in a million years.

So you ask how much it will be for her to send you a man who will "just put the cable in the back" and she says that will be £ 80, and then she tries one last time: "But really, madam, it's quite simple. Just put the cable in the back."

"Yes, yes," you say, "I'm sure it is. But just send me the man."

When the man arrives he is twelve years old. He comes into your living room, walks up to the TV, and does something with a pair of pliers that is as fast as lightning. He really does "just put the cable in the back." Then he starts to leave. You panic. "Please, don't leave," you beg. You know that the moment he is out of that door the television will stop working or you will render it insensible again, possibly by just looking at it wrong.

"Can I get you a cup of tea? Or some dinner?" Or somewhere comfortable to lie down?

The cable guy looks worried now.

You know you are looking at him like Kathy Bates in *Misery*, sizing up how strong he is and whether he will be able to resist you if you whack him over the head and try to drag his unconscious body into the bedroom. You try to work out how long he will stay out for and whether it will be long enough for you to get him tied to the bed and whether it's really reasonable to break his ankles or is that going a bit far? But you can't help it. You need this boy to stay with you forever. You know, as sure as you know anything, that as soon as he leaves the television will stop working again.

He reverses toward the door, wild-eyed. He doesn't want to turn his back on you for a second in case you grab the TV remote and club him over the head with it.

You watch him go with your stomach churning and the second he gets in his van and drives away you realize: you didn't get him to demonstrate how to turn the new television off and on.

As soon as his van has turned the corner of the street you realize you cannot switch on the television yourself. You press all the buttons on the remote and all you can get is the TV with the sound down. "I'm paying thirty-nine pounds a month for this," you scream. "And eighty pounds for the man to just put the cables in the back. And I still can't watch my TV!"

You get very, very upset and smoke a lot of cigarettes out the back door and then you decide that you can look at it another way. Sound is overrated. Sound gets you all worked up. So you watch the TV without the sound for an evening. It doesn't really work. There is only one more option. You decide never to watch television again. There's nothing on but Gordon Ramsay anyway.

You ring up to cancel the cable, but you can't cancel the cable because the cancelation line—"to remove channels or cancel your package press three"—never answers. You ring the other option— "to add channels press two"—and they answer in two seconds flat, but the bloke on that line swears on his mother's life that he cannot cancel or remove channels. "I'm not trained for it," he says, improbably.

"But you're trained to add channels," you say.

"Yes," he says, "I can add channels."

"But you can't take them away?"

"No," he says. "That's a totally different training procedure." And conveniently for the cable company's business plan, he hasn't had it. You ask him to put you through to the takeaway option, but he says he can't because his systems are down.

You say, "Well, your systems aren't down if I want to add channels are they?"

He says, "No, the system for adding channels is OK. It's just the system for putting people through to the system for canceling and taking away channels that doesn't work."

You go on like this for twenty minutes and then you give up. You have cable. You never watch it. It's just how it is.

૭৩

Sally rang in a state of great excitement. "What are you doing?"

"Trying to cancel cable."

"Again? You were doing that last time I called. And the ten times before that."

"I know. It's pretty much my full-time occupation now. I get up. I have breakfast. I try to cancel cable. Then it's time to go to bed again."

"Well, get round here now because I've got the most amazing man fitting a new floor in my basement."

"Oh no, please, not another one."

"Seriously. He's not just a carpenter, he's an artist as well. And he cooks. He's heaven."

With a sense of exhaustion and dread I pitched up at Sally's house twenty minutes later to find her breathless with anticipation.

"I've told him you're coming. He's really keen."

"Keen on what?"

I was dispatched down to the basement where I found an unfeasibly handsome carpenter laying a floor, wearing what looked like a kaftan.

He had shoulder-length blond hair, a nice smile, and was very softly spoken.

We exchanged pleasantries and I told him I thought he'd laid a lovely floor, then I went back upstairs to face the inquisition.

"Well?" said Sally.

"He looks like Jesus," I said.

"Isn't he divine? I'm having you both round to dinner tomorrow. Don't wear black."

❦

The next day, Jesus, who was also known as Nico, came up from the basement smartly dressed in a pair of chinos and a navy blue blazer. This was a little odd for someone who'd just finished sanding a floor, but I decided to gloss over it because it was preferable to a kaftan.

He was, after all, perfect in every way. He was good-looking, intelligent, kind, generous, polite, warm, humorous. His good qualities just went on and on.

After dinner we sat drinking coffee, Sally fired up a Marlboro Light, and Nico said, "Would you like to see some of my art?"

Now, this is a tricky one. I want to say my heart sank, but I know that will make me sound like a Philistine. I do like art. I like that painting by Van Gogh of the starry starry night. And I quite like *Sunflowers*, and *The Scream*, and the big fat women by Lucian Freud. And that mad pope that Bacon did. And Stubbs's racehorses, although it has to be said they don't look anything like the horses I've seen, and I've seen a lot of horses. And the Arnolfini portrait by Van Eyck. I love the bit where you look into the mirror and it sort of goes on forever. But when someone I know says, "Can I show you my art?" I panic. I would rather they said, "Would you like to look up this periscope into my colon?" I would know what to say if they showed me their colon, but confronted by their art I always say the wrong thing.

And so it was on this occasion. Nico got a large rolled-up

print out of his bag, ceremoniously unrolled it on to the coffee table, and weighted both ends down.

As he was doing this, I tried to steal a march by getting a look at it as it was being unfolded, so I could start working out what to say. It was a huge black canvas with a black shape on it, which was blacker in some places than others. It was just about as bad a conundrum as it could be.

"Oh it's wonderful," I said, feeling sick with panic. What the hell was it supposed to be? Come on, come on, there must be a clue somewhere.

I stood staring and staring as if moved beyond words by the power of the different shades of blackness. And then I realized that Nico was standing looking at it from the other way. Oh Christmas crackers.

I walked around the table and righted myself. I did this slowly, going, "Mmm, yes," as I went, to make it look like I had meant to look at it upside down first as part of an expert strategy of assessing important artworks from every angle. Nico stood back, folded his arms, held his chin in one hand and looked at it admiringly.

Then I suddenly saw something. Yes, of course! I was *this* close to saying, "Oh, it's an elephant!" when he said, "She was the most amazing woman . . ."

Dear God, that was a close one.

"Yes, I can see that," I said, thinking, "Where's her head? Where's her fucking head? Is that her head? That looks like a trunk. Maybe she has a trunk. Maybe he's painted the elephant woman."

"She posed for hours and gave so much of herself," said Nico.

"Yes, I can see that," I said again, thinking, "I wish she'd given a bit more of herself so I could see what she is." I know some people will say it's best to be honest with friends about their art, and say, "Oh is it an elephant?" if you want to say, "Oh is it an elephant?" But I disagree.

If people misinterpret what I do I feel bereft. I cannot inflict this on other people. It's only, "Oh is it an elephant?" once to me, but to Nico it's, "Oh is it an elephant?" every night for the rest of his life, haunting his dreams.

After he had explained the image to me for a long time and I had said, "Mmm, oh yes," more times than you would have thought it humanly possible, he rolled the picture carefully back up. Then he sat down on the sofa and patted the space next to him. Uh-oh.

"Tell me your dreams."

Double uh-oh.

"What do you really want out of life?"

"I don't know, do I?" I thought. I said, "Oh well, you know, this and that."

He asked me about my writing. He said, "What do you really want to write about?" As if the stuff I was writing about wasn't admissible for the purposes of a discussion on artistic fulfillment.

"This," I said defensively. "I like writing about everyday life."

"But what do you really want to do? What are your dreams?"

"This," I said stubbornly.

"Yes, but if you could write about anything, what would you write about?"

"This. Literally." Oh dear.

He changed tack. "Where would you most like to travel to?"

I told him I liked a particular village in France, in Haute-Provence, and that I go there every year. It's up a hill, in the middle of nowhere. There's absolutely nothing anywhere near. There are loads of stray cats and chickens who come to sit by the pool with me and I feed them.

"Don't you want to go to Africa, to South America?" he asked.

"No," I replied.

He started to talk about his feelings. He told me he was writing a book about the origins of Christian myths which was somehow connected to the architecture of Chartres cathedral. He began to explain why he loved this architecture and I thought, "If you don't stop talking about Chartres cathedral I'm going to poke you in the eye."

I'm too old for cultural talk. It was bad enough when I was young and idealistic. In fact, it was pretty unbearable then.

You see, when I was in my early twenties I was scarred by a terrible experience in which a guy took me to an art gallery followed by the theater all in one date. I'm not saying David Hare is hard work, but halfway through the second act I said I was going to the loo and ran away.

While this is appalling behavior, I do think there's something uniquely depressing about an overly cultured man. Men aren't meant to be cultured, they're meant to shoot big game and light bonfires in the woods.

᳇

Two days later, however, Nico was cooking me dinner. I don't know how it happened except that it was easier than dodging his texts.

Interesting and perhaps useful fact: you only have to send me about ten text messages asking me how I am before I will sleep with you to make it stop.

That is how much I hate modern telecommunications technology. I will do almost anything rather than answer a phone, send a text, tweet, update my Facebook status, or Skype someone. I prefer almost any direct mode of interaction to the virtual. It doesn't matter who it is, if they say, "Skype me or perform fellatio on me," I will give them a blow job every time.

I tried to Skype someone once. It ended with me booking myself in for a facelift. What is it with those webcams? They make me look like Freddy Krueger's less attractive older sister. I can't concentrate on the other person's face, or what they are saying, for a second, I am so gruesomely absorbed by watching my own monstrous image.

After your call, the Skype people send you one of those little surveys that asks you to rate the overall quality of your call and quizzes you for problems that might have occurred. They ask you to select statements such as, "The image was partially obscured," or, "The reception was patchy." There isn't an option that says, "My face looked so horrific I phoned the London Clinic and booked myself in for a ribbon lift, although I later chickened out," but if there was you would click it.

Nico didn't Skype me, but he sent me a series of text messages asking how I was feeling and what I was doing, which required so much input that I would have found it easier to marry him. In the end we agreed that he would come round to my house to "cheer me up" and "look after me." What is it about those two statements that is so infuriating?

I'm getting increasingly crabby about a lot of seemingly nice things that men say to women. Take "smile" for example. When a man shouts "smile" at me when I'm walking down the street it does not feel to me like a cheery greeting. It feels like a threat. Smi-yal. It even has a patronizing tune. F Sharp, D. Seriously. That's the smile jingle.

Many theories have been put forward about the whole smile-shouting thing, but for me, the smile shout is about control. Men who shout smile at you are so manipulative they can't bear to look at your face doing what it does naturally, relaxing. They want to put demands on it, make it dance to their tune.

If you were smiling, they would shout, "Gri-mace!" But of course they don't have to shout grimace because no woman needs to be told to grimace. This is because women have the weight of the world on their shoulders and are eternally disappointed. No woman smiles naturally. It's a myth. If you see a woman walking down the street smiling, she is either pretending or mad. Men know this. They know that women aren't happy. And they know it's their fault. This is why a man shouting, "Smile!" at a woman is like rubbing salt in the wound. What they mean to say is, "There's still a massive gender pay gap, you women do all the caring at home as well as flogging your guts out in a career, and most of us men are no good at all in the bedroom, so SMI-YAL!"

I'm always trying to think up the perfect answer. My current favorite is, "Make me smile, then! Go on, what are you going to do to put a smile on my face? Or are you not man enough? Is it all talk, this smile business? Or are you actually going to persuade Apple to make a MacBook that has a decent word processor on it as standard? Hmm, HMMM?!"

But I digress. Nico wasn't shouting smile, he was just threatening to "cheer me up" and "look after me" through the medium of dressing me a lobster. I suspect the cheering up and looking after was in some way indicative of a desire to control, but I couldn't quite rule out the possibility that he was just a really nice guy. If he was a control freak, it was hidden under so much kindness it was going to take ages to get at. He bought the lobsters from a trendy market, and conveyed them to my house, along with the ingredients for hollandaise, some asparagus, crusty bread, and patisserie cakes. How perfect is that? How utterly kind and generous and sensitive and thoughtful and perfect. Reader, I was terrified.

As soon as he texted to say he was buying lobster I started fretting. When he arrived I was crouching in the living room looking out of the window to see how many shopping bags he would have. He had three. This was serious. I might have to go out the back door and climb over the garden fence. "Get a grip, you stupid cow!" I shouted at myself.

When I answered the door he was charm itself. He busied himself in the kitchen unpacking the lobster. He told me he didn't want me to do a thing. "Just relax." That's another supposedly "nice" thing that reduces me to a quivering wreck. I can't relax. Give me a lobster to bludgeon, for pity's sake.

But Nico insisted. He took charge of everything and very soon a delicious hollandaise was taking shape. "Damn!" he cursed as the sauce did what hollandaises always do. (Why don't they just change the official texture of hollandaise to curdled? That way we could all cook it.)

"Don't worry," I said, enlivened by the fact that I might have a role. I comfort people who have ruined dinner really well.

"No, no, it's OK, it's coming back . . ." He was determined to get the hollandaise to stop being lumpy and was getting all hot and bothered as a result. A little voice inside me said, "What is the matter with you that you can't just let a nice man panic while he's curdling his hollandaise?"

So he panics as he curdles hollandaise. So what? Am I really so obsessed with finding a man who is super macho that I'm going to be put off when his hollandaise splits? If I am, I'm going to rule out an awful lot of men, possibly all of them.

Then I thought, "Clint Eastwood wouldn't panic if he curdled hollandaise. He would just slap it all over the lobster, lumps and all."

We talked and talked over dinner, and after dinner Nico kept talking until I was holding my eyes open with my forefingers as I propped my head in my hands. Nico wouldn't take no for an answer on anything. No matter how discouraging I was, he determined to change my mind about everything.

He was particularly insistent about taking me to South America to see the ruins of some tribe or other. He actually asked me to get my photos of India out. And then insisted on looking at all five hundred of them. I had never met anyone who insisted on looking at someone else's photos before.

In the end I said I would go to South America because it was one in the morning and I had to get him out the door.

The next day he texted and texted and I didn't return the calls. His last message was hysterical, went on for several screens, and centered on the grand themes of loss and betrayal.

Shortly afterward, Sally rang in a panic to tell me that Nico had disappeared midway through installing her imitation parquet floor. (Apparently he had modeled it on the floor in Chartres cathedral.)

"Good," I said.

"It's not good. It's not finished. I've only got half a parquet floor. And that's not the worst of it . . ."

It seemed the Canaletto hanging in the drawing room had disappeared. "Maybe he's just taken it to be valued," said Sally, trying to give the disappearing carpenter/art expert/chef/Lothario/Jesus look-alike the benefit of the doubt.

"Maybe," I said.

Or maybe any man who looks like Christ and who comes to my house and cooks me lobster and tells me he finds me fascinating and irresistible and expresses an interest in taking me to South America on the trail of the Incas is inevitably going to turn out to be an art thief.

"Is anything missing from your place?"

"You must be kidding. I don't have anything worth stealing; I pride myself on it. I certainly don't have anything that could be called art." Unless you count a huge portrait of me in an evening gown sitting on top of a mad chestnut mare in a cornfield. It's meant to evoke Stubbs and Rossetti, but the guy from Paws for Applause pet photography wasn't really up to it. I ran into the living room to check, just in case, but it was still hanging incongruously above the sofa.

3

Warm Heart, Cold Turkey

....

In which I endure numerous entirely avoidable dating disasters and discover the optimum amount of KFC needed to cure heartache.

....

A few weeks later, I was following a van very slowly down a hill toward some traffic lights. I was perfectly happy following the van slowly down the hill. Until I noticed that there was a sign on the back of the van beginning with the tantalizing words, "If you . . ." Understandably, therefore, I started trying to read the sign on the back of the van. "If you . . . came . . . dead . . . no need . . . no can . . . if you can need . . ." Finally, as we approached the lights and began to slow down, I got close enough to work it out. "If . . . you . . . can read . . . this . . . sign . . . you're too close." Ah! I see! At which point the lights changed to red, the van slammed on its brakes, and I smashed into the back of it. The driver got out and started yelling, "What the hell are you doing? Can't you read the sign?" "No! That's the whole point. I had to get close to read the sign. By the time I was close enough to read the sign I was so close I couldn't do what the sign was asking, which was to not get too close. It's a stupid sign." The van driver told me I was the only person who had ever slammed into the back of his van trying to read the sign telling them not to get so close that they would slam into the van, but I didn't believe him. I think people should be banned from putting signs on the backs of their cars, and not just ones telling other drivers how to drive. Those warning triangles with "Baby on Board!" should be illegal, too, on the basis that they are shockingly ageist. What next? "Old Lady on Board so Don't Worry Too Much!" "Ugly Fat Bloke on Board so Feel Free to Run Me off the Road!" Maybe I should have one saying, "Gullible Idiot Who Reads the Signs on the Backs of Cars on Board so Adopt the Brace Position!" I told the van driver all of this, but he didn't seem at all convinced. In fact, he was downright rude about my theory. We exchanged insurance details, and before he got back in his van he said, "Please don't drive after me trying to read the label in my underpants."

My dating life, I thought, as I drove away, is like the sign on the back of that van. I am always running into dangerous men bearing all the signs that they are dangerous. But it isn't until they get so close they are harming me that I can see they have a warning sign saying they will harm me. By which stage, they have harmed me. What is the point of that, God? Hmm? What have you got to say for yourself? Nothing, as usual.*

A day that begins with a metaphorically illustrative car crash will not end well. I should have turned around and gone home.

---

* Legal notice: God would like to point out that He was unable to reply to the author owing to an unusually high volume of calls. He would like to thank all callers for their continued patience at this time. Press one if you would like to return to the main menu. Press two to hear these options again. Press three if you need further assistance.

Instead I continued on to my lunch date with my gay lawyer friend Marcus, who wanted to introduce me to a business contact with whom he had just done a big deal. When he'd mentioned being friends with me the contact had expressed a strong desire to meet me because he liked my column. I should always refuse to meet people who want to meet me. In general, I don't really want to meet the sort of people who want to meet me. There is definitely something wrong with them. Sane people who read my column laugh, then say "that girl's nuts. I wish her well, but I do hope I don't ever run into her." Then there are men called Scott, who want to meet me. "Who is this Scott character anyway? I'm really not in the mood to meet anyone new. I hate new people. They frighten me." "You'll like him. He's a City broker; he dresses well and drives a fast car. Also, I think he might be a closet gay. I might convert him." "Brilliant. Is the entire world a closet gay to you?"

And then Scott arrived. We could tell he had arrived because there was a huge roar of a Porsche engine as he pulled up very ostentatiously right outside the restaurant. Just to make sure everyone had seen him, he revved and revved the engine many more times than was necessary to park a car, then swaggered in swinging his Porsche key ring like John Wayne toting a gun. Any sensible woman would take one look at him and think, "You have got to be kidding." But I'm no ordinary woman. I looked at Scott and thought, "You have got to be kidding. But then again, maybe I'll give it a go." He strode across the restaurant and, after spotting Marcus, swung his keys around his fingers one more time then slammed them into his holster—I mean, pocket. He sat down and gave me a look that said, "I'll deal with you later," then pretty much ignored me for the rest of the evening. I was smitten. You know how it is when you have a glass of champagne and it makes you so immediately happy a tiny bit of you subconsciously thinks, "I don't care what the newspapers say about a glass of wine a day being good for your heart, this drinking business has got to be wrong. It's way too enjoyable to be healthy." Well, that's how I felt about Scott. He made me so instantly delirious with joy that it was perfectly obvious I had stumbled on something potentially deadly. It was love, or something that felt a lot like it but sadly wasn't it at all, at first sight. Having been rudely ignored by him for half an hour I was gazing obsessively at him as if I'd been hypnotized. The sexual tension must have been getting pretty thick—and the gay energy pretty thin—because after an hour Marcus got up with a decidedly huffy air, announced that he had a meeting to get to, and left me to it. At which point, Scott had to speak to me. He gave me his card, announcing him to be "Head of Asia-Pacific" (possibly he ran a section of the ocean), and told me to ring him.

҈

I rang him the next day and pretty much begged him to take me on a date. He hard-balled at first and said he wasn't sure. He'd just got out of a long relationship and he didn't really want to get serious with anyone else. Be still my beating heart! What was he trying to do, make me want to marry him? Eventually—after I insinuated that I might jump off Tower Bridge if he said no—he agreed to a date, and a few evenings later he took me for a very expensive dinner at one of those posh Japanese places where they chop things up in front of you that you have a horrible suspicion might still be alive. He seemed to enjoy this unfeasibly while I had to keep averting my eyes. He insisted we sit at the Teppanyaki grill table so we could see the chef at his work.

"He's an artist, this man," said Scott, as the little Japanese guy threw a lobster on to the range and smashed it in half with a meat cleaver. "Aaaaagah, yes, it's wonderful," I said, cringing behind my handbag and pretending to look at my phone. "Shall we have their special beef? Chef, some beef..." "Naaaaaaa, no!" I said, diving into my bag for fear that a cow might be led out and chopped into pieces in front of me. I wasn't at all sure about this broker with a passion for extreme food, but midway through dinner he suddenly fixed me with a deep, intense stare and told me I was beautiful. I don't know why this should make the difference between thinking someone might be a weirdo and thinking about saying yes to going back to his house for coffee after dinner, but somehow it seems to.

Scott lived in a very smart house in Knightsbridge—impressive, understated, wealthy looking. But the moment I got inside the door and walked up the staircase to the living room, I knew something was amiss. The house was lit by extremely low spot-lighting, and was in near darkness apart from the corners, which were illuminated by designer lamps. At the top of the staircase was a long corridor, off of which were a series of rooms all with closed doors.

Scott showed me into the living room and asked me rather formally to have a seat. I looked around. The place was like a show home that had never been lived in. Everything was obsessively neat, shiny, and flawless. He put the chrome coffee machine on in the kitchenette area, which was on a raised mezzanine platform above the living room, and said he would be back in a moment after he'd freshened up. I sat on the sofa, but daren't lean back and relax because the rows of cushions behind me were arranged in diamond formation, three deep, in descending order of size. Something told me that disturbing the formation would upset

Scott. I could hear him in the bathroom, running water and whirring away with his electric toothbrush. Fine, he's been at work all
day; he wants to freshen up. I sat there for a while and, when he
was still whirring I thought, "Maybe I could just have a quick
look around . . ." I crept down the corridor, past the bathroom,
and stood in front of the shut door at the end of the corridor.
Something told me this was his bedroom. I turned the handle silently and the door creaked ever so slightly as I pushed it open.

I listened in the direction of the bathroom and was reassured
by the continuing whirring sound. I pushed the door open further
to reveal a large room with a colonial feel. Dark wooden shutters at
the window, a shuttered wardrobe. The bed was perfectly made, as
if by room service, in luxurious linens and throws layered many
times over, with one corner turned down, as if evening turndown
service had just been in. I crept silently over the beige deep pile
carpet and reached out to touch the shuttered wardrobe. Shuttered
wardrobes never bode well. Instinct told me there was something
terrible in there. I put my hands on the two center doors and pulled
them wide open, then I clamped my hands over my mouth to stifle
a scream. In front of me, nine identical navy blue Savile Row tai-
lored suits hung like decapitated corpses.

⁓

I reached out and turned one of them to reveal a purple silk lining. I turned the one next to reveal an identical purple silk lining.
I went on turning and turning, faster and faster, but all the lin-
ings were purple. It was horrible. (The sound of screechy violins
should be playing now for those reading on the latest e-readers.
For the rest of you—shucks, I don't know what to tell you. Use
your imagination, I guess.) At the end of the row of suits, there

was an electronic revolving rack of Hermès ties, ranked in descending order of pattern density. There were about two hundred
of them, color coded, but with gaps after each nine, so nine deep
red, nine slightly lighter red, nine purpley red, nine magenta . . .
and so on all the way round. Holy Mother of God. My eyes traveled downward. Nine identical pairs of black polished Tod's loaf-
ers were lined up on the wardrobe floor. There were also nine
little cuff link boxes on the shelf at the side, above another shelf
bearing nine belts. I gasped and slammed the doors shut.

"Are you OK out there?" he called from the bathroom, the
electric toothbrush still whirring. My heart racing, I went back
into the corridor and shouted, "Yes, just looking at your photos."
He had huge professional black-and-white prints of the same
woman hanging all over the walls of the hallway. One in close-
up, her face leaning ostentatiously on her two hands put together
in prayer, like a studio shot of Judy Garland. One of her climbing
a mountain, dressed like Julie Andrews in *The Sound of Music.*
One of her dancing, in a tutu. One of her in a bikini on a beach.
"That's my mother," he called back. "Isn't she beautiful?" Jesus,
Mary, and all the saints.

I wandered into the kitchen area, where even the sound of the
coffee percolating now sounded sinister, like the choking sound
of someone being strangled, and opened a drawer. Sure enough
there were nine knives, nine forks, nine spoons. I opened a cupboard. Nine wineglasses, nine champagne flutes, nine tumblers.
In another cupboard I found food tins, all lined up symmetrically
with their labels facing out. Who lines up baked bean tins so the
front letters are visible? I asked myself desperately. Sometimes
the nines of things were grouped into subsets of three. So there
was, for example, a pile of nine tea towels consisting of three red,
three blue, and three white. The percolator reached a crescendo.

An image of me being throttled from behind with nine Hermès ties came into my head. Then I was being smashed on the head by a tin of baked beans, the Heinz label facing forward. "Oh shit," I said under my breath. I looked around the kitchen with wild eyes. I turned and Scott was standing behind me. I screamed.

Later, as we sipped our coffee, I tried to broach the subject by saying casually, "So, I notice you have nine of everything." How crazy did that sound, just saying it out loud?

"Yes, nine is a good number." He set his cup down and fixed me with his intense stare. "Ever wondered why they say a stitch in time saves nine, or why a cat is said to have nine lives?" He leaned toward me and lowered his voice. "Not only that, if any number is multiplied by nine all the digits always add up to nine." He paused and waited for me to react to this revelation.

"Hmm!" I squeaked.

"There is a magic symmetry in nine. It's almost spiritual."

He stared at me intensely. "No, it *is* spiritual. The Hebrews refer to nine as the symbol of immutable truth."

"Hmm!" I squeaked again, before getting a grip on myself.

I coughed. "Interesting. And so you . . . have everything in your house in groups of nine?"

"Exactly."

Why didn't I run for the hills? Why was I riveted to my seat? There was something strangely compelling about him. I caught myself thinking, "Maybe he's right. Maybe this whole nine thing is the key to everything."*

* The whole nine thing wasn't the key to everything.

"I'm pretty sure he's only one percent crazy," I told Marcus. "He might be ninety-nine percent wonderful." Marcus was adamant: "You can't put up with one percent crazy. It will infect the other ninety-nine percent." "I disagree. One percent crazy is manageable. I can handle one percent crazy. Besides, he's a boyfriend. A real, live boyfriend. Do you know the odds of a woman my age finding a boyfriend? I've got more chance of being run over by a bus." "This sounds quite similar to being run over by a bus," said Marcus.

I decided I would probably have to tell Scott I wasn't interesting in seeing him again. I would. But not until I had accepted his invitation to spend a week with his family in an idyllic farmhouse in the south of France. So sue me. I needed a holiday. And this was a beautiful, sprawling Provençal farmhouse with pale-blue shutters and a serene pool area looking out onto a meadow of lavender. This surely had all the makings of the perfect romantic break. Just me and Scott, Scott's godparents, and about ten of Scott's godparent's friends. OK, it had all the makings of a nightmare holiday. So sue me. I was feeling optimistic. I thought I could handle it.

෨

House parties in the south of France are apt to take on an identical format to house parties in Kensington and Chelsea. On the first evening, I came downstairs for drinks before dinner to find a living room full of prosperous Conservative types sipping sauvignon and talking about politics and the weather. Scott's godmother, a kindly lady who, from the start, looked like she very much took pity on me for being with Scott, ushered me around the room introducing me to people.

She pushed me first toward a wiry old gentleman who was he-roically wearing the trademark red corduroy trousers of the Chel-sea set despite the heat. "Scott's girlfriend writes for the paper you know." There was only one paper as far as these people were con-cerned. The paper they all read. The most right-wing paper.

"Oh, how marvelous," he said. "Tell me, do you know Ambrose Eustace-Pilkington?"

I confessed that I did not. "Oh," said the man, looking down-cast. "Oh, well, never mind then . . ." And he walked off.

Our hostess, apparently unperturbed by this, steered me eagerly toward another guest. "Minnie dear, this is Scott's girl-friend, you remember, the one who writes for the newspaper?"

"Oh, yes, of course, I've been dying to meet you. I've been longing to ask you, do you know Ambrose Eustace-Pilkington?" I told her that no, regretfully, I did not.

"Oh, I see. Such a pity." And off she wafted, too.

To be logical about it, I could see why AEP was such a pinup in this gathering. As far as I could remember, he was the Brussels correspondent, and there's nothing that interests a certain type of upper-crust Tory more than stories knocking the European Union. I could understand only too well that no matter what I did—I might split the atom in a martini glass on a silver tray right in front of them—I would never be interesting to these people unless I produced an anecdote involving myself and sweet AEP. We didn't even have to be in Brussels eating waffles at the time. Anything would do. A chance encounter in the newsroom, a fleeting drink at the Goring Hotel after work.

But I had nothing.

I told them I knew—slight exaggeration—David Cameron, George Osborne, Tony Blair, Gordon Brown, Bill Clinton, Hillary

Clinton—well, I had met all of them (briefly)—but none of that was remotely diverting to them.

I told them I had recently traveled to Iraq and been shot at by insurgents while looping the loop in a Black Hawk with teenage gunner boys swinging from ropes out of the doors like trapeze artists with heavy machine guns. "But what news of Ambrose?" they demanded. "He really does write the most brilliant journalism about the EUSSR—ha ha haa! Are you sure you've never met him?" It wore me down. I thought about telling the next person who asked me that I did know AEP, but then again I couldn't very well change my story now, could I? And what would I say I knew about him when I knew nothing? It would look terrible if I made something up and then somebody met him and told him. I hid myself away in a corner and sipped my drink.

"Excuse me," said a tiny voice behind me, "are you Scott's girlfriend?" I turned round to face an ancient, minuscule lady in a long lacy dress.

"Yes," I said suspiciously.

"The one who writes for the newspaper?" she said in a frail, watery voice.

"Yes."

"I just wanted to ask, do you—"

"NO!"

When Scott came into the bedroom to look for me, I was busy cutting up a piece of cardboard I had found in the children's playroom.

"What are you doing?" he said.

"I'm making a sign," I said, picking up a black marker pen and beginning to write my new slogan.

"A sign?"

"Yes, to wear around my neck at the dinner table. Or I might just wear it all the time."

"You can't do that."

"I can and I will," I said, punching two raggedy holes in either side of the top of the cardboard with the end of a pair of scissors. I threaded a piece of ribbon from my vanity bag through the holes and put the contraption over my head. "There," I said triumphantly.

"NO I DO NOT KNOW AMBROSE EUSTACE-PILKINGTON," said the sign in big, thick black letters.

"I absolutely forbid you to wear that sign to dinner."

"Well, maybe just to breakfast then. Or at the door when a new set of guests arrive."

"I forbid it absolutely."

"But this is going to save so much time and stop me shouting at little old ladies, which I feel terrible about. The poor dear looked like she was about to have a heart attack. And this is very restrained, don't you think? I was going to say Ambrose Fucking Eustace-Pilkington, or Ambrose Eustace Fucking-Pilkington, or even Ambrose Fucking-Useless Pilkington, but I couldn't decide where to put the hyphen."

෴

After drinks, we all divided up into car loads and set off in convoy for "the brasserie" as they called it, explaining, "There's nothing fancy round here, but we make do." The brasserie turned out not to be a brasserie at all, but a Michelin-starred restaurant in a country club with a cheese trolley the size of my flat groaning under the weight of a consignment of unpasteurized goat's milk–based merchandise worth the GDP of Guatemala. The smell was epic. It was as if ten bodies were buried just under the floor.

I was seated between Tiny Little Lacy Lady and Red Corduroy Man, who studiously ignored me. As Scott had forbidden me to wear the sign—by turning pink, blowing out his cheeks, and threatening to explode like a balloon—I decided to apologize to Little Lacy, which was, at least, a conversation opener. "I'm so sorry, I'm just so tired. From the journey, you know."

"Of course, my dear, please don't worry about it. I only wanted to ask if you—"

"Knew Ambrose Eustace-Pilkington."

"No. Why? Who's he?"

"The Brussels correspondent."

"Oh, I never read the foreign pages. I like the columnists, especially the funny ones." And she gave me a look.

"Really?" I said, feeling the warm glow of oncoming praise begin to wash over me.

"Yes, and you know who my favorite is, don't you?"

"No," I giggled, overcome with modesty.

"Yes you do."

"No, really, you're going to have to tell me."

"Well, it's someone who writes terribly witty columns."

"I can't guess."

"Yes you can! Come on!"

"Ooh, is it Simon Heffer?" I said, determined to make her say my name. But she didn't say my name. She clapped her hands with joy and cried, "See! I knew you would guess! Do you know him?"

☙

Halfway through the meal, Red Corduroy Man leaned over. I had run out of conversation with Tiny Little Lacy Lady, having gone through all my Simon Heffer anecdotes, and was now fiddling with the new digital camera Scott had given me as a "going on holiday present."

"I say, that's a rather smart camera," said the man, who turned out to be Scott's great uncle. "Yes," I said. "It was a present from Scott."

Unbeknownst to me, Scott's great uncle was extremely deaf, and I was sitting on the side of his worse ear.

"Scott bought it as a present? For me? Oh, but that's too kind," he exclaimed, and grabbed the camera out of my hand.

"No!" I shrieked internally. "Give me back my camera, you silly old fool. I've just got myself a rich boyfriend who buys me presents. I won't let you ruin it for me!"

"No, no," I said, as discreetly as I could. But Scott's great uncle was already waving the camera around.

"Look everybody," he was shouting, "Scott's bought me a camera!"

Thankfully the rest of the guests were so preoccupied with chattering about cheese that they didn't look up. I had one more chance before he shouted again.

"I'm sorry," I said, "I've given you the wrong impression . . ."

"Hmmm? What's that?" And he started to press the buttons. As the photos I had already taken came up on the viewfinder I realized I had a far worse problem to deal with than losing my camera. If I allowed this daft old fruit to take the camera, he would soon find a series of candid shots of me posing in my birthday suit, taken by Scott as we goofed around on the night before we left for France.

I had to get that camera out of his hands right now or he was going to show nude pictures of me to the cream of West London society over the Michelin-starred cheese course. In desperation, I did something entirely instinctual. I leaned over to him and pressed my leg against his. It had the desired effect, dislodging his attention from the camera instantly, which he dropped on to the table as if he couldn't care less about it.

"Hmm, I say, is that your leg I can feel?"

Oh God. "Yes . . . ?" I said, still not really understanding consciously what my unconscious self was doing.

"Hmm, that's nice."

"The thing is, that's my camera," I said, putting it back in my evening bag.

"Scott was going to give me your camera, eh?" he said, pressing his leg back on mine.

"No, you don't understand. Scott wasn't going to give you any camera. He only gave me a camera."

"Blasted cheek of the boy. Well, I don't care. I've got a camera. Bought it in Singapore," he said rather childishly.

"But I want to ask you something," he continued. "Will you come to my room later? After everyone has gone to bed?"

As soon as we were outside the restaurant and walking toward the car on our own, I took Scott to one side: "I have to tell you something. I may have accidentally hit on your Uncle Harold." Scott looked at me as if he had no way of digesting what I had just said.

"What do you mean?"

"What I said. I may have accidentally, or in a way, accidentally on purpose, hit on . . ."

"You hit on Harold?"

"I didn't mean to. Well, I did sort of mean to. But I was doing it as a decoy."

Scott's face was getting redder and redder.

"He was going to steal my camera."

"What are you talking about? Why would Harold steal your camera?"

"He misheard me because he's deaf. He thought you'd bought the camera for him and he took it from me and was about to pass it round the table, naked photos and all, and I had to stop him. I couldn't think of anything else to divert his attention. So I may have felt him up under the table."

Scott's cheeks expanded until it looked like his face was about to explode. When he regained his composure he said very slowly, "Uncle Harold is eighty-six years of age. He's a professor of ancient history at Oxford University. He was awarded the MBE this year for services to his country. He has been on his own since my great aunt Mildred died ten years ago and you're telling me you felt him up [incredulous voice] under the table ?"

"Well, it sounds worse than it is. I mean, he enjoyed it . . ."

ᠹᠣ

After the mix-up over the camera, and me accidentally hitting on his uncle, Scott was understandably in an unstable mood as we drove home. We sat in silence as he revved violently around the corners of the Provençal roads. Then suddenly his mood seemed to change and he pulled up and parked the car by the side of the road.

"Look at that," he said, staring into a magical valley lit by moonlight. "My favorite spot."

He reached over and put an arm around me and we cuddled up. The gear stick was stuck agonizingly against my hip bone, but I didn't mind.

"I'm really sorry about groping Uncle Harold," I said.

Scott smiled. "He's a silly old fool."

Maybe it was the magical Provençal countryside, maybe it was the fact that he'd just forgiven me for groping his uncle, but suddenly I decided that whatever crazy tactics were necessary to keep Scott happy, I would learn them. So long as I didn't grope any more elderly relatives things would be fine, I told myself. And if I grouped everything in sight into sets of nine I was sure everything would be hunky-dory. No groping, just grouping, I vowed. I can do this.

༺༻

On the way back through France, we stopped off in Paris for the night. Scott had booked us into the luxurious George V, but as soon as we got there and he handed over his Porsche keys to the bellboy a dark pall fell upon his features and he declared himself exhausted from the drive.

As I flounced around the room, squealing with joy at the Bulgari minis in the bathroom, he slumped into bed, pulled the sheets over his head, and wouldn't come out. I was forced to go down to the bar and sit on my own with a cocktail. It wasn't long before the Arab sheiks were asking me if I wanted to do a little business. "Oh well," I thought, "at least they're not asking me if I know Ambrose Eustace-Pilkington."

"Are you alone?" asked a voice at my side.

"What are the chances?" I exclaimed, as I recognized the guy who lived a few doors down from me in London who walked his cats.

"Do you stay here often?" he asked, installing himself on a seat next to me and motioning to the bartender.

"No! First time. What are you doing here?"

"My mother's French. Lives near Versailles. Once a year we meet here and I take her shopping on the Rue du Faubourg."

"How lovely."

"It's just about bearable. She pays for the hotel. And the shopping. I couldn't afford it. Who are you here with?"

"Oh, you don't want to know. It's too hard to explain."

"I see. Well, everyone's got to earn a living."

"No! Not that hard to explain. Oh well, it seems easy to explain now. I'm with a boyfriend who's gone mad and taken to his bed."

"How awkward. Can I buy you a drink? It's on mother."

We drank his mother's weight in cocktails and then we went for a walk through the Paris streets. It was romantic. It was also weird. I had been hoping for a moonlit stroll along the Champs-Elysées with Scott, and here I was with the guy who lived down the road from me in South London.

"You look different without your cats walking by your side," I said.

"I suppose I look like an idiot walking cats. It's just that I lost a cat once. He went missing one day and I never found him again. It sort of traumatized me. I'm paranoid it will happen again. I love animals."

"Me, too," I said.

"Oh? What animals do you have?"

"Two horses, two rabbits, two cats. Oh, and two clown fish."

"A veritable ark. If God sends a great flood to cover the earth you shall surely be saved. You don't keep the horses in Balham I take it?"

"No, in Surrey, where I hope to move one day."

"My sister's got a place in Surrey. I spend weekends there. I love it."

We had so many odd things in common—very few people

liked Surrey, for a start—but in all the years we had lived a few doors down from each other we'd hardly exchanged two words. We might never have known how much we liked each other if we hadn't bumped into each other two hundred miles from home.

We walked and walked down tree-lined streets full of bars and cafés with twinkly lights and then we stopped walking and looked into each other's eyes. An accordion played in the distance. This was obviously where we . . .

My phone rang. It was Scott. "Where are you?" he yelled. "I've been worried sick. I've had the hotel staff looking everywhere for you. I'm having an emergency up here."

"I thought you were sleeping," I said.

"I need you to come back now. It's urgent. Something terrible has happened."

I turned to cat man.

"I've got to go."

He shrugged. "See you back in London."

"Yes, see you in Balham." I started to run away.

"Oh," I called back, "I don't know your name."

"Noah," he said, laughing.

❧

When I got to the room, Scott was sitting on the edge of the bed staring at the wall opposite.

"What's wrong?"

"The shoes," he said, wide-eyed. If he hadn't had a close-shaven head I have no doubt his hair would have been standing on end. As it was, he was puce in the face and his head stubble was kind of standing to attention.

"Shoes?"

"The shoes are in the wrong place."

I stared at the wall where I had lined up three pairs of my shoes when I unpacked my suitcase.

"But they're nice and neat," I said, protesting my innocence.

"I don't like them lined up there. I want them lined up against the other wall."

∾

I got a flight back to London. On the pavement outside arrivals I took deep, blissful breaths of the cold, slightly smelly Heathrow night air. A new beginning, I thought. All I wanted was to be alone, my own person again, in my own space, serene, at peace, calm . . .

My phone rang. A voice yelled, "I am coming inside by arrivals Sofitel opposite! Now!"

It was the taxi driver of the car I had ordered when I was waiting for my flight at the Paris airport, giving me the traditional South London homecoming. "I'm sorry?"

"I coming inside arrivals by Sofitel now!" he yelled again, sounding furious.

Did that mean he was coming inside the terminal building to meet me? Or that he was outside arrivals opposite the Sofitel? Or that he was at the Sofitel, opposite arrivals?

"I'm sorry," I said, "I didn't catch that. Where are you?"

"I am inside coming by arrivals outside the Sofitel. You go departures now opposite!"

Oh lordy. "OK, I'll be right there," I said, but I hadn't a clue where he was. I wandered from arrivals to departures and back again. I went upstairs in one lift and down in another. I took elevators; I took travelators. I went in lifts again. My shoulders ached. My new spirit of independence was crushed in thirty minutes flat of trudging around Heathrow with all my bags, alone, unloved, and the only thing I had to look forward to at the end of it was a South London minicab. Oh why did I have to get all uppity about lining up my shoes and ditch a perfectly good boyfriend? If Scott would only come back now, I would get in a black cab with him, go back to his place, and spend the evening lining up my shoes with no complaint whatsoever, I thought.

Every few minutes the cab driver rang and demanded frantically, "Where you?" Then when I said where I was he repeated a version of the same thing. At one point he demanded, "I inside?"

"I don't know, mate," I said. Where were any of us, really, and did anyone really know anything?

I couldn't tell him I couldn't understand him. But why couldn't I? I supposed because it wasn't politically correct. All the same, it seemed a bit silly that I couldn't explain myself. After all, it was the truth, and it would clear up a lot of the confusion.

We finally bumped into each other quite by accident; he was on his phone shouting, "I here in arriving Sofitel!" And I was on mine screaming, "I Sofitel now!" when we walked right past each other and heard each other talking on the phone.

I was weary. I had very little fight left in me. But unfortunately I am not the sort of person who will lie down when I ought to, so as he opened his trunk to put my bags in I said,

"I need to ask you something. Do you promise not to get upset?"

"Of course, you can ask me anything."

"If I told you I couldn't understand a word you were saying on the phone just now because of your accent—just hypothetically, I'm not saying I am saying that, I'm saying if I did say that—would you mind?"

"Of course I wouldn't mind. If it was the truth."

"Exactly what I thought. The truth cannot be wrong, can it?"

"The truth no wrong. The truth shall set us free," he said, suddenly making sense.

"Exactly. Exactly what I thought. OK, well, in that case, the reason I couldn't work out where you were just now is that I couldn't understand a word you were saying. Because of your accent . . ."

"I actually find that deeply offensive." Where did that come from? I looked round. A well-dressed businessman standing next to me who had just got out of a limo repeated, "I said I find that deeply offensive."

"What do you mean? I'm not talking to you. And anyway, how can you find it offensive? You're . . . you're . . ."

"A rich white Englishman? I'm offended on behalf of this man here," he said, making a very elaborate gesture with his arm toward my cab driver.

I puffed myself up. After putting in the research, I was on firm ground. I felt as smug as a person who has just dropped her mobile phone in a puddle seconds after taking out an insurance policy.

"Well, actually, you're wrong to be offended on his behalf," I said, pausing for effect before delivering my coup de grâce:

"Because he is not offended at all."

"I don't believe that."

"It's true. Ask him. Go on."

"All right, I will. Are you offended by this girl here offensively dismissing your grasp of the English language even though you have probably been in this country for a long time and are a hardworking member of our society, contributing to our economy and deserving of a little more respect and a little less oppression?"

"Yeeeeeah," I said, shrugging, "I wouldn't say 'offensively dismissing,' more 'haplessly misinterpreting' if anything . . ." But I still felt on firm ground, so I turned expectantly to the cab driver. The cab driver looked worried.

"I don't know . . ." he said, suddenly looking crestfallen.

"What do you mean, you don't know? You said you were happy about me not being able to understand you just now. You said if it was the truth then the truth shall set us free."

"I know, but now he puts it like that I don't feel so happy . . ."

The man smiled at him, then pulled a disgusted face at me.

"You mind your language next time you insult a person of color and ethnicity. This nation was built on migrant labor."

"Don't tell me about migrant labor!" I shouted as he wheeled his Mulberry suitcase away. "My grandfather came down off a mountainside in southern Italy! He was black as the ace of spades when he had a suntan!"

But he was gone.

I turned to the cab driver. "Can we just go, please?"

"I'm really quite upset at the oppression," he mumbled as he put my cases in the car.

"You're upset at the oppression," I said. "I'm dating a man who makes me line up my shoes."

၆ၑ

I cornered Marcus the next day. "What the hell were you doing introducing me to a maniac?"

"I thought you liked the fact that he was one percent crazy."

"He's not one percent crazy. He's ninety-nine point nine percent crazy. He made me line up my shoes."

"Oh dear."

"Yes, oh dear. Can you please confine your introductions to

people without severe mental illnesses from now on, if it's not too much trouble?"

❧

"Do not try to go out with any more men, for God's sake. My nerves will never stand it," said Sally testily. I had come back from Paris to find her in an unusually frazzled and bad-tempered state after a very rare domestic fracas. It turned out that Bobby had secretly taken the Canaletto to Sotheby's to fund the kids' university years. Nico hadn't disappeared at all, but had gone on one of his soul-searching trips, the mood to discover Patagonia having taken him while he was sawing through a particularly tough piece of parquet. He had told Bobby about his departure, but Bobby had forgotten. Sally had told Bobby about the Canaletto having gone missing, but Bobby had thought it best to let her think Nico might have stolen it in order to buy himself some time until he could get a valuation and thus present her with a more tempting proposition to sell the family heirloom. When Nico came back to finish fitting the floor two weeks later, Sally had just put the phone down, having reported the matter to the police.

"Darling, I tell you, he couldn't have been sweeter about it," said Bobby to me now, as Sally dragged murderously on a Marlboro while tweeting that her marriage was over.

"Honestly, dear heart, that man really is Jesus Christ come again. Talk about turning the other cheek. He said he couldn't have cared a fig for Sizzle accusing him of being an art thief. He said, 'What's a little wrongful arrest between friends?' Isn't that heaven? Are you sure you couldn't bear to have sex with him, angel? He'd be a frightfully good husband, I'm willing to bet on it."

"Quite sure," I said.

"Hasn't poor Nico suffered enough?" snarled Sally.

"Really, Sizzle, you're being a perfect pain. If you carry on like this I'm going to have to put you over my knee and spank you."

"Bor-ing," said Sally, tweeting a link to a picture of the empty space where the Canaletto had been.

∽

It should have been easy to ditch a man who made me line up my shoes but it wasn't, strangely. After I stopped ringing Scott, and he didn't ring me, I started to feel a bit weird. I was all alone, I realized. Very, very alone. Possibly forever. I started to reflect on how I had come to this point.

All I can say is, I blame the internal satnav. You know, the one that malfunctioned when my teenage sweetheart David was waving me down all those years ago as I set off on the superhighway of romantic failure, trying to get me to take the turnoff marked "Happiness."

I might well have taken it, if the darned satellite navigation hadn't been faulty. It never tells me where my exits are until it's too late, and then I miss them and it starts barking at me to "turn around when possible." But by that time I don't want to admit I've gone wrong. I want to prove to myself that the extra miles haven't been a waste of time, taking me out of my way, so I keep on. And on. And on. There's bound to be another exit coming up sooner or later, I tell myself. And I bet the next exit gets me there even quicker. Ooh, here's one now! "Keep right."

Your happy ending disappears further and further into the rearview mirror, but you can't turn now. You can't ever turn. You know if you turn around you will have to drive for miles in the other direction and you may never get there, and anyway you may as well just accept you've missed your turn. So you keep going and you keep going, as the road gets ever more impassable, and before you know where you are you're trying to drive a truck through the garden of a cottage in Chipping Campden. And yes, I've let my metaphor get out of control. I'm aware of that, thanks.

∽

After a few weeks, Ricky Moon, star of reality TV Show *Bow Belles*, professional wearer of Dolce & Gabbana tight trousers and inventor of the catchphrase, "Fuck you!" grew tired of hanging off the arm of a handsome, debonair, wealthy, kind, intelligent, articulate man and announced to *Yeh!* magazine that he was actually straight. It caused a huge hoo-ha and his father threatened to disown him, but Ricky declared that he could no longer hide his true feelings for fellow cast member De-Shaznia Winters and the pair were snapped on the red carpet of the TV Choice/Reality Star of Britain awards.

At last, Simon was available for carbohydrate-free dining with yours truly.

We went for breakfast at the Wolseley, where we both ordered eggs Benedict, mine as they came, his with all sorts of special cadences, including no chives because of his allium intolerance.

"Is that a real thing, or a made-up allergy for professional purposes?" I asked, as the waiter did some especially loud under-his-breath tutting.

"It's real, thank you very much," said Simon, giving me a smoldering look as he sipped sexily from his decaf cappuccino.

Being with Simon was heavenly. Every woman in the room eyed me with envy of murderous proportions because he was so good-looking he made your womb ache.

"So, what's happening in your love life?" said Simon. It was his favorite subject.

"Still with Scott."

"Oh dear. How absurd of you. Well, I've got myself a new man."

"Already? You've only been split up from tight-trouser boy a week."

He leaned in close. "I can't say much because it's top secret and we don't want to get in all the papers, but he's currently starring in a top West End show and he's an unbelievable Adonis." He started messing about with his BlackBerry and before long the picture of an unbelievable Adonis flashed up. "Lucky me, eh. I think this could be The One."

"This is unbelievable. Why can't you be single for just five minutes?"

"What's the matter with you? You should be happy for me."

Yes, I should, if I weren't planning to make you have babies with me. I sipped my mineral water. I supposed that if he married the star of the West End's most camp musical they might use me as a surrogate.

"So, when are you going to get a nice boyfriend? Still getting cold feet every time you think how fabulous your life is going to be without a mad man in it and how you won't be able to spend hours moaning about how sick you feel from the stress? You know your problem? You need to drag yourself into the twenty-first century. You need to go online."

Oh god, please no, not the online dating lecture. I will do anything to avoid the online dating lecture. I will go online dating rather than listen to the online dating lecture.

"Fine, I will go online," I said.

∾

The people who swear by online dating will tell you that all the world's problems have been solved by it. They make finding a partner on the Internet sound as easy as switching on the kettle in the morning. "Oh, just go online," they say, as if one need only fire up the MacBook, click on Match.com, and hey presto, there's your happy ending.

If I hear the phrase "I met my husband online," one more time I will scream. What happened when I went online could be sub-titled Fifty Worst Dates. However, I will spare you most of those and just give you the edited lowlights.

There were countless twenty-year-old college boys who were very excited about the fact that I was nearly forty and could teach them things. Evidently they believed that something magical happened to a woman as she approached middle age that made her a qualified sex instructor. These I messaged back politely to say I was sorry to disappoint them but I knew nothing interest-ing whatsoever to do in bed, apart from eating club sandwiches while watching old episodes of *Columbo*, so it was probably better we didn't meet.

Out of the ones I did meet, there was a funny little man with eyebrows that stood on end who took me to see a David Mamet play, which was almost worse than the time I had to run away from the date who took me to see a David Hare play, but not quite. There was a good-looking guy called Nick who said, "Oh," when I introduced myself as his date. I walked into the deserted bar where we had arranged to meet, ordered a drink, and stood there waiting. And he walked in, looked around, walked up to the bar, ordered his drink, and stood right next to me sipping it, checking his watch and looking nervously at the door until I said "Er, I think I am the woman you are supposed to meet." At which point, he looked me up and down, visibly deflated by about five inches with disappointment, and said, "Oh."

But the worst by far was the advertising executive who broke wind.

The Farting Man was a bit like the Smoking Man from *The X-Files*, only not as sexy. The Smoking Man was mysterious. The Farting Man had no mystique at all once he had discharged his various emissions.

He was very good-looking. He was cultured, and intelligent. According to his online resume, he had a high-flying career with one of the leading ad agencies and was obviously a high earner.

The reason he couldn't get a girlfriend, however, was that unless the dating site had scratch-and-sniff technology you couldn't prepare yourself for his only flaw.

Within seconds of me approaching him in the lounge bar of a hotel he dropped his first cluster bomb.

"Parp!" it went.

Nobody tells you when you are a little girl dressing up in bed sheets and your mother's high heels, pretending to be a bride, that one day you will go on a date with a handsome man who breaks wind. It is most definitely not in the script. And yet it happens. But because no one discusses that it happens, there is no template for dealing with it.

I know, for example, that when a handsome prince goes down on his knee and produces a glass slipper, the thing to do is to squeeze your tiny foot into it.

When a handsome man goes down on one knee and farts . . . no, I've got nothing. Not a single clue as to how to respond to that.

I approached the table, smiled, said, "Hi, you must be Richard," and he stood up, went "Parp!" and I drew a blank.

What the hell?

I told myself it might be nerves. I felt sorry for him. I decided to give him the benefit of the doubt. I insisted on buying him a drink and flatly refused every time he looked like he was getting up to buy me one. I did everything possible to keep him riveted to the chair so that he wouldn't go "Parp!" again.

For the record, this is not the right response. If your date greets you by breaking wind, just turn around and walk straight back out.

But because I'm such a sucker for a pity case I decided to not only sit out that date but to go on another one with him. "What is the matter with you, you stupid moron?" I screamed at myself in the mirror as I prepared for this totally extraneous second date.

The next time we met, it was in a restaurant and I was braced for all sorts of gastric complications. But there were none. This time, he was perfectly normal, digestively speaking. It wasn't until the end of a very pleasant meal, with some rather diverting banter, that things went awry.

The waiter placed the bill in the middle of the table and we both sat staring at it like it was an unexploded bomb.

Now, call me old-fashioned, but I think a man should pay for dinner, notwithstanding the fact that we are all equal now. Fine, so a lot of women earn more than men and shouldn't expect special treatment or ask for favors, etc., etc. But dinner is different.

And the reason I think that is this: in order to get myself on a date, as a woman, I have had to spend in the region of £ 100 and sometimes ten times that depending on the seriousness of the prospect.

Hair styling, including having my roots done, can cost the lion's share of that, but then there is often a new outfit to be bought, along with new items of makeup, spray-tans, manicures, pedicures, and waxing. Above all, waxing. No woman can go on a date nowadays without making sure she is good to go in the regions of her body normally governed by the Forestry Commission because, as we know, things move pretty fast in modern dating.

The man, meanwhile, has only to pull his best shirt and underpants out of the closet and, hey presto, he's set.

The least the man can do, therefore, is pick up the tab for dinner. Especially when the tab is only £60, as it was on this particular evening.

But the tab sat in the middle of the table, and the Farting Man and I stared and stared at it and sat with our hands on our laps until finally he picked it up like a doggy-poo bag and said: "Hmm, well, I suppose I did have the steak . . . and a glass of wine . . . and you drank mineral water, and had chicken . . . which was three pounds less . . ."

And he pulled out of his pocket a horrible little dog-eared wallet and fished out of it the exact money that he owed for his meal, right down to the last penny. And he put the notes and loose change down on the table and looked at me until I took my wallet out and made up the difference.

"Keep the change," he said to the waiter, after I put down about 50p too much.

❧

"Yuk," said Sally. "The farting I could deal with. But the tiny little wallet and the check-dividing stuff, no way."

It was funny enough when I was with Sally laughing about it. But when I got home and sat in my lonely flat and thought of my dating disasters a strange thing happened.

On the basis that anything was better than the Farting Man, or the Man Who Said Oh, I rang Scott.

This action can be explained by the Theory of Dating Relativity.

The Theory of Dating Relativity is a bit like Einstein's Theory of Relativity only instead of dealing with Space and Time, it deals with Dating and Desperation. It states that the severity of the Dickhead one is prepared to date at any one time is equal to the number of Dating Disasters one has had, multiplied by one's Age, to the power of 2.

Thus: $D = DDA$ squared.

Scott didn't answer. I left a voice mail. And a text. And when Scott didn't get back to me, I became distraught. This was pathetic. I was scared. I was scared I was going to be alone forever.

Something I can only describe as cold turkey set in. I don't mean cold turkey in a poetic, metaphorical sense. I mean in a literal sense. I lay in bed shivering and sweating and scratching my skin and getting up only to eat toast before crawling back under the covers to moan and groan.

෯

After a few days, I got up to go and buy takeout KFC, which I forgot to eat, then put in the fridge, and then, days after that, devoured with gusto. This is one useful thing about relationship breakups: they force you to eat all the out-of-date stuff in the fridge. Freed from the fear of poisoning, liberated by a great sense of not caring whether you live or die, you tuck into a piece of takeout chicken, still in the soggy paper box on the third shelf down four days after you bought it, and make the following startling discovery: it tastes amazing. Better than it did when you bought it, better even than the day after you bought it. In fact, it seems to have got exponentially better for each day it has been shriveling in the fridge. It's like opening Pandora's box to discover that there is nothing better for cold turkey than cold takeout chicken. I've done a bit of research on the Internet and I'm afraid I cannot get official clearance to recommend eating leftover chicken takeout for anything longer than four days, which is a shame, because I suspect that after five days it tastes sublime.

Happy people don't know this, you see. Happy people in happy relationships don't get to discover what four-day-old takeout chicken tastes like. I pity them; I really do. The poor, blinkered idiots.

"What the hell is happening to you?" said Sally after I made it to her house one night for some rescue salad.

I was rubbing my arms as I sat poking at a plate of rocket, watercress, Parmesan, and quails eggs. "I don't know. I feel all itchy." We sat in silence while I ate and scratched and checked my mobile phone every ten seconds for messages. "I hate to sound dramatic, but I'm going to have to call him or find another boy-friend, or do something to make me feel like I'm not going to be alone forever. Or my white blood cells are going to atrophy and my entire body is going to start rejecting itself."

"Don't be ridiculous. That's not going to happen." But she didn't look convinced.

⟋⟍

Elizabeth Hall was billed as the best relationship therapist in town. She would tell me what was wrong with me in seconds and then she would put it right, was the way Simon sold her to me. She had helped many of his celebrity clients who, he announced proudly, were among the most fucked-up people on the planet.

She turned out to be a brassy fiftysomething Australian lady with big, blond hair who took one look at me as I stumbled into the consulting room of her large London home and said, "Siddaaaan doll." As I looked around for a chair by her desk, she sighed as if this were all mind-numbingly routine, and pointed me to a really uncomfortable hard plastic chair in the middle of the virtually empty room, miles away from her desk. I plodded over to it and sat there, marooned like a four-year-old in kindergarten on the naughty chair, staring across the vast sea of room while she, sitting behind her big important desk, looked me up and down silently and didn't say anything. I looked at my watch. This was costing me £150 an hour. I started timing my money disappearing.

The most alarming thing was, I could see through the window into the garden where a man I took to be her husband was chopping wood furiously, as if he were imagining the fallen tree sections were someone's head. Possibly hers.

"These are mad axe-murderer people," was the thought that went through my head.

After about £20 worth of nothing she pulled her glasses down to the tip of her nose, peered over them, and said, "Gotta pin?" When I hesitated for several seconds, trying to work out why I would need a pin—was she going to make me perform acupuncture on myself?—she tapped the desk to denote a spare pen and a scrap of paper and made me walk all the way over to get it. Then she started reciting homework orders.

She told me to order a long list of books from Amazon with psychobabble titles by authors with first names like Melody and

Pia. And she gave me a leaflet of something called "Positive Affirmations," which I had to recite every morning and evening and which were, without exception, totally unfathomable. For example, "In my heart I AM the wisdom of the universe."

"What does that even mean?" I asked her. "Never moind," she drawled in her rough Aussie patois. "Ye daaarnt needa knaiiiuuu."

I left her feeling none the wiser. But by the next week she had stopped the itching. And the week after that she had me keeping down solids.

Then she let me in on a secret: "You wanna knaiiu why the world's gone med? Why there are so many crazy people out there?" She was wearing a kaftan this time, and kept putting her hands together in the prayer position and bowing slightly while playing twangy twangy music on her iPod.

Her husband was still in the garden chopping, sweat pouring from his head.

Knowing why so many people were med, I mean mad, seemed like a useful thing to know, so I nodded. She pointed to the back of her neck. "This."

"I'm sorry?"

"Knaiiu what this is?"

"Your neck?"

"That's the amygdala gland, doll. Right there in the back of yer nick. It's the gland that governs yer reactions. Know what's wrong with yer reactions?"

I shook my head. "All the instant technology we use has fucked 'em up. People are reacting too quickly to everything. And they're reacting to things they oughtn't react to at all. They can't not react. They've got overactive amygdalas."

It was kind of a bummer that my life seemed to have narrowed to a choice between a man who grouped objects into sets of nine and a therapist who believed there was a second brain in the backs of our necks making us crazy, but I tossed a coin and went with the gland lady. On the basis that you fight fire with fire I could see how fighting craziness with something equally or possibly more crazy might just work. And indeed, it did seem to be working.

After a few weeks in Dr. Hall's expert care, I started to enjoy life again. In fact, I felt so good I went online and posted a new profile photo of myself in tight riding breeches.

What was I thinking?

のの

Like Monty Python's Mr. Creosote I told myself: just one more wafer-thin date.

He advertised himself as a "go-getting sporty type" who wanted "someone special with whom to share the good things in life." But when he turned up he was an accountant called Terry.

I met him outside Sloane Square station.

"Shall we go for dinner?" I suggested.

"I've already had my dinner," he said, clinging to his backpack.

"Drink, then?"

"I don't drink alcohol."

"Coffee? Tea? Milkshake?"

Over frappuccino in Starbucks he told me that his favorite thing to do was row a boat on the Thames. I told him I once took a rigid inflatable out off the coast of Sardinia, which was fun. "I don't like hot places. The sun exacerbates my alopecia," he said.

The only good thing to say about Terry was that by the end of the evening, I was more than happy to go home alone and prepare to live alone my entire life until I died alone, lying alone undiscovered for weeks, until I was eaten by my own cats.

∾

Dr. Hall didn't want to know I had "relapsed" online. "I can't hilp you because you are resistant to mah methods," she said exasperatedly when I phoned her. "I may be able to put you in touch with a guy who can hilp you, but he's very expensive and he practices from a teepee in his back garden in Brighton."

"What does he do?" I could barely hear her for the sound of squawking and panpipes in the background. She had evidently moved on to rainforest wisdom.

"Cranial."

"Cranial?"

"Yeah. It's the only thing that'll hilp you now."

"How is this happening?" I asked Sally as we pored over *Heat* magazine and munched a mélange of peppers, deviled chicken pieces, and beetroot. "Apparently I'm going to need a lobotomy. Elizabeth says cranial is the only thing that can help me now."

"Don't be stupid, she means cranial massage."

"Oh. Will that help me?"

"I shouldn't think so."

"She says I've got to go to a guy who practices inside a teepee in his garden in Brighton and charges three hundred pounds an hour."

"No you don't. You can get it at the Shangri-La opposite Victoria station for £50. Only be careful they don't try to give you a happy ending."

"A happy ending would be good," I thought. Obviously I meant the sort where I walk off into the sunset with a man who is neither an art thief, nor a neurotic shoe-tidying maniac, nor a compulsive farter, nor a boating enthusiast with a backpack. Nor, if it was at all possible—although I accept this was a bit nitpicky—a man who walked his cats every day. I'd settle for someone who just walked cats, say, on weekends. Was this too much to ask?

4

A Girl's Guide to Running Away

In which I go on holiday with a silly person who makes me drive her car into the sea (that's my story and I'm sticking to it).

"No please, not Gigi. Anyone but Gigi."

I begged Sally not to make me go on a girl's shopping day with the richest, silliest woman in London.

"I like Gigi; she's fun." (It was pronounced Giggy, not Gee-Gee, which seemed to make her more annoying somehow.)

"She's not fun. She's stupid. There is a difference."

"Come to mine at eleven. We'll take my car. I want to go to Biba and Cath Kidston and a few other places down the bottom end."

Down the bottom end meant down the bottom end of the King's Road. We never said where we were going to go any more specifically than that because we never had the energy or intuitive flair to shop on any other street, apart from visiting Topshop and H&M in Knightsbridge, occasionally. I also once took Sally to Ikea in Croydon, where she bought the EU Daim bar mountain from the Swedish food shop, but that's another story entirely. (Does the EU still let things pile up in "mountains?" Possibly not. Those were the days, eh?)

At 11 A.M. I was sitting around Sally's breakfast bar but there was no sign of Gigi. At 11:45 we heard a cab door slam and a commotion outside—"Why is there never any bell on this house?"—and a fist thumped the door. Sally lit a cigarette as she went to answer. "For God's sake, Gigi, the bell's where it always is, on the right-hand side of the door, at eye level," she said, through gritted fag-smoking lips.

"There is no bell, I can assure you. I have been searching for it for the best part of half an hour, so I should know. I was about to send you a text."

Sally and Gigi mwah-mwahed and in walked Gigi, a vision in Versace jeans and big jewelry. She was also making a strange yelping sound. "What's that noise?" said Sally. "Is that your ring tone?"

After it "rang" for three minutes while Gigi searched through her enormous Balenciaga bag for her phone it became evident that it was not. "Ah no, I remember what it is," she said, lifting her right hand, which was looped inside something. Trailing behind her, panting on the end of a silver lead, was a scrappy little dog. It was one of those indeterminate pint-size crossbreeds that looked like nothing on earth.

"Isn't it just *the*?" said Gigi. "It's a toy cocka-malti-poodle-dor. I had to send to somewhere called Doncaster to get it. There are only ten of them in the country. Two thousand pounds."

"You two know each other, don't you?" said Sally, gesturing to me in case Gigi was having one of her amnesiac moments and lighting a new ciggie from the end of the old one. If you smoked, the stress of Gigi made you chain-smoke. If you didn't smoke you were a bit stuck. You had to chew your fingernails, or hyperventilate.

Gigi mwahed the air in my general direction: "Of course we do. We are practically blood. We had an extraordinary time watching the burlesque penis juggler at The Box in Soho the other night."

"That wasn't me, but never mind," I thought. At least she recognizes me as someone.

"What's its name?" I said, gesturing to the dog.

"It's not an *its*. It's a *he*. And its name is Ten."

"Ten?"

"Ten. Ten. Ten!" she kept saying, as if trying to convince us of the brilliance of the moniker. "Numbers are the new fruit, remember. Aren't they Tenty-poo."

Apparently, after the era of Apples and Peaches, the trendsetters were turning numerical. Posh started it off, of course, with Harper Seven. Even so, Ten seemed a little dry for a dog's name.

"Yes, there are only ten of them in existence in the world. So I called him Ten. Do you see?"

Sally stubbed her fag, pushed us out into the street, then squashed us mercilessly into her Mercedes A Class before we trundled off to the King's Road looking like an illustration from a Roald Dahl story.

To make matters more claustrophobic, Sally insisted on playing a CD the kids had left in the car. "I love this club music; it's so cool!" she screamed over the colossal din.

Gigi placed her hands over Ten's ears and looked out of the window while I held my BlackBerry close to my face and texted anyone I could think of to take my mind off things. It must have looked like a scrap-metal machine had crushed up the whole of Chelsea and made it into a small, condensed parcel.

On the King's Road we made slow progress as Ten couldn't walk very fast and Gigi had apparently brought the wrong handbag for the purposes of carrying it.

"It simply will not fit in a Balenciaga," she said, as the poor little thing strained at the leash toward a dropped half sandwich as we crossed the King's Road. "You are remembering to feed it, aren't you?" said Sally.

"Yes I am, what sort of fool do you take me for? I am feeding it special formula bicky-wickies in the morning, poached fish for lunch, and lightly grilled chicken breast for dinner."

"It eats better than I do," I said.

Sally and Gigi bought bags full of designer dresses and I bought a Cath Kidston mug with a cowboy on the side, which was half price in the sale. We could barely fit in the car with all the bags and even had to use the space above our heads. It wasn't until we got halfway back to Belgravia that Sally said, "Where's Ten?"

Gigi screamed. Among the many other handles she had in her hands, she was holding a lead at the end of which was an empty collar. Ten had given her the slip.

Sally slammed on the brakes and pulled over on a double yellow. We leaped out of the car and ran back along the King's Road.

Ten was lying in the road outside a shop called The Arrogant Cat, ironically enough.

Gigi sighed and put the collar and lead in her bag, as if it were about as inconvenient as discovering you had left your shopping bags in Peter Jones.

There were only nine cocka-malti-poodle-dors in the world now. And one cocka-malti-poodle-squash.

☙

Some people are rich and just happen to be stupid and some people are stupid rich. Gigi was stupid rich. I could not work out whether being so rich had made her stupid, or whether being so stupid had made her rich, but the two were definitely connected.

The next week she turned up to brunch at Sally's with an identical dog to Ten.

"I thought you said they were a limited edition?" said Sally.

"They are. This one is completely different. Can't you tell? It's got bigger ears and a smaller tail. This one is a cocka-malti-shitsu-dach, with some Lhasa apso."

"Is it called Eleven?" I asked, innocently enough. I genuinely assumed it might be.

"Don't be absurd. Of course it's not called Eleven. What sort of a stupid name would that be for a poor little dog? It's called Cha-Cha."

As Sally served food and tweeted, and Gigi fed Cha-Cha little scraps of Parma ham and mozzarella, I told Gigi about Scott, for want of a better conversation idea.

She was unexpectedly brilliant about it and suddenly began to exude a kind of world-weary wisdom. "Darling, darling," she said, raising a hand to stop me telling her any more with a look that said it was all too predictable. "Men are like little children; it really is too tragic. You are better off on your own with a dog. What do you need a man for anyway? Apart from a bit of . . ." And she whistled.

"Christmas and vacations," I said.

"I'm sorry?"

"It's Christmas and vacations when you need a man. I can't bear spending either the summer or the festive season without someone to at least pretend I'm in love with. And now summer's approaching and I've no one to go on holiday with. Before long it will be Christmas and I'll have no one to go shopping in the snow with and snuggle up to on long, winter—"

"Oh my God, stop it now, you're making me feel sick. Christmas with a man? A big fat slob eating and snoring and watching television? Please. Vacations? Men on vacation are too tiresome for the opposite reason, always wanting to climb hills and play tennis and look at cathedrals. And anyway, a man is for life, not just for Christmas and vacations. Once you've got one you're lumbered with him. Forget it. You must come to Saint-Tropez this summer with me."

She caught me at a low moment. I should never have agreed to go somewhere that upmarket. I am cursed when it comes to supposedly idyllic European holiday destinations.

When I went to Sicily once, for example, my hotel was downwind of an oil refinery and sitting on the beach you couldn't tell whether you were tanning from the sun or the hot smoke belching from the petro-chemical factories.

I was with my fiancé of the time—you remember Jim?—and after arguing pointlessly with the manager for our money back, we decided to get in the car and drive until we found somewhere nicer. We drove the length and breadth of the entire island for two weeks. Every day we got in our car and drove and drove. We crossed bandit country. We went through Corleone, which was, to be fair, everything you would want it to be. There were no shops or bars open, the streets were deserted, and people stared menacingly at us as we took pictures of ourselves grinning and holding our thumbs up like idiots in front of the Corleone sign.

We stopped in eerie seaside resorts where there weren't any people on the beach or in the bars. We went to town after town where doors slammed shut and curtains twitched. We tried to book into hotels, but they wouldn't have us. "We're full," they would say through the intercom on the electrified gates.

When we managed to breach the barbed wire perimeter of a hotel and got as far as the front desk it was obvious they weren't full so they had to take us in. As my fiancé was getting the bags from the car I foolishly tried to check us in on my own. The hotel manager eyed me with deep menace. "Who is vouching for you?"

"What's that?"

"What man is guaranteeing you?"

"I'm not a washing machine, you know," I replied.

My fiancé came to the desk and said he would "guarantee me," whatever this meant. We handed the manager our passports and after reading them both he shook his head. "You are not married?"

It was the same all over Sicily. In terms of female emancipation and sexual equality, it wasn't quite as enlightened as Iran.

Sicily also has a weird thing going on with pedestrians. They seem to be able to walk out into the middle of the road, right in front of your car, and demand that you don't run them over. You can be driving along at sixty miles per hour on what passes for a main road and a little old lady will just walk out in front of you. And when you screech to a halt and half catapult yourself through the windshield she won't thank you for avoiding her by inches; she will stop and shake her fist at you.

I am always amazed by how many people of impeccable taste adore the destinations I have found traumatic and grueling.

Saint-Tropez is one of those places that sounds as though it must be at least half decent because of the sort of people who go there. People like Joan Collins for example. Yes, you reason, the French Riviera can be brash and expensive—Cannes is way more trashy than Cancún—but there must be something nice about a place that attracts a classy broad like Joan. After all, Joan has traveled the world. Joan has been on *Dynasty*. Joan knows a good holiday destination when she sees one.

No, no, no. Do not fall into this trap.

I don't know what Joan Collins is doing when she is in Saint-Tropez, but she must spend the entire time lying by the pool in a rejuvenating face maskthat doesn't have eyeholes. There's no other explanation for how hideous this place is. I rate it as worse than Blackpool by a country mile. If I never see another Nikki Beach or Cinquante-Cinq full of rich people in white linen I shall die happy.

Also, never go on holiday with Gigi. If you meet Gigi and Gigi asks you, which she will, believe me, at the drop of a hat, do not say yes.

It didn't help that Gigi was going through a rough patch. Euphemisms aside, she had hit the bottle. Generally speaking, one shouldn't go on holiday with a friend who has just hit the bottle unless one intends to hit the bottle oneself. In which case, it might be very jolly.

On this occasion, I wanted to eat healthily, swim, and read improving literature. Gigi, meanwhile, was looking forward to going bonkers.

When I arrived at Nice airport she was waiting to pick me up in a huge, black four-by-four. She giggled manically as she heaved my bag into the backseat. I told myself she was just pleased to see me, but then she swerved all over the road as we pulled away from the terminal.

She was, it emerged, both drunk and stoned.

We had an hour's drive to the villa in the dark and she drove like a crazy person all the way. She veered over three lanes of motorway for half an hour, then she almost veered over the edge of every bend as we climbed through the hills in the pitch black.

The next morning she announced that two more friends would be coming. We drove to the station to pick up the first of these friends, who was Swiss—let's call her Petra. She looked like a very nice girl as she walked toward the car, very pretty, well dressed, demure, as if she played a lot of tennis and got taken to country clubs by boys with floppy hair. But when she got into the backseat, leaned forward, and started to talk, I could have got drunk on her breath. She had evidently topped herself up nicely on the journey.

Friend number two—let's call her Izzie—had just arrived by taxi at the villa when we got back. Izzie was thin and short with wiry curly blond hair, and was wearing a brightly colored kaftan dress and mad shoes; she looked like a thin Sarah Jessica Parker. So, pretty damn thin, in other words. As she showed no obvious signs of being blind drunk I decided I liked her immediately, relatively speaking. Alas, this was a misjudgment. Izzie might not have been blind drunk but she had a complex eating disorder *and* chronic fatigue syndrome.

Truly, people should only be allowed to have one or the other of these two things. Both together is too much for anyone to cope with. Let alone me, on vacation.

Izzie's eating disorder made its presence known as we sat down to brunch on the terrace that day and she started to explain the seemingly pointless and quite baffling combinations of things she depended on eating together, or not together.

For no reason I could think of, for example, she could not eat tomatoes and bread together. However she did have to combine, or die, olive oil with salt in a bowl.

She spent the entire brunch explaining these things to us. And the entire afternoon by the pool. And the entire evening.

When somebody finally got her to change the subject, it was

to talk about *why* she had to combine certain foods: to combat her chronic fatigue.

She had suffered with chronic fatigue since she was a teenager when she had been laid so low with it she had taken to her bed for two years. Two years? I'm sorry, but I don't buy that. I'm not arguing with chronic fatigue syndrome as a concept. I'm not saying people don't get clinical exhaustion and take to their bed for years, or even die of it. I'm just saying that I didn't believe that thin Izzie had been bedridden with fatigue for two years.

For one thing, she kept leaping about. She was constantly on the move and never sat still. She kept springing up from her seat to do yoga or Pilates or tai chi or Riverdance. Anything, so long as it involved jumping up and doing something.

She kept saying, "I'm so exhausted, SO exhausted." But she had so much nervous energy she made me feel dizzy just watching her. She couldn't sit still for two minutes, never mind lie in bed for two years.

Also she had a look in her eyes that said, "I like mischief." She was someone who messed with people for a living and she was messing with us now. I'm not claiming I have supernatural powers or anything, but I will say that I could see into that girl's soul and she was one manipulative bitch.

If she had been bedridden with fatigue, I bet any money she snuck out a few times when no one was looking. Right after her adoring family had sat by her bedside for a while, or a friend had brought her chicken broth, I bet she waited till the door shut, ran to the window to see if they had really gone, then got dressed, called a cab, and went to Harvey Nicks for a mooch around the shoe department and a glass of bubbly in the top-floor bar. I bet she even flirted with an Arab before hotfooting it home to be in her sick bed in time for evening visits from the concerned multitudes.

I wanted to tell her I didn't buy it. As we were sitting by the pool in this gorgeous villa filled with Francis Bacon portraits overlooking the French Riviera, I did nothing but fantasize about how I would tell this girl she was a fraud.

"You don't look to me like you've got chronic fatigue. Are you sure it's not hyperactivity disorder? Because it's easy to get those two mixed up." "Maybe if you sit still for a while you won't be so tired." "Have you thought about lying down on a sun lounger as a way of combating your exhaustion? It's a bit unorthodox, but it might just work. Or does it help to jump up and down?"

By the end of the second day, I was getting nowhere with my attempts to confront her. She was impervious. I, on the other hand, was pooped. On the third day, I couldn't lift my head from the pillow. I didn't have the strength—physical, mental, emotional, or moral—to go downstairs for breakfast and face mad Izzie eating bran flakes in organic coconut juice and rattling on about how exhausted she was. There was no doubt about it: I had chronic fatigue fatigue.

⁊⁖

After hanging around the pool all day, Gigi decided we should go down into Saint-Tropez for an all-nighter to celebrate Petra's birthday.

Having seen what Saint-Tropez had to offer briefly the previous day when we'd visited the Cinquante-Cinq for a late lunch followed by a posing stint at Nikki Beach, I begged to excuse myself.

Lunch at the Cinquante-Cinq had been traumatic. I had never seen so many people looking like Elle Macpherson in one place. It was terrifying. All the women had impossibly long, lean legs, perfect tans, and salon-blow-dried-that-morning honey-blond long hair. All the men were fifty plus, slightly paunchy with red faces and shoulder-length hair. Absolutely everyone, male and female, was dressed from head to foot in white linen. Except for the children, who were dressed in impossibly crisp Petit Bateau–style nautical wear. Walking into all this white linen, blond hair, and navy-blue-and-white stripes was like being swallowed up by a Ralph Lauren summer-special photo shoot for *Vogue*. As relatively normal people with cellulite, bank accounts taxed by mainland authorities, and gaudy summer beach dresses that had been randomly picked out of our jumbled-up suitcases a few hours earlier, we stuck out like sore thumbs. The obsessive compulsive in me wanted to remove myself because I was ruining the color scheme.

Evidently the maître d' agreed. He shook his head aggressively and tried to shoo us out when we asked for a table. Then Gigi told him who her father was and he nodded his head excitedly and shooed us back in, claiming he had, of course, been joking, "Ahahaha, ahahaha!"

Gigi told me not to be so sensitive as I grumbled all the way to the table. Apparently this was par for the course in Saint-Tropez.

"If you are going to take mortal offense every time a maître d' chases you away from a restaurant until you tell him the name of a rich person you are related to, you are going to spend a lot of time looking for somewhere to eat at peak hours," she said haughtily. "Come on, this is fun, isn't it?"

I looked around like a spoiled child. How was this fun?

"Please, for me, try and enjoy this. It's my treat," Gigi pleaded.

When I looked at the menu I couldn't feel good that anyone I knew was paying. It seemed immoral to take this much money from anyone, even a girl whose father was so rich he had a personal assistant who had a personal assistant. Gigi said she wanted to order the crudités for €50. "Fine," I thought, "*you* spend fifty euros on some raw chopped-up vegetables that have cost the owner one euro, tops."

As we chomped, a fine mist of cool water sprayed on to us from the ceiling. "Isn't it brilliant," said Gigi. "They spray you with a mineral spritz to keep you cool."

"I bet it's wee," I thought, most unbecomingly.

I texted Sally under the table: "I fcuking hate st. tropez." She texted back, "go bamboo club coco beach stud muffin gays serve sardines n french fries ask for karl say u know theo." She was no help, no help at all. She failed to see the bad in anything.

After lunch we tried to go for a stroll along the beach, but couldn't find a bit of it that was open for free strolling, so we paid what I can only assume was what Sally would call a "stud muffin gay" €20 each to let us into one of the private sunbathing areas.

This I could only stand for ten minutes as it was next to an abomination of a private members' club, which emanated thump-thump-thump music and was full of rich kids in long shorts, whooping.

"Isn't this just *sooooo* relaxing?" said Gigi, as we perched on our €20 sunbeds and watched rich, young people lord it over us by drinking mojitos in Vilebrequins and tiny little bikinis that had to have been sewn by the minuscule hands of specially captured pygmies in the Upper Volta.

"Just tell me when you're ready to go," I said, gripping the sides of my sun lounger and staring determinedly out to sea.

❧

The next day, therefore, when Gigi insisted we go to a nightclub that was really difficult to get into to meet more rich people her father knew, I begged for her indulgence . . .

"Please, I cannot do nightclubs," I pleaded.

"You're ruining this holiday for me," she said, tears welling in her eyes. "You won't enjoy anything. Why are you like this?"

Why indeed? I know I'm a dreadful stick-in-the-mud when it comes to having fun, but I do try to let my hair down sometimes. My ability to delight in eating club sandwiches in bed while watching reruns of *Columbo*, as I've explained before, is legendary. Having fun in Saint-Tropez, however, was just beyond me.

Gigi threw a full-on tantrum. She was a hell of a sight standing by the pool in her designer bikini, weeping bitter tears of disappointment, no doubt fueled by memories of childhood abandonment—her father left her mother when she was very young, then married again five or six times, littering upmarket residential areas of the world, from Mayfair to the Côte d'Azur, with his various offspring—half brothers and sisters of hers who reduced her inheritance every time they reached eighteen.

Now she had a girlfriend who didn't care for her enough even to get drunk, snort coke, and dance to Euro-pop in a private members' club in Saint-Tropez. No wonder she stood there crying and crying. She'd had it rough. Petra and Izzie looked at me accusingly.

"OK, fine, I'll go," I said, if only to wipe the stupid looks off their faces.

It was agreed that as the only one who didn't want to get drunk and take copious amounts of recreational drugs, I would drive us down to town in the four-by-four and drive back again when they were done partying. If at any point I was desperate to come home, it was agreed that I would be allowed to leave early and drive myself back and they would get a taxi.

The first problem was that the four-by-four was automatic.

It's not immediately obvious why a car where you have to do less is actually more difficult to drive, but people like me who like driving with a shift are incapable of driving an automatic. I feel there is a parallel with life generally. For a shift person to become an automatic person successfully, they have to suppress all their instincts for taking control and allow events to take their course.

Don't try to make life, or the car, do anything it doesn't want to. Just sit there and every now and then flip the lever on the left into the D or P position. Keep your foot on the accelerator at all times, except when pressing the brake in an emergency. I always forget this. I'm sure the ideal way to do life/drive an automatic is to flip it into D, point it down the hill into Saint-Tropez, open a copy of *OK!* magazine, and read about Kerry Katona.

As it was, the four-by-four choked and stalled until the girls in the back were screaming abuse at me for throwing them around and messing up their hair.

We lurched into town not very stylishly and I pulled up and choked into a car park, where we handed over a sum of money that would probably have rented me a small cottage in Sussex for the entire year.

As befitting my new status as driver, the girls didn't open the car door themselves but waited until I got out and opened it for them.

Petra, who had been slugging from a bottle of Veuve Clicquot all the way, fell out of the backseat, and staggered about for a few seconds, as if someone had just shot her in the back. Just when you thought she was going to fall down dead, she managed to right herself.

She staggered a few paces behind us as we walked into the town square, past the yachts moored in the harbor. Then she came up behind me and put her hand between the straps of my backless dress and stroked my bare back as we walked.

"You're zow lovely," she whispered slurringly in my ear in her Eurotrashy posh Swiss German accent, then she felt her way down toward my bottom.

One stoned, spoiled rich-kid friend. One eating disorder chronic fatigue friend. And one drunk lesbian friend with a crush on me. What, precisely, had I done to deserve this?

෨෧

I only lasted three hours in the nightclub before I gave up. I tried to find them to tell them I was leaving, but I could only find Petra, who was standing on her own in the middle of the dance floor pouring with sweat, swaying from side to side with her eyes closed. A tanned Nikki Beach–type was eyeing her like a fox eyeing a chicken in a particularly flimsy pen. It was only a matter of time before he pounced.

Another tried to stop me as I ran out.

"Hey, baby, whassup?"

"I'm too old for this," I shouted at him.

"Hey, baby, whassup?"

I think he only had one sentence of English, economically designed to meet all Saint-Tropezian eventualities.

I was so agitated when I got back into the car that whatever skills I had mustered to drive it earlier totally deserted me. I slammed the thing that should have been a gear stick backward and forward in an effort to get it out of parking mode and then I tried pressing all the pedals. I had been staring down at the thing that wasn't a gear stick screaming obscenities for a long time when I looked up and realized I was rolling forward toward the harbor edge. I slammed the thing that wasn't a gear stick up and down but nothing happened. I pushed a pedal that should have been a brake and we speeded up.

I wound down the window and shouted at a passerby to *"m'aidez, vite parce que je ne peux pas conduire les automatiques!"* But he seemed more concerned about ushering women and children out of my path. "Somebody *m'aidez!*" I screamed, as the car approached a gap in the yacht moorings. "I heard someone shouting about *"une folle anglaise."* There was only one thing for it: I pulled the keys out of the ignition, grabbed my handbag, opened the door, and bailed.

When I had recovered from the fall, it was just in time to see the huge black rear of the Beemer disappear over the edge of the sea wall.

∽

I took a cab back, beeped open the gate with the beeper on the car key ring, let myself into the house, and crawled up to bed. I pulled the covers over my head and prayed for something to come between me and the inevitable confrontation with Gigi— possibly death.

When they got back Gigi stormed up into my bedroom. "How dare you leave us like that without telling us you were going. We rang and rang but you didn't answer your phone. We spent hours looking for you. We thought you were dead. You're so selfish.

Don't you ever think about anyone but yourself?" It's true, I told her. I am selfish. I think mostly about myself, I admit it. I panic at the least provocation and I don't hold my nerve in difficult situations. I hate putting up with discomfort and I'm not good at handling drunk people. I often forget to check my phone when I storm out of places upset. What I didn't say was that I drive cars off sea walls.

She obviously hadn't checked the garage. No one had noticed the car wasn't there.

They sat up for most of the night drinking red wine, smoking pot, and talking about me. At one stage I went to the top of the stairs and shouted down, "I am still here, you know. I can actually hear what you're saying."

If it was this bad before they discovered the empty garage, imagine what the backlash would be like when they discovered the missing BMW?

As I lay in bed listening to them it was clear there was only one thing for it: I had to leave. I still had the keys to the Beemer, which had the gate beeper on it so at least I wouldn't have to climb over the barbed wire fence.

When I got up the next day they were sleeping off their hangovers, so I cased my surroundings and worked out how I would do it. I hadn't fled a really big holiday since I ran away from Scott in the middle of the night in Paris, but there had been numerous more minor Code Reds so it wasn't as if I was completely out of training.

I had to stay focused and remember what I knew. The basic steps: pack quickly; leave quietly; e-mail about sunk BMWs later.

The evacuation, however, was fraught with complications that considerably tested my advanced holiday-fleeing techniques, and

I want to pass on what I have learned. So, as promised, here are my top tips for vacating vacations:

If you are staying in a private villa, always work out when you arrive where they keep the keys or gate-opening zapper. Also, is the fence electrified? This could be vital if you are forced to take drastic action after a late-night drunken argument with your hosts. I was locked in behind electric gates, and although I had a gate beeper, I had no idea how the gates opened from the inside when a cab rang the bell. Thankfully the cleaner arrived at 8:30 a.m. and was able to point me to an entry phone in the kitchen. Therefore:

Make friends with the staff. Cleaning ladies are essential allies for nervous types who run away from holidays. Don't worry if you don't speak the lingo. A cleaning lady could still make all the difference to your escape plan. Often these vital people will have inside knowledge of the family you are staying with and may be unsurprised that you are proposing to leave. Throw yourself on their mercy and beg them to call you a cab. If you are particularly angry with your host, tell the cleaning lady something shocking about them—for example, last night they snorted copious amounts of cocaine. She will not iron their clothes properly for weeks in disgust. When it comes to spoiled rich people, revenge is a dish best served creased.

Tip everyone. Tipping is your way of winning the argument before your friends get up out of their alcoholic stupor and start telling their side of things, or lying as it is more conventionally known. Remember, time is on your side in this respect if you storm out early in the morning before they get up. Palm the cleaning lady a huge backhander, then tip the taxi driver €20 when he drops you at the harbor, while crying about how awful your hosts have been. Most holiday destinations are small towns and the taxi driver will put it about that you have been badly wronged. Your aim should be to have the entire resort talking about how mean, inhospitable, and/or depraved these people are by the time you reach home.

Be prepared to travel by land, air, and sea. You will not have time to arrange the most efficient, inexpensive, or luxurious mode of transport. You must get on board whatever is moving in the general direction of where you want to go, even if that is a pleasure boat or a donkey. Therefore:

Pack light. I've said this before and I'll say it again, if you are a bolter like me, do not travel with anything that you cannot carry yourself in one bag or a suitcase on wheels.

If at all possible, and if you are near one when you decide to evacuate a holiday, take the TGV. It is the gold standard of emergency transport. It is fast, clean, comfortable, and stops everywhere. And they don't even ask you to buy a ticket. French stations make no fuss about having a ticket before you get on board and there are rarely conductors. I walked the entire length of the train from Saint-Maxime to Paris looking for a conductor and demanded he make me buy a ticket because it was such a good service. It is also worth noting that train travel affords you the time to make some initial jottings in a notebook about your experiences for the purpose of your later memoirs, should you become famous. Or perhaps you are already a D-list celebrity and you want to keep the details fresh in case an opportunity arises to appear in a *Daily Mail* feature about holidays from hell. Perhaps you're a minor politician and have a blog that needs filling with "what the lack of a ticket inspector means for the crisis in the Eurozone." Or maybe you just want to sit on the TGV and tweet for eight hours about the state of the toilets and the buffet service. It really is your call.

Do not dismiss the idea of a ferry. It may sound counterintuitive, but ferries provide an excellent transportation option for running away. I once walked out of a job as a nanny in a terrible resort called Lignano in northern Italy, and the ferry to Venice, while full of sunburned German people being sick, was a godsend. No one can drive after you when you are on a ferry, thus making it the ideal way of giving an irate summer-holiday employer the slip, or anyone else you are leaving in the lurch for that matter. It is also very satisfying from a spiritual point of view. Watching the wretched place you've left disappear until it's a dot while the sea crashes dramatically around you and then seeing the place you are going to, where everything will obviously be better, appear on the horizon is fantastically cathartic and one of life's great "up" moments. It almost makes it worth having the horrible experience you are fleeing in the first place.

Throw money at it. While there are doubtless savings to be made by taking public transport across borders, you cannot expect to travel cheaply when you are in a blue funk. In the race to get home before having a nervous breakdown you must be prepared to spend anything. If you arrive at the Gare du Nord you may need to get the Eurostar, and the Eurostar from Paris to London is not just expensive at short notice; it is gut-churningly expensive. It's cheaper to charter a jet than pay the last-minute fare on a train from Paris to London. But unless you are Mark Cuban, or know someone who is Mark Cuban, you will not be able to scramble a jet, so pay it you must.

Book a holiday to get over the holiday. Do it soon. Falling off a holiday is like falling off a horse. You must get straight back on or you will never do it again.

5

The Gamekeeper
Is Always Right

....

In which I try to fill the yawning gap in my life with a trail-
riding holiday that inevitably doesn't go according to plan.

....

Your friends may not agree with you about getting straight
back on the holiday bucking bronco.

"I just think you should stop going on holidays," said Sally.
"I'm not sure I can take the stress of another one."

To be fair to her, she had had to pick up the pieces after my
traumatic trip to Saint-Tropez by counseling me at length over a
series of enormous salads. It was the same when I ran away from
Scott in France. I was in delayed shock for weeks and was horribly high maintenance.

"But I really need to get away," I whined. "That last holiday
was worse than useless. I need to erase it from my mind, and there's
only one way to shift the memory of a bad holiday and that's to
have another holiday."

An opportunity suddenly came from nowhere. A few days later, while out horse-riding with three of my girlfriends, one of them said, "I've just been sent a catalog for one of those trail rides. It looks brilliant. We box up the horses and drive to Oxfordshire and stay in this farm, and then the next day we ride until we get to another place and we stay there overnight. And so on until we're back to the start again. It's only five hundred pounds all in and we get to ride across some beautiful countryside."

What could possibly go wrong with a nice gentle riding holiday in Oxfordshire? How could this fail to be relaxing, healthy, wholesome, and fun?

"Let's do it," I said.

The gamekeeper at the farm where I keep my horses couldn't wipe the smirk off his face. "So, let me get this right. The four of you ladies are going to box up your horses and go on a trail ride across Oxfordshire?" he said, taking a long drag on his roll-up.

"Yes, and what of it?"

"Got a map, have you?"

"Yes, we've got a map. Lots of maps, actually. Detailed ones."

"And a compass?"

"I'm sure we will have a compass, yes."

"Maybe you should take your satnav."

"Look, what is this? Just because four women are going on a riding holiday does not mean we are going to get hopelessly lost."

"Right you are then."

"I mean it. We know what we're doing."

"Of course you do."

He picked up his gun, stubbed out his cigarette, and got up from the stable yard tearoom table to go.

"I'll speak to you later then. When you call me from a field to come and pick you up."

"We will not be calling you from a field to ask you to come and pick us up. We will be fine."

But deep down I knew that wouldn't be the case. It was an ill-starred trip that started with a warning from the gamekeeper. As any fool knows, the gamekeeper is always right. In the ten years I had kept my horses on this particular estate, the gamekeeper had never once been wrong about anything. From the weather to the exact whereabouts at any given moment of every last one of the thousand pheasants in his dominion, the gamekeeper knew everything.

With one look over a stable door, he could tell you if a horse with colic would make it through the night. He could look up at the sky and tell you at what time, to the nearest minute, it was going to rain. He could forecast crop failures, economic down-turns, and the outcomes of general elections—the gamekeeper was the only person I knew who had seen the recession, the fall of banks, and the British Coalition government coming. When he sniffed the air he could predict thunder, or he might just say, "We'll be getting one of them hung parliaments, I reckon."

You messed with the gamekeeper at your peril. Legend had it that terrible things had happened to people who had tried to stand in his way. It was said that a dog walker once defied his orders to put his Jack Russell on a lead as they walked near his pheasant pens.

"That's a nice hat you're wearing," the gamekeeper is said to have opined as he approached the dog walker.

"What hat?"

"This hat," he said, letting rip with his shotgun and picking up the furry carcass to demonstrate its head-covering capacities.

༺༗༅

We packed a lot of extraneous stuff, including a pack of cards to play rummy and the satnav, which wouldn't, of course, work in the middle of a field, and at the last minute, almost on a whim, I put a roll of stretchy horse bandage in one of my saddle bags. "We won't be needing that," I thought cheerily, "but it looks professional to carry it."

We loaded up the horses and set off on the M25.

When we arrived at the farmhouse, just outside a pretty village near Newbury and surrounded by racing gallops, our host was waiting in the driveway to guide the horse lorry in. He was a tall, wiry old man with a huge hearing aid standing out from the side of his head.

It turned out his wife was away—we weren't told where she'd gone—and she had left him and their son-in-law in charge of attending to the B&B guests. She had prepared our dinner before leaving—a big, hearty chicken pie—and the father and son busied themselves in the kitchen heating it up.

After settling the horses in a paddock for the night with their buckets of feed, we came inside to eat our dinner.

The son-in-law, a City type who looked very out of sorts in the farmhouse kitchen, ushered us into the dining room and his father asked us what we would like to drink.

The choice, which would be the same in every farmhouse we stayed in over the next few days, was water, orange squash, or Liebfraumilch. I hadn't realized that the embarrassing German wine of my childhood was still in circulation, but over the next few days I would discover that it festers proudly in the sideboards of old England.

My girlfriends looked at each other shiftily. I could tell everyone really wanted a glass of dry white wine. All except Sonia who, from the look on her face, wanted a stiff drink. Sonia, a former TV presenter, still retained a considerable skill for the sort of charming straight-talking that had made her a killer interviewer. "Do you have any vodka?" she said commandingly as we all tried not to look at each other and giggle.

The farmer stared at her for a moment before shouting, "What d'you say?"

"Vodka!" shouted Sonia. It really was too incongruous: the four of us sitting in a creaking farmhouse demanding Stoli. Thank goodness she hadn't asked him for Red Bull as well.

"Vodka?" he mused, turning to his son-in-law. "Vodka? Do we have any vodka, Jeremy?"

The son ran his hand through his floppy hair and darted back into the kitchen. The sound of cupboard doors banging open and shut went on for some time, then he came back looking even more flustered.

"No vodka that I can find. Did Jean ever say anything about where she kept the vodka?"

Sonia could easily have let them off the hook at this point, but she kept staring and smiling, the way she did when she was waiting for a celebrity to get so uncomfortable with a live TV silence that he would tell her he was having an affair.

The old man opened the sideboard and started pulling out bottles of curdled Advocaat and dusty Chiantis in baskets. Even Sonia relented at this point. "Oh honestly, don't worry, it doesn't matter," she said reassuringly. The old man and his son sat down.

The chicken pie was delicious and the Liebfraumilch went down like lemon squash. It was turning out to be a thoroughly enjoyable meal. Then the old man started to tell us his stories.

I couldn't make out much of what he was saying, and we couldn't interrupt to ask him to repeat things because he was so deaf he couldn't hear us speak when he was talking.

As he spoke, the son carried on eating as if he couldn't hear him.

The story seemed to have something to do with what it was like living on the farm during the Second World War: "... huge crater round the back there ... airman tangled up in his parachute ... wild pigs in the woods in those days ... Jean and I were just married ... she'd been engaged to that Bradshaw fellow from over at Critchley Park ... but of course he couldn't get it up ..."

We all looked at each other. Had he just said what we all thought he'd just said? I nudged Judith, who shook her head to signal that she was in trouble.

"... broke off the engagement and ran away with me ... we were at it all night ..."

Surely not? Judith made a squeaking sound.

Sonia, who was used to this sort of thing, was concentrating very intently and seriously on him and nodding sympathetically, in order to get the next bit of the story out. She kept saying, "Oh yes. Well, of course! I mean, you would do, wouldn't you?"

My other friend Julia stared into her plate and pushed her food around it methodically, as if it was all she could do to maintain the concentration she needed not to giggle.

"... all these pigs in the woods, you see, dozens of them wandering around ... dug this blinkin' hole and fell in ... but we couldn't work out where the bombs were coming from ..."

He went on like that for the whole meal—two hours in all—and no one else said another word. At the end of the evening, it was clear that his wife had in all likelihood run away and left him, possibly to take up with the Bradshaw fellow again, forty years later. She didn't care that he couldn't get it up any more. He wasn't deaf and he didn't go on and on about the war. She hadn't given a stuff that there were B&B guests coming. She'd just packed her things and left.

After dinner, we retired to our bedrooms, two to a room, and spent most of the night giggling. I shared with Judith and we couldn't sleep for hours as we whispered like schoolchildren. I really could have done with a good night's sleep before we started our trail ride, but we were way too overexcited. I'm aware that a bunch of women in their forties giggling all night is just sad.

The next morning the daughter was in the kitchen frying bacon and eggs. "Tea or coffee?" she said as we all appeared. Sonia gave one of her looks. "Oh God, no," I thought, "please don't ask for green tea, or organic Earl Gray, or a cup of hot water with lemon and ginger."

Thankfully Sonia relented and made do with coffee. "Have you got any muscovado sugar?" she said, before hastily taking it back. "Nothing, no, fine, I've found the sugar here."

"God, this is wonderful, isn't it?" Julia said as we all stood outside the back door sipping our coffees and dragging on Marlboro Lights.

"Oh it's delightful," said Sonia.

"I wonder if the horses are OK?" said Judith.

We couldn't see them from the back door, but we hoped they were in the paddocks somewhere. We were unused to looking after them as we had them in full livery. Our normal routine was to drive to Surrey from our homes in the city, turn up at the stable yard, and everything would be done for us. All we had to do was get on.

Now we were in charge. The horses were our responsibility. We were very focused on this tremendous challenge and determined to prove to ourselves, the yard owner, and the gamekeeper, when we got back in one piece, that we were up to the task. Before we even thought about our bacon and eggs we stubbed out our ciggies, put on our wellies, and trudged out into the paddocks to find our horses and give them their buckets of nuts. "Look, they're still here!" said Judith as we all mentally ticked off, "Don't lose horses in the night."

Afterward we sat around the table to eat our breakfast. The old man was still talking about the war. It was entirely possible that he had not gone to bed and had been telling the same anecdote since we left him after dinner.

". . . before we had time to do up our trousers the Luftwaffe were flying over . . . had to run the gauntlet of the pigs . . . I was very drunk . . ."

We set off with our saddle bags sensibly loaded with essentials. I was carrying ibuprofen; a spare T-shirt; a fold-up raincoat; a pen and paper; my copy of the map; my mobile phone; the portable satellite navigation device from my car; some mints, in case someone fell off and lost a horse and needed to lure him back; a bottle of fly spray; antihistamine; plasters; a bottle of water; and the roll of stretchy horse bandage, which I definitely wouldn't need but was just taking to look professional.

Over the course of the next three days, I used only one of these things. Can you guess which it was?

Judith had a compass hanging around her neck on a sort of necklace. Julia wasn't carrying anything because she didn't want to ruin the feeling of freedom by being encumbered by stuff. I wouldn't say we were entirely sensibly dressed. Sonia was riding in a skimpy little Alice Temperley lacy vest top, so she could tan properly, and Judith had a new pair of very strange baggy pink riding gloves on that came nearly up to her elbows and looked like rubber dish-washing gloves.

"Why are you wearing washing-up gloves?" I asked her as we set off.

"They're high-tech summer riding gloves," she said defensively. "They're the latest thing. Haven't you seen them before? They're lightweight and specially designed to absorb sweat. They're a bit big because I couldn't get them in my size."

I couldn't see them catching on.

The idea was that we would follow the trail on the maps sent by the riding holiday company until we hit a pub stop for lunch, then we would ride on again to another prearranged farmhouse stop that evening.

At some point during the day, the people at the last place, the old man or his son-in-law, would put our bags in their car and drive them to the next stopover. Then we would stay at the new place overnight and the people there would carry our bags to the next place while we rode for another day, and so on.

It all sounded very doable, and it would have been doable if we'd been sensible, and not daft as brushes and ditzy and kooky and flaky and useless.

We started out from the barn, walking up a hill, with the farmhouse behind us. "Where are we, you know, on the map?" I said feebly as we started to trot.

I should have persisted with this line of attack, but I assumed somebody had looked at the damn thing before starting out. In hindsight, this was foolish, as I had very definitely not looked at it, because the very sight of all those squiggly lines and symbols made me hyperventilate. I should have assumed that the other girls had not looked at it either.

And so we set off from the farmyard exuberantly, all of us knowing only that we were heading for a village called Woolley—which, as plans go, was a bit woolley—and all of us assuming the others knew how to get there. As we cantered off across a field we were all perfectly happy in the knowledge that someone else knew why we were cantering in that particular direction. At the top of the hill, we stopped and took stock, but the sun was shining and the corn was blowing and it was all too picturesque. Still nobody got the map out.

"It's obviously this way!" said Julia, who was a free spirit with a natural instinct for directions. "Come on, girls! Let's go!" And we all whooped and galloped off again.

We had been galloping with glorious abandon across fields for about ten minutes, I would say, when we realized we were going in the wrong direction. When you gallop for ten minutes you actually go quite a long way. If a horse at top speed does up to forty miles per hour, that's seven miles by my reckoning. Seven miles in the wrong direction would be an orienteering challenge for a Duke of Edinburgh award winner, but for four blond women with no map-reading skills it was tantamount to being dropped out of a plane over the Hindu Kush.

We realized something was up when we came to the end of a stubble field and had to pull up and consult the map. We should have had a left turn on to a bridleway, but it wasn't there. We couldn't right ourselves or go back as we had come too far, so we had to improvise.

We knew we were near the Ridgeway and we knew that the Ridgeway was a straight line, broadly speaking, so all we had to do was get to the Ridgeway.

But the map no longer correlated with where we thought we were. And that was when the skies turned black and a torrential rainstorm came crashing down on us. "I suppose if we survive I might get a column out of this," I thought, grimly.

It's at times like these that people's true characters come out.

Friend number one was thoroughly inspired by it all. "What an adventure!" she kept exclaiming. Friend number two developed an addiction to the compass, which she hung around her neck and consulted ceaselessly: "We're facing north . . . we're still facing north . . . we're facing northeast . . . we're facing south . . ." All of which was impressive but, as we didn't know where we were on the map, whether we were pointing north or not was utterly without consequence. Friend number three came up with all sorts of extreme suggestions for cutting through woods and jumping fences in order to right ourselves. As for me, I proclaimed that the end was nigh. "Oh, no, it's like *The Blair Witch Project!*" I wailed. "We'll never get out of this alive!"

Somehow we managed to right ourselves and rode on to our pub stop. We had gone horribly out of our way, so by the time we reached the Queen's Arms at East Garston it was 4 p.m. We had to rest the horses for two hours before we could start out again, and by that time they had dug up an entire pub garden with their hooves and we only had a few hours before dark.

The friend who claimed to be enjoying herself declared the threat of sundown a huge excitement, while the girl with compass addiction resumed her endless search for north. Just when we thought we were nearing our B&B, we asked a dog walker where we were, and instead of telling us we were half a mile from Woolley, he looked at our laminated map and said, "Oh, I see you've got the Queen's Arms on your route. Well, that's just down there." Yes, we had ridden for two hours in a complete circle. Which, of course, was straight out of *The Blair Witch Project*, as I'd predicted.

I flagged down a farmer driving by in his tractor and garbled hysterically, "You've got to help us! We're four stupid women and we've been riding around for eight hours and we're going insane and I don't know how you're going to do it but you've got to get us to Woolley!" The poor man explained exactly where we had to go, but I wasn't having it. "Do you have a mobile number?" He nodded at me with his mouth open. "Give it to me. When we get to the next bridleway junction I'm calling you to make sure we're taking the right turn." I must have convinced him of our utter incapability because we had only gone a few paces when we heard him coming up behind us in his tractor. He waved us to the side of the track, put the tractor in front of us, and escorted us through his fields all the way to the point where we could actually see our destination. I trotted happily behind our knight in shining overalls, enjoying myself for the first time that day.

Even the horses seemed to know when our destination was in sight. My poor Irish mare was exhausted, but she steamed down the home stretch into the entrance of our overnight stop, a huge, sprawling farm, where the farmer's wife was waiting for us. She was one of those unflappable country types whom nothing seems to faze.

"We're so sorry we're late but we've been riding all day, we got horribly lost and had to follow a tractor here!" Judith explained as we dismounted.

As I got out of the saddle my legs were so numb that when my feet touched the ground I couldn't feel them, so I kept going and collapsed on to my knees. I remained there like I was praying for several minutes, until Sonia pulled me up.

"Oh never mind, you're here now. Come inside for something to eat," said the cheery farmer's wife.

"What would you like to drink?" she asked, setting a bottle of Liebfraumilch down on the table. "There's white wine, water, or orange squash . . ."

Oh dear. Sonia, blond hair standing on end, replied quick as a flash, "Do you have any vodka?" I didn't blame her this time, mind you. We all needed one.

"Vodka?" said the farmer's wife slowly, as if she hadn't heard that word in years. "Vodka, you say . . ." And she got up and went to a sideboard that was identical to the sideboard in the last farm-house and started bringing out curdled bottles of Advocaat again.

This time none of us took the pressure off. We needed hard liquor. Let her ransack the house for it, and if there wasn't any, we would be sending her out to the liquor store.

"No, no vodka." Sonia looked like she was going to cry. "Oh wait a minute, what's this?"

And she pulled out a bottle of the poshest, trendiest-looking vodka you have ever seen. It wasn't curdled, or in a basket; it was some sort of special-edition Absolut, complete with a gold seal and ribbon round the neck.

"Yes," she said, putting her half-moons on and squinting at the label, "I think this is vodka; it was a Christmas present from someone, I can't remember who now. Or did we win it in the raf-fle at the Conservative Association summer fête . . . ?"

Sonia looked like she was going to snatch the bottle out of her hands and open it by smashing the top against the table.

As the farmer's wife poured the vodka into little sherry glasses, we tucked into our starter of baby mushrooms in cream-and-brandy sauce on toast. I hadn't eaten food like this since my mum started collecting Robert Carrier recipe cards for a hobby in the seventies. It was delicious. Julia, however, was fidgeting and eyeing the table. "Actually, I think I'll have a glass of Liebfrau-milch if that's OK. What?" she said to us as we giggled. "I'm getting into it."

After dinner we played cards, and then we did the brave thing of taking out the map and trying to look at it. We decided that tomorrow we would do a short ride and come back here. We asked the farmer's wife if this would be OK and she was delighted. We were welcome to use this as our base and then ride back to the first farm on the last day. That way we would almost halve our chances of getting lost again.

The farmer's wife showed us upstairs. There were three bedrooms this time, so two of us would be able to have our own room. "Sort it out for yourselves," she said.

For some reason, of all the combinations of people and rooms that were discussed as we made our way along the hallway, nobody suggested pairing up with me. "Well, you've been a pain in the arse all day," I said to myself. "You panic at the least provocation; you bail at the first sign of trouble; adventure doesn't interest you; you rarely rise to any occasion; you're neurotic; you complain. And now your friends are fed up with you, quite understandably." I went to the room furthest from the others and didn't even bother to call goodnight. Inside I collapsed on to a big lumpy double bed in my jodhpurs and shut my eyes to go to sleep.

And then it started. I yawned. Nothing unusual about that. Then I yawned again. Still nothing odd, really. Then I yawned again. "Fair enough," I thought, "I am pretty shattered." Then I yawned again. This was a bit odd

I rolled over in the big creaking bed and tried to get comfortable. Then a series of big gaping yawns shot out one after the other, making me emit involuntary "Aaaaaaaaaah" noises. This was extraordinary. Before I knew it, it was an hour later and I still couldn't sleep because I couldn't stop yawning for longer than a few seconds.

One after the other they came until my jaw ached and my eyes watered and I was almost in tears from the effort. I had heard of people who couldn't stop hiccuping, but this was something else. I forced my mouth shut and tried not to let it open, but that just made for an even bigger yawn. I tried yawning spectacularly to let it all out, but that only made me yawn more.

I yawned all night, sleeping fitfully in between bouts of serial yawning, and the next morning I awoke to find myself still yawning with gut-wrenching intensity on average every six seconds.

I leaped out of bed in a panic and rang my mother. My mother is the first port of call for all hypochondriac emergencies, of which there are lots. Hypochondria is second nature to me. I don't fight it. I live in permanent thrall to it.

My father answered the phone and received the obligatory, "Quick! Put Mum on!"

"Yes?" she said in her half-weary, half-optimistic voice, as if a tiny bit of her hoped that one day I might ring to tell her something cheerful or ask how she was.

"You've got to help me. I can't stop yawning."

"What?"

"I can't stop yawning. What does that mean?"

"You're tired."

"No. It's not normal yawning. I've been up all night yawning."

"What were you doing yesterday?"

"Riding all day, got lost, panicked a lot . . ."

"Oh dear. You're overwrought. You must calm down and get some rest."

"I can't calm down! I can't stop yawning! I'm going to yawn for the rest of my life, like those people you hear about who can't stop hiccuping! Aaaaaaaaaah—you see, here I go again!"

Judith was knocking on my door. "Are you ready to go? We've all had breakfast."

"Yawning's not going to kill you," shouted my mother.

"That's easy for you to say. How do you know I'm not going to yawn until my heart gives out?"

"Hello? Are you in there?" Judith was still knocking.

"Mum, I need you to phone the doctor."

If my mother had a pound for every time I'd rung her and told her to phone one of the local doctors in my small hometown she would be a rich woman. Actually, that's not strictly true. She'd probably have about £750, but that's still a lot. You could go on holiday with that. Or buy a new sofa. Or at least have the old one re-covered.

"I'm not phoning the doctor. Phone *your* doctor."

"I can't phone *my* doctor; he doesn't exist on the phone. If you phone a doctor's office in London you just get put through to a recorded message that sends you round and round in circles until there is no longer a problem for them to deal with because you have committed suicide through frustration. I need you to phone one of your doctors."

"Oh for goodness sake, I'll phone your doctor. There must be someone there. What's the number?"

We always go through this. I hung up and sat on the bed, and the next time Judith knocked on the door I opened it, stuck my head out, and said I wasn't well. "I can't come today. I've got an upset stomach."

"You didn't drink that much, did you?"

I wanted to say, "No of course I didn't," but then I thought, "Fine, that will do as an excuse." It was less embarrassing to tell everyone I was hungover than that I had yawning sickness.

"I can't drink, you know that. And last night after you all went to bed I snuck downstairs and finished off the vodka and the Liebfraumilch. I'm really embarrassed. Please don't tell anyone."

"OK, don't worry," Judith whispered conspiratorially. "I'll make up some excuse."

I sat back down on the bed and did some yawning. Ten minutes later my mother rang back.

"Right, I got through to a very helpful recorded message which told me to ring another number which told me to ring somewhere else called NHS Direct. There was a very nice woman there and I told her all about it and she said you're to go to the Emergency Room."

"No! They always say that. That's why I told you not to phone them."

I slammed the phone down and Googled "can't stop yawning" on my BlackBerry. I love the Internet. What did we do before we could instantly look up whether the weird stuff that's happening to us is happening to anyone else in the universe?

"Can't stop yawning" elicited legions of crazy people talking about how much fun yawning was, including quite a few who sounded like they were doing it for sexual excitement and some who had found drugs that kept them yawning on purpose because they were enjoying it so much. And then, amid the craziness, this gem, on a site called Askville.com, from someone calling himself Dr. Strangelove:

> I was watching the Discovery Channel and they had a whole show just on yawning . . . I can't believe I sat and watched the thing . . . must have not had anything to do. Anyway, "they" have not figured this one out yet but there are some strong ideas on why we yawn.
>
> One is that when we were primates (and I don't believe that we were primates), yawning was a form of communication. In order to communicate danger, small primates today

will yawn to express to other primates that there is cause
for concern. Scientists believe that this is a primitive reac-
tion that has been passed down from our "primate" ances-
tors.

At that moment my mother rang. "Right, I've spoken to our
doctor, and he says your brain is trying to get more oxygen.
You've been shallow breathing. You need to breathe deeper and
slower."

"No, it's not that," I said. "It's because I got so frightened
yesterday I've regressed into a gorilla. I'm trying to warn off . . .
aaaaaaaaah . . . predators."

"Oh for goodness sake. Go and take some deep breaths."

I watched the girls ride out of the yard from my bedroom
window, then when the coast was clear I crept downstairs. The
farmer's wife intercepted me in the hallway. "Are you all right?
Do you want some breakfast?"

"No . . . aaaaaaaaaah," I said, putting my hand in front of my
mouth surreptitiously. "I'm fine thankyouuuuuuuurrrrrrrrrrrrr . . ."
She gave me a look. I think she'd worked out that I was the odd-
ball who was going to be trouble.

It was a blisteringly hot day, so I got the mare in from the field
where she had spent the night and put her to bed in a cool stable,
where she gave the most enormous horse yawn, showing off her
humongous teeth. "Don't you start!" I said. Then she propped one
of her back feet against the other, gave a big sigh, and fell asleep. I
settled down in a chair in the yard and resigned myself to yawning
myself to death, but after a while I must have dozed off. When I
woke it was eight hours later, the girls were back from their ride,
and I felt reassuringly refreshed. I got up from my chair and

waited. Could it be? No. It was not to be. "Aaaaaaaaaah," I said, as I resumed my frightened gorilla routine.

During dinner I was yawning so much I could barely eat. "Gosh, you are tired, aren't you?" said Sonia. "You've not stopped yawning."

When people said the word "yawning" it made it ten times worse. I was going to have to tell them I couldn't ride back tomorrow. But how could I tell them? I couldn't. I would have to bail. But how could I run away from a holiday on a horse? I couldn't call a taxi to come and pick up me and a horse and take us to the station. And I couldn't demand the girls take me back in our lorry. It would ruin their holiday. I would have to call a specialist horse-transport company. But those outfits needed weeks of notice. There was nothing else for it. I would have to get up the next day and join them for the ride back.

This was no mean feat. It's very hard to ride a horse while yawning compulsively every few seconds.

The mare sensed immediately that something was up and took considerable advantage of my weakness. She pulled me along at a breakneck pace, streaming out in front of the other horses and trying to fulfill her life's ambition, which was making sure her nose was just in front of all the other horses' noses at all times.

We got lost, obviously. At one point we went the wrong way round a racing yard and ended up on a gallop track, with racehorses careering past us and jockeys screeching abuse. As we trotted back past the yard to find the bridle path we had missed I heard a trainer inside an office building shouting, "There are a load of old women galloping around my racecourse!" Something about that struck me as funny, although I'm sure it should have been horrifying.

In the end, through a combination of stopping and asking and getting random strangers' mobile phone numbers, then calling them when we got lost again, we made it back.

When we could see the farm where the old man and his son-in-law lived at the bottom of a hill in the distance we were ecstatic.

In the excitement we forgot our riding skills and allowed the horses to bunch up as we sped on. Judith's horse squashed right up into Julia's horse's bottom and there was a great squeal as Judith's horse got kicked. It was a bad kick. A flap of flesh hung down from his front right leg and blood spurted out as if an artery had been severed. To a panicker like me it looked fatal—I would have sent him to the slaughterhouse as soon as look at him—but thankfully everyone else stayed calm and sensible.

Judith leaped off and applied pressure. Julia, who had been a nurse once, flushed the wound with a bottle of mineral water and started tying a handkerchief around it. Then I remembered the stretchy bandage. I got it out of my saddle bag and dismounted to take it over.

The sight of the bright-red blood against the horse's dark leg made me feel horribly faint and sick, so after handing Julia the bandage I sat down in the grass, still clutching the mare's reins, took my riding hat off, and put my head between my knees.

Behind me, on the end of the reins, the mare fidgeted and started jousting with the other horses nearby. Then one of the horses kicked the other; I don't know which. It all happened very quickly, as these things do, but a hoof connected briefly with my head and, before I knew it, I was lying back in the grass. It was only a glancing blow, but it left me seeing stars. It also took a very small chunk out of my scalp, so when I came round Judith and Sonia were holding me steady as Julia dripped water in the wound then wrapped some leftover stretchy bandage round my head and under my chin until I looked like a character from a Benny Hill sketch.

Judith was fussing. "You poor thing, are you all right?" But I leaped to my feet, a look of great joy on my face.

"Oh thank God!" I cried, gripping my comedy bandaged head and staggering joyfully about. I had stopped yawning.

໑୭

When I got back to London I decided that what I really needed more than anything, more than another holiday certainly, was a morale-boosting dinner with Simon.

We met at our favorite Kensington brasserie. He looked ravishing. We both ordered steak frites. He gave his instructions for no garlic or onions and as always the waiter brought him one with melted garlic butter on top and a generous sprinkling of onions in the garnish.

"What's that?"

"It's a beurre blanc sir."

"But I didn't order a beurre blanc. I can't have garlic. I have an allium intolerance. Please take it away and bring me one that's completely plain."

If Scott had done that it would have been terrifying, but when Simon did it, it somehow managed to be elegant and sophisticated. He had this wondrous, old-fashioned restraint, like a fifties movie star. He reminded me of Cary Grant.

"Are you sure about this allium intolerance?" I asked.

"Quite sure. If I eat garlic I start sweating and my gums explode in blisters."

"Fair enough."

I also wanted to say, "Are you sure about this gay thing?" But

I didn't. I would work on him more subtly with a view to challenging that one.

His boyfriend, a young movie star of some standing, had just left him and he was heartbroken.

"Men are awful," I said. "Awful. Women are much nicer."

He didn't get the point. "Yes," he said vaguely. "So how's your love life?"

"It doesn't exist. I will qualify for sainthood soon, or at least martyrdom. If I carry on like this for much longer I'm probably going to become a virgin."

"Like Doris Day," he said, pouring out the fizzy mineral water.

I kept wanting to say it, to ask him if he would be mine. "How do you fancy compromising yourself entirely and living a lie?" I wanted to ask. But I just couldn't find the moment.

The waiter came back with the steak minus beurre blanc and there was a protracted discussion about whether he had simply scraped the beurre blanc off or whether the chef had cooked him a fresh steak.

"*Mais oui, monsieur,* is new steak. *Bien sûr* new steak. Not old one. *Absolument non, monsieur.* Old one in bin. Completely wasted. Down the pan, while the poor people in Africa starve to death. Can I get monsieur anything else? A side order of blood diamonds mined by orphans in Angola perhaps?"

"How rude," said Simon, as the fair trade waiter stormed off.

6

The Other Other Woman

In which I meet a rich, influential older man who sweeps
me off my feet (and even hints that he might leave his wife).*

"*Can you get* yourself to Battersea heliport?" It's very hard to
turn down a man who asks you out on a date involving a helicopter. Even if he is married. And twenty years older.

It just seems a bit churlish to say no. How would you say no?
"I'm really sorry but I can't let you fly me to lunch in a custom-
built Sikorsky tomorrow because I'm busy. Yes, I really must in-
sist. I've got urgent ordinary person's things to attend to."

I thought about saying that. Then I thought, "Life is short. I
can keep my dignity and moral integrity or I can find out what
it's like to be flown to lunch in a helicopter. In the name of all that
is wrong and yet somehow enriching, I choose knowing."

We had been introduced to each other by a friend who ran a

---

* For maximum enjoyment this chapter should be read in conjunction with
Wagner's "Ride of the Valkyries" (which your e-book will now play, unless it's
still malfunctioning).

charity we both supported and who sat us next to each other at a dinner he had arranged to further the aims of this organization. Instead of talking about how we would help the charity we immediately sized each other up and had one of those moments where something passes between two people and they decide, very definitely, if subconsciously, that one day they will sleep together. All this happened, I would say, within the space of about 1.5 seconds.

For the rest of the dinner we ignored everyone else at the table and talked only to each other. It was quickly obvious that for reasons neither of us really understood, or wanted to understand, we longed to tell each other our most intimate secrets. I told him about Scott and the shoes and he told me some stuff about his marriage and how he was basically just rattling around in this big country house with the dogs.

I had heard of him before I arrived and was sufficiently impressed by who he was to have made a mental note to try to talk to him even if I wasn't sitting anywhere near him, so when he told me his marriage was over I thought, "Hmm, interesting."

It was a slow burner. After dinner, we exchanged business cards and e-mailed each other off and on for almost a year and then, when I told him it was over with Scott, the e-mails became more frequent. Even so, it wasn't until I got back from my riding holiday with the girls that he sent me an e-mail asking me out on a date. Not just any old date. The sort of date where he thought it was a bit shabby of him not to send a car to pick me up to get me to the helicopter.

As I say, this posed a small moral conundrum. I would quantify it as no more than that. It took about ten seconds to resolve. Once I had decided to sell my principles down the river, the next, more taxing problem was what to wear. I ran around my flat for several hours pulling clothes from cupboards and screaming about how I had literally nothing to wear on a helicopter. I wanted to phone my mother and ask her, but I realized I couldn't do that because I could not answer the "ooh, who . . . ?" question. When she asked the "ooh, who . . . ?" question the whole facade of needing to go to lunch in a helicopter so badly that it was OK to do it with a married man would have disintegrated and I would have had to confront the reality of the enterprise full on. And I didn't want to do that.

So I settled on a dress that I thought my mother would like, which looked a bit like the sort of thing Liz Hurley might wear in a helicopter.

"Why do single women get involved with older men?" I asked myself as I painted my toenails. "Because there aren't any single men," I answered. "What's a nice girl like me doing getting excited about an assignation with a rich, married man?"

I told myself I was not going to invest emotionally in it, that I could keep it in perspective and not get too hopeful, but before I'd even painted my last toenail, I paused my ablutions to dig out last month's *Hello* to look at a photo shoot of the rich married man's wife "relaxing in her Belgravia home." I searched the pictures for evidence of her cruelty and obvious madness, thinking, "I can get him to leave her, no sweat. She's got an eighties hairstyle."

"Look," I exclaimed, as I found the killer evidence. "She's got all the books on the bookshelves arranged according to the colors of their jackets!"

But of course, deep down, I knew he would never leave the wife with the eighties hair. Never, ever, ever, would he leave her. Even if she did color-code her books.

"Why do single women get involved with married men?" I asked myself again. Because married men are the only men who chase women. Seriously, when was the last time an available man offered to take me to lunch, never mind on a helicopter? Single men never chase me, ever. Married men are the only ones so desperate to get what they want that they pursue it properly, using a helicopter. Ergo, if you want to be flown around in a helicopter you've got to engage in a dynamic that involves guilt and manipulation. Yes, that's it. I've worked it out.

Then I was fine about it. I had reached a place where it all made perfect sense. I had reached a place where I was not only good to go on a date with a married man; I deserved to go on a date with a married man. I had to go on a date with a married man. So I painted my nails and moisturized my legs—why do women moisturize their legs for special occasions?—laid my dress out on the bed and then stuck my head out the back door and smoked a million cigarettes, all of which tasted suspiciously like guilt.

ô©

When I get out of the minicab at Battersea heliport, a handsome, uniformed pilot is waiting at the entrance to shake my hand and usher me toward the helicopter, where he says "He" is waiting. I don't know much about the lives of the rich and famous, but I can just about work out that people who are referred to by their staff as "He" are big knobs.

"He's already on board," says the pilot. "Please, come with me."

The helicopter is huge and dark, shiny blue. I can't see "Him" until we get through the hot, swirly, thudding air and the door is opened, and there He is, sitting with his helicopter headphones on reading a copy of the *Times*, looking like this is the start of an ordinary lunch outing. He smiles and looks genuinely pleased to see me as I sit down on the beige leather seat next to him and fasten my seat belt. I spend a long time trying to work out what he is saying before I realize he's telling me to put my headphones on. What an amateur. I arrange the headphones so they sit nicely on my hair, then we talk over the intercom. Unfortunately, there is a delay of a few seconds. This is precisely the sort of thing I am unable to cope with. "This is lovely, how long have you . . . shhhhh some coffee? . . . shhhhh some coffee in the drawer . . . sorry? . . . shhhhh get here OK? . . . shhhhh what's that? . . . shhhhh come by cab? . . . shhhhh some coffee . . . shhhh sorry? . . . shhhh there's coffee in the drawer beneath your . . . shhhh . . . sorry? . . . shhhh beneath your . . . shhhh . . . sorry? . . . shhhh . . ." and so on.

I suppose rich people must conduct intimate conversations like this all the time, but I find it a very difficult medium in which to flirt and be sexy. And I do want to flirt and be sexy.

I notice that every time the pilot comes on the airwaves and calls him "sir" I fall ever more deeply in love with him. When the pilot says, "We'll be on our way in a few minutes, sir, just waiting for clearance," for example, I feel an actual flutter in my undergarments. Never having been out with a man who travels by helicopter before I hadn't realized that the connection between male wealth and female sexual attraction is so visceral. "Interesting," I think.

We take off and follow the curves of the Thames then, after what seems like seconds, we are flying over rolling countryside. It is fantastically exciting. I look across at him looking out the window, and then down onto the distant green squares of English fields and feel the urge to scream, "I love the smell of rich man in the morning!" But I don't, because that would be embarrassing. I settle into the rhythm of the helicopter's "d-d-d-d-d-d-d-d-d-dudder" and the effect is pleasingly hypnotic.

I look over at him again and notice that he is wearing a very nice navy-blue linen suit, open-necked shirt, and no tie. He has just the right amount of chest hair showing. Not many men get that right. I also decide that he has expensive hair.

"... shhhh fifty billion pounds off the footsie ... shhhh hedge funds selling ... shhhh Governor of the Bank of England ... shhhh debt crisis ... shhhh price of gold ... shhhh U.S. Federal Reserve shhhh ... lunch with Obama shhhh d-d-d-d-d-d-dudder ..."

After a while I decide to stop interrupting him. I am only saying things like, "Shhhh oh yes, I quite agree shhhh," anyway. I have nothing very substantive to contribute on the matter of what he should say when he next sees the leader of the free world, and after a while he gets into such a monologue that he doesn't seem to notice I have given up trying to join in the conversation.

He talks all the way, virtually nonstop, pausing every now and then to look rather abstractly out of the window: "... shhhh ... disaster if we don't do the deal shhhh ... knife edge shhhh ... my shares are virtually worthless shhhh ... d-d-d-d-d-d-dudder ..." I am fairly certain he is telling me his troubles, but I can't be sure exactly what these troubles are, so I can't really say anything useful. A few times I try to say something mundane but sympathetic like, "Shhhh ... poor you ... shhhh," but he doesn't notice.

We land in front of a huge country house hotel and the pilot shuts down the engines and opens our door.

As I get out of the helicopter my dress billows and I feel pleased with my choice of outfit, remarking to myself that I doubt Liz Hurley could have done better under the circumstances.

When we get inside the restaurant, however, Liz Hurley is actually there. She is wearing something far nicer than the dress I'm wearing, and which I thought looked a bit like something she might wear. She is wearing a dress a lot like the dress I nearly wore but ruled out on the grounds that it was not like something she would wear.

Hurley's dress is a pink, chiffony number. The more I look at it the more I wish *I* had worn my pink chiffony number. It doesn't seem to occur to me that it is best we are not in the same outfit, that in a contest between me in pink chiffon and Liz Hurley in pink chiffon, there can be only one winner.

The waiter shows us to our table, which is the table next to Hurley's. I spend so much time looking behind myself at Hurley at the next table that I spend almost no time looking across the table at him. This must happen all the time in restaurants with helipads. So much so, in fact, that they really ought to have a system of little mirrors on the tables so the diners can look at Liz Hurley without turning round and ignoring their dates. I make a mental note to mention this to the maître d' before we leave.

The genteel silence and clink clink of the restaurant is slightly abstract after the flying noise. I can still feel the d-d-d-d-dudder going through me, like a phantom limb after it's been cut off. I feel woozy.

I wonder what the pilot is doing. "Will he get lunch?" I want to ask, but I imagine this is precisely the sort of question I am meant specifically not to ask.

As we look at our menus I realize I haven't said anything interesting since we left London, or indeed anything at all, really. It seems extraneous and pointless, somehow, to say what I would normally say to a date. Something about the drama of the morning, how one of my house rabbits chewed my phone charger, or how the minicab driver who drove me to Battersea tried to persuade me to run away with him to Islamabad, then overcharged me by £1:50. Or how my neighbors are driving me mad in the night because they don't have carpet in their bedroom, and they have noisy sex in an iron bed that bangs against the bare floorboards and makes extremely loud squeaking noises. All of these things seem mundane and irrelevant after our journey in the helicopter. But it doesn't matter because he continues his monologue. There seems to be no end to it, and he really doesn't appear to mind in the slightest that he's doing all the work. There is something terribly gallant about it. I like the fact that all I apparently have to do is keep breathing.

During a lull in the monologue, after we order our food, I remark on the wonders of modern helicopter travel. He tells me that helicopters and private jets start out as a luxury but quickly become essential. This is because once you have them, and get used to using them, you cannot live without them, and then it's a question of running them as a matter of necessity. After you have got used to a helicopter, a black cab seems like slumming it. Private flight is therefore not a treat, but an everyday burden to be maintained, like a minicab account. I nod sympathetically, but who am I kidding? He continues. The Sikorsky eats up a couple of hundred thousand pounds a year in running costs. I nod and pull an understanding face. I want to shout, "Great balls of fire! I could pay off my mortgage with that!" But I don't. Because that would be embarrassing. Over the starter, I remain largely silent because I am busy working out that lunch has probably cost him a few thousand pounds in helicopter fuel and air-traffic charges. And that is before I even look at the dessert menu.

I am used to men who want to split the bill at the end of a steak dinner at TGI Fridays so situations like this make me feel a little light-headed.

I have to look behind at Hurley to orientate myself. I fret that she might be making brilliant conversation as well as looking pretty in pink, but she's not. She's just smiling really widely and giving her lunch companion gorgeous, adoring looks. That's genius, I think. And I turn back round and smile really widely and give my lunch companion a gorgeous, adoring look.

"Are you all right?" he says, putting his hand on my arm. "You haven't got an earache from the flight have you?"

I decide to stop trying to be Liz Hurley. It's never going to work. It's silly on many counts, not least because the real Liz Hurley is sitting three feet away, doing very well being herself thank you very much and not needing anyone else to be another one of her. I must simply be myself and if he doesn't like it, well, at least I've been flown to lunch in a helicopter once in my life.

But at the end of the date, after we are installed on our beige leather seats and the engines are thudding, he looks at me rather sweetly and intimates that he's really enjoyed himself. ". . . Shhhh really glad you came . . . shhhh do it again . . . shhhh was that Liz Hurley? . . . shhhh overdressed for lunch . . . shhhh pink dress . . . shhhh very poor taste . . ."

When we landed at Battersea, he was most put out that I hadn't got a car waiting and insisted I take his. I would normally regard a chauffeur-driven car as a treat, but as I sat in the back watching the streets of Battersea Rise give way to Clapham North Side I felt a vague and unsettling feeling of despair. Why was it taking so long to get anywhere? Why were we sitting in so much traffic. Then I realized. We weren't going *over* things. This was the same traffic that just this morning had seemed perfectly reasonable. The problem was I was no longer content with perambulating at ground level. After a day with a helicopter at my disposal I had crossed some sort of line. "What's taking so long?" I hassled the poor driver as we crawled across Clapham Common obeying the thirty-mile-per-hour limit. I fantasized graphically about flying over the top of the cars in front. I hoped I'd be able to get back over the line again, because this was unbearable.

⟲

The next morning I was woken by incessant text messages that made my mobile phone vibrate under the pillow, where I had pushed it in a vain attempt to make the ringing, and indeed all other forms of reality, go away.

I looked at the most recent text blearily: "Call me!!!" The others said, "I can't get you!" and "Where are you?!" They were all from Sally.

I pressed her number and she answered in one ring. "Ohmygod, where have you been? I've been ringing you all morning. Have you seen page three of the *Telegraph*?" This could only be something really important.

"Liz Hurley's back with Shane. She was photographed with him yesterday. She's wearing a hideous pink dress. Or it might be fabulous. I can't decide . . ."

"Oh yeah," I said, trying to roll myself sideways out of the bed, slightly panicking now. Sally would consider it the height of treachery that I had not kept her informed in real time by text and BBM. "I think I may have been there."

"What?"

I collapsed in a heap on the floor and struggled to my feet. "You know," I said, as I wandered unsteadily down the corridor to the kitchen. "The date I told you I was going on with a married man. He took me to this place, can't remember where. We went by helicopter so I was totally disorientated. And she was at the next table. I feel strange. I think I've got a helicopter hangover. Is there such a thing?"

"Did you see him?"

"Who?"

"Shane!"

"Not really. I was too busy worrying about whether I should have been wearing what she was wearing."

"Ohmygod, you are, like, literally the worst star spotter I know. You could not be more useless. Oh, that's *Tatler*, I've got to go. I'm writing a piece on Brazilian hair spas."

℃

On our next date I tell Him I think he is a big cheese. He laughs and says, "A *grand fromage*, eh? No, I'm not a *grand fromage*; I'm what you would call a medium *fromage*. Something like a Camembert or Époisses." We laugh.

I tell Sally, and the next time she calls me she says, "How's your medium *fromage*?"

The next time she calls me he has become my MF. It's easier than using his real name in phone messages because, apparently, no one can be sure these days whether someone is listening in. I change his name in my phone just in case Andy Coulson has worked out how to intercept texts.

After a few weeks it becomes clear that this is a one-helicopter-ride relationship. After we have been seen together in one high-profile place we can't afford to be seen together again. Two helicopter rides and we might end up being gossiped about in a D-list celeb magazine, although, having said that, there are worse things. Instead we go to little local restaurants and then one night he drops me at my house and, as we stand outside, it occurs to me that I ought to ask him in.

We stand on the pavement and I look at him and try to will him to kiss me. I'm not entirely sure if he fancies me. Maybe he's just doing this because he's mindlessly bored being at home alone with the dogs. Or maybe he wants to make himself feel younger—in which case, I'm amazed that someone with as big a frown furrow above her nose as me can make anyone feel any younger. He says, "Have you got your key?" It's caring, romantic even, but reminds me a bit of what my dad might say.

For some reason, I find this appealing. I think it's because I like things to have multiple uses. I'm very keen, for example, on bottle openers that have ring pulls on them; reversible jackets that have another pattern on the other side; those little Longchamp bags that fold up and fit inside another bag. OK, so that's not a multiple use, but you see what I mean. I like versatility.

A boyfriend who can double as a father is economical. It covers bases.

The next time, I decide to ask him in and throw caution to the wind. We have tea and then he says he really ought to go and we stand in the hallway and giggle. It is clear that he is weighing up whether to allow this to go to the next stage. So I lunge at him because I can't be bothered with the uncertainty anymore.

Before I kiss a man who is twice my age I cannot imagine what kissing a man who is twice my age will be like. Then when I kiss a man twice my age it is somehow exactly as I imagined kissing a man twice my age would be. It's like normal kissing, only a bit more restrained. It feels like what movie kissing looks like.

I quite like it. The next date we end up pulling all our clothes off hurriedly and leaping into my bed. Before I have sex with a man twice my age I cannot for the life of me imagine what having sex with a man twice my age will be like. Then when I do, it is exactly, down to the last little detail, as I think I must have imagined it. It feels a bit like what movie sex from the black-and-white era looks like. It cuts to the chase and is a lot less hassle than sex with younger men.

For reasons I cannot quite fathom, my affair with the married man has made me the envy of my girlfriends, even though I do not tell them who he is.

My elegant "have-it-all" friend Lydia, who is married with two teenage children, seems to think my life is so exciting that we must meet every Wednesday at Pizza Express in Balham so that I can update her on every detail.

She hardly says a word for the duration of these meals. She just sits and listens to me tell her what happened when I was with him. As what happens when I'm with him is mainly what he says to me, this means I just repeat what he says to me to her. Luckily for her—and me, as it's very therapeutic—she finds this fascinating.

We get the same table every week and order the same pizza. The waiter knows us by name, sees us coming, and gets our bottle of sparkling water ready before we can even sit down.

One week Lydia decides to jack up the drama a bit. She arrives wearing a divine black-and-white Chanel dress and sits down with a particularly conspiratorial smile.

"I've been thinking about what you said last week," she says, "about how this man told you he was doing a big deal with an oil company in the Middle East. And how he played golf the other weekend with George W. Bush. You've got to be careful. Copy any e-mails he sends you to a secret account. Keep all the texts." She leans toward me. "Because if it goes wrong, *They* could bump you off."

"Siciliana with a mixed salad?" says the waitress, who appears with impeccable timing to take our order.

"Yes, thank you. With a Romana base," says Lydia, smiling politely.

"Bump . . . ?" I say. I can't concentrate on my pizza order.

"Would you like a mixed salad to share today, ladies, or two mixed salads?"

"Yes. Two," says Lydia calmly, smiling confidently and handing her menu back to the waitress. "And can I also have an orange juice?"

She smiles and smiles until the waitress has taken the menus and the unused wineglasses and gone away, then her smile disappears in one foul swoop and she turns back to me and says, "These people are ruthless. *They* wouldn't hesitate to get rid of you if they thought you knew too much."

"Who are *They*?"

"*Them.* You know . . ."

"No, I don't."

Lydia leans forward, lowers her voice, and says, very slowly and dramatically, "The . . . Establishment . . ." Then she sits back, raises her eyebrows, nods, and winks.

"Oh don't be ridiculous. The . . . Establishment is not interested in me."

"Don't you believe it," she says, winking again.

೧◯

We meet in small restaurants. We go back to my flat in Balham and go to bed.

He never stays over. He always rings the same local cab firm for a taxi and says, "Hello, this is . . ." and gives his full name.

"For an international man of mystery you're not very worldly, are you?"

"Hmm?"

"You shouldn't really tell the taxi firm your real name. Or at least just say your first name."

"Oh shit, you're right. Bloody hell."

This, more than anything, makes me think he's never done anything like this before. I start falling for him in a big way when clearly I shouldn't. I become fixated on the idea that he might leave his wife, and then get more and more disappointed that he obviously isn't going to.

He's always busy playing golf with George W or Obama, I never see him, and all he does is text me endlessly. We hardly ever meet, and when we do I can barely contain myself. Shouldn't *he* be trying to get *me* into bed? Why am I the one doing all the chasing here?

ᘓᘔ

When I get to Pizza Express I flop down on to my seat. "Oh my God, I'm so exhausted. I hate my life. I can't bear this any longer. I'm so lonely. Everything's terrible. Not only is he never going to leave his wife, he's never going to find time between rounds of golf with Obama to have sex with me."

Lydia gives me a withering stare. "You are hilarious. Look at you, most women would kill for your life."

"What? What life? My life's awful. Terrible. Hideous. Chaotic. Really, it's not exciting. It's just a mess. It's all over the place. I don't know whether I'm coming or going from one minute to the next. The man I love is not only married but constantly tied up playing golf with the president of the United

States, and when we do see each other it's a snatched assignation."

"You lucky thing," says Lydia.

"Me? Lucky? You're lucky. I want your life. I want to go back home tonight to a big family house in Dulwich, to a husband and kids and a big pile of washing up and homework and normal stuff. And instead, what do I get? An affair with a leading businessman who flies me around in a helicopter, then hides me away and visits me in secret every now and again, when he's not playing golf with the leader of the free world."

"You lucky thing," says Lydia.

⁂

In his stand-up show *Never Scared*, Chris Rock says there are only two options in life: married and bored or single and lonely. Most people spend their entire lives looking for a sneaky third option, but it doesn't exist. Married and bored, or single and lonely. That's it. There ain't nuthin' else, people. You have to pick one of them.

Lydia and I were living proof, if proof were needed, that Chris Rock is the foremost social commentator of our age.

His brilliant analysis totally nails it. The reason why some people can't get married is because they don't have the mental resilience and reserves of moral courage needed to withstand the boredom.

I have a very, very low boredom threshold. Boredom terrifies me. Whereas, when I get lonely I just stare out of the window for a few seconds pondering the futility of life, then I'm fine.

The second I get bored I panic, as if my oxygen supply is running out. I break out in hives. When I'm really bored my white blood cells start rejecting themselves. I love a good story. But when someone tells a long anecdote that opens out into several other anecdotes that are necessary to give the original one context my chest tightens and I feel like I've woken up in a coffin in which someone has buried me alive. Men are the biggest culprits at blow by blowdom in my experience. Women are criticized for being gossips, but men are the worst offenders when it comes to relaying mundane routine information in minute, mind-numbing detail.

I once had a male lodger who used to describe everything he did, pretty much a few minutes after he did it, as if it were all totally unusual and fascinating. "Oh my God, right!" he would say. "I just got out of the shower and wrapped myself in a towel and walked into the kitchen and made a cup of coffee and then you came in!"

"Maybe I just have a lower boredom threshold than everyone else," I said to Sally as we sat at her breakfast bar with our laptops writing articles and eating giant chocolate buttons from a huge Kilner jar. "Maybe it's just as well I'm not married."

"But you're missing out on so much fun. Marriage is like a really long sleepover with the person you love most in the world. It's like having your best friend to stay for forty years."

She made it sound so tempting and easy. For a second I thought, "I could do that," then I remembered that Sally and Bobby actually liked each other, whereas I chose men I couldn't stand to be in the same room with for more than an hour.

"But you have to do a lot of other stuff, right? You have to listen to men telling you things."

"Yeah, you do have to do that."

At this moment Bobby appeared, as if by magic, and started telling Sally about how he couldn't find his passport.

"You see, I don't see what that's got to do with you," I said.

"It's in the bedside drawer on my side of the bed," she said, sending Bobby trotting away happily.

"It's not really a sleepover, is it? When I had friends stay over when I was a kid they never asked me where they'd put their passport. Also, if they did irritate me, I told them to shut up and go to sleep. If they were banging on about their new Commodore 64 I would tell them to be quiet or I would tell Mum. With a man you can't do that."

"What's a Commodore 64?"

"A computer."

"Jesus, how old are you?"

"It's out of date, Sizzle," said Bobby, coming back into the room, mournfully reading his passport. "Here, I'll leave it on the table then I'll do something about it tomorrow. I'm going upstairs to watch television."

"I don't like the way men have to tell you what they're doing as they're doing it or just after they've done it," I said, warming to my theme.

"All men do that. I bet MF does it." That was just it. MF was the worst.

"Yes, MF does do it. He tells me where he is with pinpoint accuracy in real time. "I'm at Terminal Five about to board a plane; I'm walking through arrivals at JFK; I'm at the hotel; I'm at the UN; I'm at the restaurant; I'm back at the hotel; I'm with Dubya; I'm in bed." And just when I think the messages might start getting interesting it's, "Night night, speak tomorrow," by which he means, "Night night, I'll text you my bearings tomorrow." Then the next morning it's, "I'm leaving the hotel; I'm getting in a cab; I'm at the office; I'm having lunch with 44 (that's his code name for Obama); I'm leaving the office; I'm at the restaurant with 43 (that's his code name for Bush Junior); I'm leaving the restaurant; I'm in bed, night night; I'm leaving the hotel; I'm at the club; I'm having breakfast with 41 (that's his code name for Bush Senior) . . ."

"Jeez . . ." said Sally, who sounded both impressed and bored.

"I don't care how many American presidents he meets in a typical working day. It's like having a relationship with a GPS signal."

"All men do that," said Sally as Bobby put his head over the banister of the mezzanine and shouted, "Sizzle! I'm watching the most amazing television show about a man who only eats bananas. The poor chap is completely yellow." And he disappeared back into the TV room.

"Why? Why do they do that?"

"I don't know. I think it's something to do with Heidegger. If a tree falls in a forest and no one is around to hear it, does it make a sound?"

"I think that was George Berkeley."

"Well, anyway, something hasn't happened unless someone has seen it happening. And with men, something hasn't happened unless they have told someone it has happened, preferably their wife. I think it's probably about their relationship with their mother."

It was a gripping theory, and a great comfort to know that I was not the only one suffering. All the same, I didn't want to be one of those people who had an entire relationship on text, Facebook, and Skype, with MF simply telling me everything he did a few minutes after he did it. I wanted to actually meet up and make physical contact with him at some stage, if only once a month. As the Good Lord once said, man cannot live by text alone.

Finally, MF stopped texting me what he was doing, got back from New York, and invited me on an actual, three-dimensional visit to his country estate. And a day of hunting.

Fox-hunting is my favorite thing in the world. Please do not ask me to account for the fact that it was supposed to have been banned in Britain under the Hunting Act 2004. We get round it by sticking some fox guts we prepared earlier in a sock and dragging that around before setting the hounds on to chasing it. I would prefer to do it the traditional way, when we made ourselves useful by killing the vermin as we went along, but the lefties won't have it. They prefer we shoot the vermin first, then pretend to chase it, rather than chase it then kill it. So there we are. To the lefties who are pleased about this (because they want to kid themselves that they are preserving said vermin because it looks "cute" and has a fluffy tail and should therefore be allowed to flourish in all its disease-ridden splendor so it can rip chickens and household pets to pieces) I would simply say this: all the animals on your plate have also died, and you're not asking me about them.

I would also say that chasing foxes across fields and jumping huge hedges is tremendous fun and you don't know what you're missing out on, you miserable hypocrites. In fact, it's the most fun you can have in this country. If we Brits can't have black-run skiing locally available like the French, then we must have something thrilling to do in the great outdoors. Otherwise we will all turn into couch potatoes watching Gordon Ramsay on Sky. Oh yes. When all the left-leaning antihunt campaigners are clogging up NHS waiting lists with their type 2 diabetes and their blocked arteries I will still be fit and healthy, so there.

I turned up at his estate in a mood of high excitement, wearing a tight pair of breeches and my best black hunting jacket.

"It's only a scruffy day," he said, coming out on to the gravel drive as I got out of my little car. He was wearing tweed. I didn't care. This was not the time to be casual, even if it meant wearing something that was slightly outside the dress code for an early season, weekday meet. I've long ago given up trying to cover up the fact that I'm arriviste. Let the swells wear shabby chic. I'm a middle-class girl from a small town in the Midlands, and when I go to meet a load of rich people in a posh place I push the boat out. So shoot me.

The house was swarming with staff. Elevenses, or whatever it is posh people call morning snacks, were laid out on the table of a sort of semi–dining room next to the kitchen. I stuffed my face with everything as I am apt to get weak after three hours in the saddle.

He tutted as he eyed my crumpled-up hunting tie. "Come here, you haven't got that right."

I chewed a big mouthful of cheese sandwich as he straightened it.

"There, that's better."

The stable girl who showed me to my horse gave me a funny look. Maybe she was worried I couldn't ride. "Will she be all right?" I asked as I looked at the huge bay mare.

"She's called Venus," said the girl, who was in her twenties, blond, and pretty.

"Sorry, he didn't tell me what her name was."

"He doesn't know what any of his mares are called," said the stable girl, a look of hurt on her face.

"Well, thank you, er . . ." I didn't want to say that I didn't know her name either.

"Lucy," she said with a clenched jaw.

As we rode out of the yard I looked back and she was filling a hay net. Something about the way she slammed the hay into the net just didn't seem right to me at all.

Venus was a good horse. I knew I would be OK when she gave a great buck as we set off. I'd rather have a horse with a bit of life that will go over a hedge like it's on rocket launchers than a quiet thing that wouldn't say boo to a ditch.

After a while we were galloping over fields with the wind in our tails. MF would hurtle off and I would try to catch him. It was so much fun I could barely get my breath. We flew over the fences like maniacs, competing with each other to be the first over. He would gallop past me and take a flying run at a hedge. I would jump the hedge, then chase after him, and when he was still looking round to see if I had caught up to him fly over the next fence and pretend I couldn't see him. Every so often, when we were side by side, he would shout, "How's the mare?" and I would say, "She's called Venus!" And we'd gallop off again.

When we got back the horses were covered in sweat.

As we clopped into the yard, the stable girl was singing along to the radio. "You broke my heart, you broke it in two . . ." she sang to herself rather enigmatically as she came to help us dismount. "I never knew, love was so cruel . . ."

She took my horse with a look of disapproval. "Nice day?" she said enigmatically. "You made me cry, now I'm through with you . . ." she sang under her breath, her eyes looking distinctly watery as she got him down off his horse.

I thought at first she was cross because we'd sweated the horses up, then she took his horse and a look passed between them.

"Oh my God, they're doing it!" I thought.

Later, curled up on the sofa together in front of an open fire, the maid and the butler dismissed, I said, "You don't have to keep it from me that you're at it with Lucy, you know."

"Lucy who?"

"The stable girl."

"Don't be ridiculous."

We lay there in silence for a while, the evening light fading, the logs crackling.

"You can tell me if you are."

"Look, for the last time, I'm not at it with the stable girl, whatever her name is."

"Her name is Lucy."

"Well, I'm not at it with her."

"Fine. But I just want you to know that you don't have to hide it from me that you have another woman. Other than me, I mean. I thought we were friends, that we had no secrets. I'd like to think you could tell me."

"I would tell you. We don't have any secrets. You're the only one."

I changed tack. "Look, I don't want to be the only one. I like to think you have other interests. It frees me up to have a good time when you're away. So if you could see your way to telling me it would be helpful."

"Well, I'm sorry, but I don't have anyone else apart from you, so please feel free to have a good time when I'm away, but I can't make you feel any better about it."

I changed tack again, this time snuggling up against him. "I find it quite sexy actually." I pulled his shirt undone and breathed in Czech & Speake's No. 88 cologne. "Mmm, the thought of you playing the field turns me on."

"Does it?" he said, kicking off his slippers.

"Mmm. You must have just a few little stories for me . . ." And I made a saucy face, to the best of my ability, which wasn't great but seemed to have the desired effect, "because I just love hearing all about what you get up to . . ."

"Hmm, do you now?"

"Yes. Come on, tell me everything. All your naughty assignations . . ."

"Well," he said as he started to nibble my neck. "There was just a small incident in New York with an heiress. I had to really. She was the daughter of a colossally rich oil baron who was investing a shitload of money in the business. I didn't really feel I could say no. The oil baron might have withdrawn his offer." He reached up under my shirt.

"Ooh you naughty boy," I said, maintaining the sexy voice. "So me *and* the woman in New York then."

"Yes," he said, warming to his theme as he pushed his head under my shirt. "And the stable girl."

"Oh for heaven's sake!" I screamed, leaping up from the sofa and pulling his head with me so that he rolled on to the floor.

∾

I slumped down into my chair in Pizza Express.

"I can't believe my expectations are now reduced to being hopeful that I might be a man's favorite mistress."

"Being the favorite mistress of a man who plays golf with three presidents isn't bad," said Lydia, flashing her eyelashes. "And I bet you definitely are his favorite mistress, you know. That Lucy girl sounds particularly insipid to me."

"It's all too confusing. Who's the other woman? Is it me, or one of them?"

"You're the other woman. And don't let anyone tell you different."

"I *am* the other woman. Siciliana with a Romana base, please. And a side of garlic bread."

"That's the spirit."

7

Please Hold. Your Life May Be Ruined for Quality and Training Purposes

In which I decide to single-handedly set the world to rights, even though I cannot work out where to put my wheelie bin.

One of the qualities my older man particularly likes about me is my inability to do what he calls "the simple things."

He checks on me a lot because he says he's worried that I don't seem to be able to cross the street without falling over.

Or negotiate a pay-by-phone parking meter, or put my recycling out without being fined by the council, or drive to a friend's house for dinner without getting prosecuted for parking in a bus lane. He thinks it's marvelous that I manage to make a few quid by writing my struggles down in a weekly magazine column, but he remains baffled by the question, "How come these things are always happening to you?"

I tell him these things are always happening to everyone. "They don't happen to me," he says.

I tell him that this is because he has staff. I am a normal person living in a two-bedroom flat in South London. I have to do battle with Lambeth Council and Network Rail and the man who times how long you've been in the supermarket car park so he can fine you if you go over the limit, even though you've only gone over the limit because you've been in there so long spending the money that is keeping said supermarket going.

I have to go to shops and ring call-centers and deal with people who say things like, "Is it for yourself?"

The only difference between me and the rest of the losers in the world who also have to do this is that I have zero tolerance and am unable to put up with any of it. So I do the stupid thing of arguing with the buggers and getting myself into all sorts of trouble.

Actually, can I just say, the misuse of the reflexive pronoun is quite possibly the most depressing thing that is happening in our world right now. OK, it's not, but it's damned annoying.

Every time a poor deluded soul says to me, "Is it for yourself?" I say, "Do you mean, is it for you?" Sometimes, just to be really facetious, I say, "Do yourself mean, is it for you?"

This is because I see it as my public-spirited duty to set the grammatically bewildered on the straight and narrow. It's no good just moaning about the decaying fabric of Western civilization. If you want to make the world a better place you've got to fight to the death against bad grammar, especially bad grammar masquerading as something a bit fancy.

I'm pretty sure "Is it for yourself?" is meant to make shop assistants and call-center staff sound highbrow. I fear that they think they are making themselves sound special by saying "is it for yourself?" But how dare they attempt to lord it over us with this ungrammatical hyperbole. "If yourself would just calm down I'll be able to deal with yourself shortly . . ." says the clueless dolly-bird at the bank.

"You! The word's you!" yourself screams, before they throw yourself out on to the street for verbal abuse.

"I'll tell you what verbal abuse is . . ." Yourself is now bashing on the windows of the bank, setting off the panic alarms. "It's the strangling of the English language so that basic, easy, innocent phrases such as "How are you?" become "How is yourself today? Can I ask yourself whether yourself would like to discuss a new mortgage for yourself?" And then the police come and cart yourself away.

"Have you anything to say for yourself?" they say. "Thank you!" you say. "Finally, someone who understands the reflexive pronoun." After which, of course, they lock yourself up.

MF often asks me, "If you hate living in the hustle and bustle of the city so much, why don't you move? You could go and live in the Surrey countryside where you keep your horses." He's right, of course. That is the logical solution. And I do threaten to move to the small leafy commuter haven of Cobham several times a day.

But if life were logical David Cameron would have solved the deficit by now.* Life isn't logical. It's complicated and contradictory.

I don't move because I've become dependent on the misery. Excited misery. That's what I call living in a suburb of South London. There's never a dull, or particularly pleasant, moment.

And before you say, "Ah but you're such a high-maintenance

---

* I shall deal with why David Cameron has not solved the deficit in my next book: *Fiscal Conservatism and the Decline of Keynesian Economics.* (Just kidding. I know my place.)

fusspot," I know it's not just me who has these troubles with modern existence. I was driving home from dinner one night when Sally rang.

"Come quickly! Bobby's trying to fill in a passport application form!"

When I got to the big blue front door of their house in Belgravia I could hear a commotion inside, a sort of screaming, howling noise and the banging and crashing sound of large objects being hurled against walls. I rang the bell and Sally opened the door instantly, ashen-faced. "Oh my God, he's been like this all afternoon, ever since he got back from the Passport Office, and it's getting worse.

"He's been trying to fill it in for, like, seven hours now. I've tried helping. The kids have tried helping. None of us can do it. It's insane. I'd just got him to bed and then he got up and insisted on trying again. Then he went really berserk . . ."

Bobby was in his boxer shorts and a T-shirt, hopping up and down in front of the kitchen table, on which was spread out the passport form and all the passport-form explanatory notes. There was also a bottle of Glenlivet and a full-to-the-brim glass, about ten pens, in various states of vandalization, and a lot of A4 sheets full of rough scrawlings, which were obviously his practice answers.

Bobby's hair was standing on end as he bent over the form. He stood gripping the edges of the table staring intently down. Every now and then he would read a bit out loud and then launch into an expletive-strewn rant, which would start in a horribly hushed sarcastic tone, then grow louder until he was yelling himself hoarse. For example, "Do I have any medical conditions? Yes, I've got a fucking medical condition. High blood pressure, heart palpitations, epilepsy, dyspepsia, and a fucking hiatal hernia!" Then he would stab the form with his pen so hard the pen would snap in two, leap back from the table, spin around, grab the nearest thing, and throw it across the room.

He looked like King Lear on the heath. He had been driven mad. One of Britain's finest classical actors, educated at Oxford and the Royal Academy of Dramatic Art, literate and articulate beyond measure, driven to the point of foul-mouthed lunacy by trying to fill in a standard British passport form.

He ran his hands through his silver hair as if he were about to tear it out, then shook his fists at the ceiling, then held up the form and read aloud: "If the answer to Question Three is no, go to part A of the relevant subsection. What fucking subsection, you arse wipe?"

The expletives grew ever more inventive and obscene until he threw his arms wide to the heavens, let out a great howl from the depths of his soul, and screamed at the form, "I hate you, you mother-fucking spunk-bubble!"

Sally dragged deep on a Marlboro Light. "I'm going to have to slip him a sleeping pill."

"Spunk-bubble?" I whispered, horrified. West London had not heard the likes of it since Bobby was rehearsing for a David Hare play.

"I know. They don't realize what they do to people."

After Sally and I had successfully drugged Bobby with a crushed-up Temazepam in a glass of Glenlivet and dragged him by his feet to the living room sofa, where we laid him out and covered him in a blanket, I pondered this question on the drive home: What is the world coming to when the most intelligent among us cannot fill in a passport form? How are the ill-educated coping with this bureaucratic hell? (OK, so that's two questions, but I'm all about value.)

As I arrived back home and surveyed the collection of different colored bins standing proudly in my front garden I thought, "And another thing. How do the educationally challenged among us make sense of the guidelines on where and when to put out their wheelie bin?"

I had a private education. I have nine General Certificates of Secondary Education, four A levels, an upper second class Bachelor of Arts degree from London University, and a postgraduate diploma in journalism. I have worked as a journalist in some of the world's most challenging trouble spots, including Northern Ireland and Iraq. I have managed to file copy even while crouching under a camouflage net in Afghanistan's Camp Bastion, with both my laptop and satellite-phone exploding in fifty-degree heat. However, I cannot for the life of me understand the way Lambeth Council requires me to put out my bin.

I have had detailed instructions. The leaflet from environ*mental* services (with the emphasis on mental) explained that the bin must be put out at some point on Wednesday night, not before 8 p.m., and before 8 a.m. on Thursday morning. It must be brought back in "promptly" once the bins have been emptied on Thursday. If it is still found on the pavement at some unspecified point during the day there will be trouble.

Consequently, I creep outside my house after nightfall on Wednesday, as if I am about to get fired on by pro-government forces.

Sometimes I think about putting it out as I leave my house in the evening for a dinner date, but that is usually around 7 p.m., so even though it feels like a good and sensible time to put the bin out, I try my hardest not to succumb to the deceptive feeling of common sense.

I leave it until I come back, when it is past midnight and my neighbors are all in bed and the sound of the huge wheelie bin being clattered out across the pebbled front garden on to the pavement is extremely deranging and a nuisance. Because this is the way the council wants it to be.

The next morning, I have to keep watch to see when the garbagemen have been, then I go out and bring the bin back in again. If I forget about it and go to work earning money and paying taxes I may fall foul of a bin-checker coming round to find a stray trash can left in the street. So I don't go to work or to the shops to contribute to Britain's economy. I sit in my living room waiting to see when the bin is emptied, so that I can then bring it straight back into my garden. Because this is the way the council wants it to be.

When I go on holiday I get red warning tags on my bin because I have not put it out properly.

The dilemma I face is whether to leave a note on the bin saying I'm not there and risk inviting burglars, or to not go on holiday.

While I feel sure the council would very much like me either to get burgled or cancel my holiday, I cannot be sure which one it would enjoy most, so I plump for not going on holiday.

Seriously. The trauma of organizing someone to put out my bin every Wednesday night when there is nothing in it now means I think twice about going away. I have to pay my cleaner to come specially on Wednesday evening after 8 p.m. to do it, or when I get back from holiday I have two red tags of shame tied to my bin, reminding me and all my neighbors that I am an environmental criminal who has failed to present her refuse for collection in an appropriate and morally acceptable manner.

But this paranoia is nothing compared to the terror of checking what is inside the bin now that we have an entire department at the town hall devoted to checking people's trash cans.

I live in fear of my neighbors or a passing drunk throwing the wrong kind of rubbish into my trash, something that might be deemed recyclable if the rubbish wardens check. And I often end up bent over the bin, half inside it really, with my head deep down in the garbage, sorting through the soggy bags to make sure there aren't any milk cartons or wine bottles inside.

It would be nice if this was just my paranoia and neurosis, but it's not. I once left a garden sack out for collection and got a warning tag accusing me of "contamination."

I peered into the sack for a long time before I spotted a tiny scrap of cellophane lying on the very top. It was no more than two centimeters across and had clearly blown on to the top of the sack as a passerby opened a cigarette packet in the street.

The refuse collectors had not thought it appropriate to flick the two-centimeter scrap of cellophane out of my bag, an action that would have taken all of one second, but *had* thought it appropriate to attach to the bag a large sticky-backed plastic "Contamination!" notice, measuring seven centimeters by five centimeters, warning me of the breach of protocol, an action that probably took a good deal longer than one second and used up a great deal more of the earth's resources. They then left the bag unemptied and standing outside my house gathering more street debris for a further two weeks until the next garden collection, the night before which I virtually took out every leaf and twig to ensure the bag was completely "uncontaminated."

This is how we live now. I pondered all of this as I got out of my car and walked toward my house. I pondered it as I noticed my bin was slightly askew and I started maneuvering it to make it exactly parallel with the garden wall. I pondered it as I opened the bin and had my habitual quick peek to check that the girls in the flat upstairs hadn't put any contraband inside, such as plastic shampoo bottles or chocolate milkshake cartons. And then, as I disappeared over the edge, balancing with my head right down inside the bin, as usual, I lost it. "I'm a civilized person, reduced to the status of a bum!" I screamed, as the full absurdity of my position hit home. Nobody heard me, of course, because I was buried upside down up to my waist in a wheelie bin, talking to an audience of putrid bin bags.

By the time I righted myself the handsome single guy who lives two doors down was standing watching me as he took his cats for their evening constitutional. "You all right?" he said as I fished my Tod's handbag out of the bin.

"Yes thank you, just checking the rubbish. It's bin day tomorrow," I said primly. I have given up trying to flirt with my neighbors. They know too much.

"Napoleon! Bismarck!" he shouted, as he wandered off down the street. It was hard to decide which of us was stranger.

The next day I made a decision. As with all my important decisions, I texted it to Sally before it was even fully formed. "Am gonna run for office and be balhams answer to sarah palin!" It wasn't just that I thought I would look good in rimless specs, although admittedly that was most of it. I also wanted to do something to help my community, and by that I meant the privileged middle classes. Someone had to speak up for us. Someone had to put an end to the injustices we were suffering on a daily basis. And if that meant me dressing up in sharp little suits and wearing my hair in a half beehive, then so be it.

With the ever-worsening refuse collection situation, a tipping point had been reached (pun intended).

I had become radicalized. It wasn't just the bins, or Bobby's passport form. The parking situation needed bringing to the attention of the European Court of Human Rights. It was positively inhumane. I was still traumatized by the horrific events of the previous Christmas . . . I had been about to drive north to be with my folks, and in order to heave my heavy bags and gift-wrapped presents into the car I pulled it out of its parking bay and alongside the motorbike bay right outside my house.

The street was deserted. Everyone had left London for the holidays. I opened all the car doors and the trunk to start loading. I turned back to the house to get the first bags, and when I came back with them a man on a moped with his face wrapped in a black scarf had appeared from nowhere and was photographing my car with a tiny camera. He didn't even bother to put a fine on the windscreen. It was all done digitally. He just snapped it, and drove off at speed, like a smash and grab.

Now, this got me thinking about a lot of things. Most pertinently, it showed what could be done if the political will is there. "Imagine," I thought, "what could be achieved if we paid these little moped snoops a generous commission to ride around cities looking for troublemakers?" What if every time a youth—or yoof, as they are officially known, or yoot (in the vernacular) or yoots (plural)—smashed a window or dealt drugs on a street corner, a masked man on a little moped appeared and took a photo of him?

I'm not saying it would always result in a prosecution, but at least the authorities would be hounding the right people. If all the parking wardens stopped checking cars and started checking hoodlums we could turn this society of ours around!

This is the sort of thing I would campaign for if I was elected as a local councillor. I obviously had much to offer my community as a slightly eccentric right-wing zero-tolerance maverick.

As a gentle warm-up for my debut in local activism, I picked an issue I thought would be straightforward enough. I stood on the corner of my street getting people to sign a petition against a huge sign saying, "Welcome to Lambeth." What could be simpler?

It cluttered the pavement, blocked our view of the park, and served absolutely no purpose, except to advertise the local authority.

"Excuse me, sir," I said breezily to a kindly looking elderly man, "would you care to sign my petition against this horrible sign, which is spoiling our view of the park and serving absolutely no purpose, despite costing you, the taxpayer, a thousand pounds. That's a thousand pounds of your money wasted. And you weren't even consulted."

The man looked up at the sign. "What's wrong with it?" he said grumpily.

"It's a waste of money, sir. Your money. It's an example of the overbearing state."

"Is it?" he said, looking up at the vast municipal sign looming over him, before shaking his head and walking on.

Maybe I'd just got a dud one. I stopped a young guy with iPod wires coming out of his ears. "Excuse me, mate. Can I interest you in signing this petition? This sign cost a thousand pounds of taxpayers' money and it serves no purpose whatsoever."

The guy pulled one earpiece out and looked at the sign. "Mmm. I don't mind it," he said. "It's telling us where we live, isn't it?"

"Yes," I muttered, as he walked off re-plugging himself, "in case you forget where you live, you moron."

"Excuse me? I wonder if I could interest you in signing a petition against this useless—"

"No thank you!"

"Excuse me? Would you like to protest against this hideous sign which cost—"

"Not today!"

It was the same whoever I stopped. One woman was furious that I should be trying to keep her council tax down. "Are you a

Tory, then?" she said, eyeing me suspiciously. "What have you got against Lambeth Council?"

"What haven't I got against them?" I laughed. "They're awful."

"No they're not," she said, pulling her organic shopping bag further on to her shoulder. "They're just trying to do the best for everyone in the community."

Was she for real? Had she had a full frontal lobotomy, or was she a member of the Lambeth Council corporate communications team? Worse was to come.

After about an hour, I was counting my pathetic little list of signatures when I looked up to see a young girl walking toward me with a look of fury on her face.

"What are you going to do about my poor father?"

"I'm sorry?"

"He's in a wheelchair and he can't get about because of these pavements."

"Eh?"

"Look at them! Just look at them! They're all uneven. They're a disgrace. What have you got to say for yourself? You should be ashamed."

I looked down and the pavements were indeed very uneven.

"Well, er, I don't know . . ."

"You don't know! God, you people make me sick. Have you any idea what my father goes through every time he wants to leave the house?"

"No, I, er . . ."

So she told me. And as she did a little crowd of outraged people formed around her, determined to hold me to account for the human misery and suffering I was visiting on the disabled. "Are you all right dear?" asked one old lady as the girl began to cry tears of anger and frustration. "I'm just so exhausted," she explained tearfully. Soon she was being comforted by a posse of public-spirited people baying for my blood.

Every time I tried to stop a passerby to ask him or her to sign my petition, the girl would shout, "Don't do it! Why should we help her when she won't do a damn thing about these pavements? My father's in a wheelchair . . ." Gasps.

After a while there was a little protest group standing next to me, campaigning for rights for the disabled. "What do we want?" shouted the girl.

"Better pavements!" shouted the group.

"When do we want it?"

"Now!"

It was a relief when the token madman with badges all over his lapels and a floppy canvas hat came up to talk to me.

"Couldn't agree more," he said as he signed my petition with mad, loopy handwriting. "What's your e-mail? Can I send you my reports?"

"What's that now?"

"I'd like to show you my research. I've uncovered a major scandal involving Lambeth Council and gerrymandering. They keep people poor deliberately, you know. Have you ever wondered why South London looks like it does?"

It was a good question. "I try not to think about it too much, but yes, I think it's a valid issue."

"They could pour money into it if they wanted to. They could make it look better. Why don't they? Eh? That's what you've got to ask yourself."

I was too tired to argue. I could have made up an e-mail address but I thought I owed it to him to read his dossier of evidence. At least he was fighting the fight. I gave him my e-mail and he wandered away talking to himself.

"Excuse me, are you aware how dangerous this street is for children to cross?"

What fresh hell was this? A gaunt-looking woman with straggly hair and three children hanging off her was standing at my elbow.

"We need a pedestrian crossing. When are we going to get one?"

"Madam, if you would just sign this petition."

"But what about the zebra crossing?"

"Well, if the council hadn't spent a thousand pounds on this pointless, ugly signpost we could have had a zebra crossing." I was quite pleased with that.

"But what are you going to do about getting the crossing put in?"

Before long an angry group of mums with strollers had gathered.

"We need a crossing!" they were all shouting. "What about our crossing?"

The queue of people waiting to harangue me was now stretching down the street. I kept shouting out that I was not a representative from the council.

"What are you doing here then?" shouted one of the angry mums.

"Don't believe her. She's lying to us. She won't give us our crossing. She doesn't care about our children's lives!" shouted another. "Boo!" they all yelled.

I kept thinking, "What would Michele Bachmann do?" But the only answer I could come up with was that Bachmann probably never campaigned to get something as prosaic as a signpost taken down. Would Palin have bothered? Probably not. I was coming at this from entirely the wrong angle. Nobody cared about principles and saving money. They wanted stuff that cost money, the more money the better. Like shiny new zebra crossings with flashing lights or the total refurbishment of the city's pavements. I would have to rethink my entry into local grassroots politics.

◌◌

Thankfully, the protestors got fed up and dispersed after a while. At sundown, after the last of the commuters had walked past on their way home from the station, mostly refusing to sign my petition, I gave up and slunk home.

Despite the horror of my first foray, my local campaigning ambitions remained very much undimmed. This was because there were just so many battles to fight, and so many faceless, and indeed nameless, fascists to rail against.

There was the small matter of one Mr. O, in particular.

Mr. O was a bureaucrat who had written to me to reject my appeal against a parking fine imposed on me for stopping for seven seconds on a bit of faded zigzag line at 8 p.m. in a deserted street when I was on my way to Lydia's house for dinner.

I had appealed on principle. The principle being this: dinner at a friend's had gone from costing me nothing to costing me £60, just because I had a headache on the way causing me to stop outside a shop to buy water and ibuprofen. If that isn't an infringement of a person's civil liberties I don't know what is. So I wrote to the council and told them so.

The letter I got back, signed "Mr. O," said I had no grounds for appeal on this basis. The only grounds on which an appeal would be granted were as follows: you were not there at the time. The car was not yours. You are an alien from outer space and have now returned to your home planet fifteen million light-years away.

There was nothing about getting a headache and having to pull over. Because that actually happens.

The letter also included a long lecture about how morally repugnant I was. I had, Mr. O claimed, willfully broken the highway code. No, I had not. I had simply got a headache and pulled over in the dark outside a skanky old corner shop to buy a packet of extremely expensive painkillers. In the process I had been nabbed by a camera on a defunct zebra crossing and stung for £60 by some thieves calling themselves council officials. If there was any justice in the world, *they* would be getting hauled before a court for breaking the law, not me.

Quite apart from all that, why did the head of parking appeals sign himself Mr. O? What was his surname? Why was he hiding? In the last paragraph, Mr. O invited me to phone an 0845 number if there was something about his letter I did not understand.

So I did. "I'd like to speak to Mr. O, please."

"Mr. who?"

"Mr. O. He's written me a letter and says to call him if there's something I don't understand, which there is."

"Well, that's no good, is it?"

"No," I said. "It's not. Do you know Mr. O?"

"No."

"So how come he can write me an official letter and hide his identity?"

"It doesn't seem right, does it?" she said languidly.

She suggested I send the council an e-mail complaining. I

might as well send the man in the moon an order for two portions of egg fried rice.

But I did. I sent the e-mail protesting in legalistic terms about the infringement of my human rights. It's the only language they understand. I fancied that when the e-mail was received it went straight into a file marked "troublemakers," where I have my very own subcategory under my surname.

I complain so much I am starting to get into a rhythm. The peak of the complaining season for me is when I go in person to the council headquarters to renew my parking permit.

It's a part of my social calendar, as set in stone as a day at the races, to turn up at a place called Gracefield Gardens in Streatham once a year to have a really good rant at some really useless lefties.

But the last time I did this I got in horribly over my head.

When I arrived at the fabulously well-appointed building in otherwise totally neglected Streatham, it was virtually empty. Only three people were sitting on the designer seats in the waiting area and, what was more, there were eight members of staff sitting behind a long row of gleaming desks. Eight servers to three customers is the sort of ratio even Lambeth couldn't fail to turn to its advantage, I thought, as I settled myself in for a medium wait.

I took a ticket from the expensive-looking machine, which told me I was number fifty-six, and sure enough the huge flat screen on the wall declared that number fifty-three was currently being served while the estimated waiting time was five minutes.

What happened next was extraordinary. As the minutes ticked by, the number of customers being served exponentially decreased until I slipped from being third in the queue to fifth, then seventh, then tenth, then fifteenth. Then my number dropped off the screen altogether.

In fifteen minutes, the estimated waiting time went from five minutes to one hour fifty-five minutes. There was no escaping the incredible truth: where there had been no queue, Lambeth Council had managed to conjure one out of thin air. I don't think David Blaine could have done any better. Never have so many members of staff made so little service go such a short way around so few people. It was a wonder to behold.

I strained every brain cell to try to work out how they were pulling it off. I decided to focus my eyes on the blank-faced operators sitting behind the desks to see if their actions provided any clue to the illusion.

After a while, I worked out that a pattern seemed to be at work. After dealing with a customer for a few minutes, the operators would wander away from their desk and stand doing nothing in a corner. Often a few of them would stand together in the corner talking, or offering each other candy or comparing their nails. Then they would walk back to their customer and resume serving them.

After each customer had been dealt with, they would take an even longer break of about ten or fifteen minutes. This they would spend wandering around the service center very slowly and aimlessly, at times stopping to stare out of a window or glance at their watch.

Suddenly it hit me: the poor lost souls must be fulfilling some sort of workplace repetitive strain injury prevention target. They had obviously been ordered not to press the buttons of their keyboards or sit in their chairs for longer than a few minutes at a time and to take generous screen breaks to ensure their health and well-being. Clearly they had also been told that dealing with the general public was emotionally exhausting and that they should not attempt to hold a conversation of longer than thirty seconds

without taking time out for "mental stress relief." Whether this
helped them or not I have no idea, but the net result was that I
ended up spending an hour and a half trying to read the tattoos
on the arms of a girl sitting on the ergonomic waiting bench next
to me. One of them bore the legend "Sean Tequan," which I concluded was either a rap star or the father of her child, or possibly
both, because the toddler in her arms was wearing a pacifier held
round his neck by a massively thick, solid gold chain. I sat staring
at this item for a long time and invented the term "binky bling."
Such things are entertaining if you're stuck in a reversing queue.

"What are you in for?" I asked Mrs. Tequan, attempting to
strike up conversation.

"Re-'ousin' innit," she said, as little Sean Tequan Junior sucked
his solid gold binky.

She wasn't alone. The only person getting served was a lady
at one of the counters who was complaining loudly about re-
'ousin." Apparently the re-'ousin' had been promised but hadn't
happened, and she was demanding that it now take place this
afternoon.

"You 'ere for re-'ousin?' she asked, as little Sean Tequan
Junior slapped her face to amuse himself.

"Nah," I said, "I've been re-'oused. I live 'ere, innit."

She nodded and said, "Oh yeah?"

When I finally got served, it was by a woman who typed in
the license plate of my car so randomly, and with such incredible
lack of attention to where she was putting her fingers, that she
got every single digit wrong. She didn't read it back to check and
so as she went to issue me with a permit that had nothing to do
with me, I had to scream at her to stop.

"But you've got all the letters and numbers wrong," I said.

"Oh, yeah!" She laughed and started randomly bashing the keys again with all her fingers at once.

On reflection, I don't think this was because she was stupid, but because of workplace stress injury guidance stating, "Do not try to press any key with one finger. This will increase your chances of RSI by 0.001 percent."

I am only human and I couldn't take it. After watching her stab randomly at the keys with one finger for another ten minutes I exploded.

"For God's sake! I just want to park outside my own house. Is that too much to ask? I don't want you to give me anything, like a house, or 'ouse, for example. I want to give *you* something. One hundred eighty pounds to be precise. To allow me to park outside my own house, or 'ouse, which I've already bought, and which I pay lavish taxes on. To you. And I'm willing to give you more money now. For this permit. On which basis, I think you should just get on with it, if only to get my one hundred eighty pounds."

I thought this line of argument would appeal to her. It did not.

As if by magic, a frighteningly large woman came out of an office next to the desk I was seated at. The door had been invisible until that moment. It seemed as though she had walked out of the wall. "Could you come with me, please?"

"Fine," I thought. "I may as well go all the way this year and have an argument with the supervisor."

Inside the tiny office it was gloomy and dark. The shutters were closed tight. A solitary lamp burned dimly on the supervisor's desk.

She sat down and disappeared into silhouette. "Please," she said, pointing to a chair. I could just make out that she had leaned right back in her seat and was sitting very still, watching me. It was macabre.

"I understand you've been having some trouble," she said, slowly, thoughtfully. Too thoughtfully. Still, I reasoned, maybe I was going to get some help. Maybe there was someone in this place who was on the side of the tax-paying citizen after all.

I told her the story of the past hour that I had spent laboring to be served in a line of just three people while eight members of staff sat around, eating candy, filing their nails, and being damnably rude to me.

"Oh dear. That is terrible." She spoke very slowly and very deliberately. Something about her reminded me of those films where a seemingly kind Gestapo officer befriends a newly imprisoned member of the Resistance, only to turn on him suddenly and hose him down with freezing cold water. When was she going to turn? I didn't have to wait long.

"Right," she said, picking up a pen. "Your name, please?"

"Why do you need my name?"

"You've made a complaint. We're going to need your name."

"Look, I'm not the one who's done something wrong. It's those girls out there. You're paying them and they're not doing anything."

"Yes, I know, and they will be spoken to, believe me. But before we can take action, we need your name, address, and telephone number.

∞

I used to say I didn't care if I was on an official list of subversives. I used to say I didn't care if there was a file on me at the local council detailing how I subjected officials at the parking center to "verbal abuse" and stood on street corners stirring up local opposition to road-sign policy.

I used to say, "It's a good job I don't want to adopt a baby or these people would have the power to ruin my life!" Then I got old and wanted to adopt a baby.

It was an idea that took shape as my search for a man grew ever more labyrinthine. After the madness of Scott, and the infatuation with the gay nutritionist, and the affair with the older man, my friends started to counsel me in the direction of going it alone.

"Why don't you adopt?" said Sally. And Lydia, and Sonia, and Judith, and Julia.

"I don't want to adopt. I want to have my gay best friend's babies."

"OK, fine," said Sally. "That's plan A. But let's have a plan B. You know, just in case a devastatingly handsome gay celebrity nutritionist doesn't want to have a baby with you, let's have a backup plan."

"But Simon *is* my backup plan."

"I'm saying let's have another one."

"What, you mean like a backup backup plan?"

"Exactly," said Lydia. "Just in case you don't find Mr. Right, or walk off into the sunset with MF, which I'm sure you will."

"But adopt? Are you sure?"

"Yes," said Sonia. "You should definitely adopt. I can see it now, it's absolutely what you're meant to do."

All of a sudden my friends were on fire with inspiring stories about successful single female adopters.

"I knew a woman who adopted this adorable . . ." became the standard opener in the leading topic of conversation. Suddenly, according to my girlfriends, every successful woman who had ever lived had adopted at least three, and up to ten, children, all of whom had grown up to be brain surgeons or astronauts at NASA.

Even women that I thought had their own children were now revealed to be adoptive mothers. "Oh no," Sally would say, when I cited an older woman we knew who'd produced a brood of children, "they're all adopted."

If I was a little skeptical of these stories, it was only because it was the same when I first mooted the idea of having Simon's babies by IVF.

Suddenly, everyone knew a kick-ass woman who had had a baby with a gay man and/or a baby by IVF at the age of forty-five, or fifty-six, or ninety-three. A lot of them seemed to have gone to India or Peru and come back with quadruplets.

Who were these women? I suspected they didn't exist.

In the end I agreed to make inquiries about adoption just to get everyone off my back.

Then, when I was next weepy about my single, childless status and a girlfriend snapped back, "Well, you could always adopt," I could be ready with the reply that I had tried and been rejected.

"I want to inquire about adopting a baby," I said to the adoption helpline at the council.

"Is it for yourself?"

"Does yourself mean, 'Is it for you?'" I said, and we were off.

Eventually I ascertained that the only route to becoming a prospective adopter was to turn up at an adoption social evening at the town hall, where a talk would be given, and if I was still interested I could then apply to have an interview.

There were only three of us in the room when I got there. The random sad single woman who gullibly believed the world had gone so mad that a loony left-wing council might give her a baby—dear God, is this really me standing here?—and a couple holding hands and looking smug and sitting on the far side of a huge round conference table. The reason they were looking smug, I hazarded a guess, was because he was black and she was white.

From what I had already gleaned from reading the literature, being a mixed-race couple makes you Posh and Becks on the adoption circuit. This is because most of the babies waiting for adoption in London are mixed race and the officials don't like putting them with completely white people, or completely black people, in case completely white or completely black people corrupt their heritage, or turn them completely black or completely white, or something. In any case, for whatever reason, they were looking for people whose skin was a very specific shade, or who represented all the shades between them, as my rivals did.

When the social worker giving the talk walked in and saw them she visibly swooned. She plied them with warm orange juice and potato chips from the buffet table and gave them a heap of booklets to read while they were waiting for the talk to start.

Then she walked over to me and asked if I was looking for the dancercize class taking place down the hall. Single women are in the bottom caste of the adoption system. Local authorities are required by equality legislation to claim that they are pleased about single women applying to adopt, but really even the left-wing ones wish they could shoo us down the hall to a singletons' keep-fit class, where we will hopefully meet a nice man and stop making such a nuisance of ourselves.

"OK, then," said the social worker, who was nice in a bossy sort of way, "let's get started . . ."

And she began explaining what sort of children come into care. Babies found in plastic bags outside supermarkets were the lucky ones. They hadn't been harmed too much. But the other children, well, they had pretty much had the worst that life can throw at a person. As she detailed some of the abuse situations, the tears started to well in my eyes. A little girl of three had asked the policeman who rescued her from a squalid, deserted house if he would like a cup of tea.

I felt the tears running down my face. I cry at the least provocation at the best of times. I cry at romcoms, I cry when my local supermarket discontinues my favorite goat cheese. So give me something genuinely sad and I'm inconsolable. I didn't know how much more of this I could take.

The social worker started to explain the adoption process. At this point, the only process that seemed valid to me was a process whereby these poor babies were given straight away, no questions asked, to nice middle-class people. People, for instance, like me.

Then the Posh Spice of adoption piped up, "Sorry, can I just interrupt you there." She tapped her pen impatiently on the table. "Can I just check, when you say we'll have to wait a while for a child, how long exactly? Because we're thinking about IVF. So we need to know. I mean, if this is going to take ages, it might not be worth our while."

She was what I would call—and this is a technical term—"A Horrendous Middle-Class She-Devil." If she had been a bit less awful she might have been a bitch, but she wasn't. She was worse than that. She was every reason why social workers have to spend sleepless nights worrying about the sorts of people they are placing children with. Never mind the ones who are going to beat them up and lock them in a cellar; there are also these complete idiots who want a ready-made child as a cheap alternative to IVF.

The social worker told the HMCS that she would not only have to go through a long and rigorous application process, but that even if she was accepted she might have to wait a long time before a match was found, and that even then it would be difficult. These children had problems.

"What sort of problems?" asked the HMCS.

The social worker started to explain. "Some of them are so damaged that they can't show love. You mustn't expect rewards from adopting a child." The tears started to run down my face again.

The HMCS was unimpressed. "I heard that schools give priority to adopted kids, so when you're applying to a good school that's oversubscribed you can actually jump the queue?"

"Well, I don't know about that. I don't think so," said the social worker, starting to look a bit rueful.

"Hmm," said the HMCS, making a note on her pad.

Her boyfriend or husband stared into his lap and every now and again tried to shush her or plead with her to be quiet and listen.

"Don't shush me!" she would say to him with a look that said, "If you don't shut up, I'll cut your dangly bits off in the night when you're asleep."

The social worker finished her talk with a run-through of what would happen if we successfully managed to adopt.

"And then, we give you two hundred pounds to help you buy a few things for the baby. We know it's not much, but it's really just a gesture, you know, from us to you to wish you well on your way."

The HMCS all but exploded: "Two hundred pounds! You're kidding. What are we supposed to buy with two hundred pounds? I was in a store the other day and the cheapest decent high chair was seven hundred pounds."

When the talk was over and the HMCS was packing her

notepad into her biodegradable designer bag, the social worker turned to me. "So, are you still interested?"

"Huh?" I said, still wondering what happened to the three-year-old who made tea.

"You should apply. I think it's definitely worth you having a go. I placed twin girls with a single woman the other week. It can happen, you know."

I suppose in contrast to the HMCS it hadn't been difficult for me to look like a responsible prospective parent. I felt uplifted. Maybe, just maybe . . .

◌

I cleaned the house until I couldn't find anything left to clean, so when the adoption lady arrived I was pretty high on bleach.

She introduced herself cheerfully as "Corsa, like Vauxhall Corsa." I had a feeling this did not augur well.

She was small and busty and had come with a little suitcase on wheels, which contained her laptop. As soon as she got inside the house she exuded disappointment. As we walked down the hallway to the kitchen she poked her head into each room and gave it the once-over. "Ooh, it's not as big as the Williamsons' place, is it?"

"I'm sorry?"

"The Williamsons. At number fifty-three. They're a few doors down from you. I placed Rosie with them."

It struck me as a bit rum that (a) she was being rude about my house and (b) she had just told me that my neighbors' kid was adopted. I was pretty sure they were meant to have been "empowered" to make the choice as to whether they told me that themselves.

I showed her into the kitchen and her beady eyes went everywhere. "Hmm, no, it's definitely not as big. Which is strange really, isn't it, because these houses all look the same from the outside. But this one is quite pokey compared to—"

"Would you like a cup of tea?" I said, trying to draw her attention to the inspiring range of organic, free trade herbal beverages neatly stacked on the shelf above the kettle.

"Coffee please," she said.

As I fumbled with the *cafetière* she said, "Oh no, just instant."

"I'm afraid I don't have instant."

"Oh," she said disapprovingly, "well, then I'll just have tea. You do have normal tea, don't you?"

Schoolboy error. The organic herbal teas and Colombian coffee beans obviously made me look exotic and experimental, a total basket case.

"Now, this is really just so that we can get to know you; it's nothing formal or anything, nothing to worry about." And she got out a huge laptop and started punching in everything I said. I'm pretty sure she typed in "Sugar?" and "I think that may be a bit strong so let me know and I'll add more milk."

"Now, how would you describe your ethnicity?" she said cheerfully, typing all the while.

Oh dear. I had hoped I might have got at least a few positive points across before we came to the crunch. I took a deep breath. "White . . . ?" I said, feeling doubtful for some reason. "She looked up and stared at me. "Just white?" she asked.

"Y-es."

"Hmm," she said, and she stopped typing.

I realized what was happening, of course. If I didn't find a bit of black in me somewhere this interview was going to be over before it had begun.

"No other ethnic influences?" she chirped. "For example," she prompted, "I would describe myself as British-Asian."

"Yes," I thought, "that's because you are British-Asian. I, however, am not British-Asian. I'm British-British."

"British-English?" I said, digging deep.

She grimaced and turned up her nose. Come on, come on, there must be something. Suddenly I had an idea.

"Hang on, my grandfather was Italian. My mother's half Italian. That makes me a quarter . . ."

"Yes, we get a lot of European children," she said joyously, typing faster. She had cheered up considerably. "Well, Eastern European, but who's arguing . . ."

Not her, obviously.

It wasn't just my heritage that fascinated her. Everything I said seemed to have an exorbitant amount of significance attached to it. Everything I said was also wrong.

For example: "So, why do you want to adopt a child?"

"Well, I think I could offer a child a really good home. I've got a lot of love to give."

"Do you think children are there so that you can feel you've got something to love?"

"Er, no, it's just that I feel I would like to give something back."

"So, this child is a sort of project, is that it?"

"Oh, God no, I just er . . ."

In the end she only stopped typing when she was satisfied that I had dug myself a big enough hole so that I would never get out.

"Let's dispense with all the things you think you ought to say. Why do you really want to adopt a child?"

"Because I, er, just thought it would be nice to be a mother."

"I see." She seemed satisfied now.

"And what do you think being a mother entails?"

"Oh, er, being there for a child. Love . . ."

"You haven't said anything about discipline. It's not all a bed of roses, you know."

"Yes, that too. Firm boundaries, that's very important. And a sense of right and wrong."

"Right and wrong? Are you religious?" Her beady eyes were narrowing again.

"Eh? No. Well, a bit."

"What religion are you?"

"Roman Catholic."

"Hmm."

Oh God, why hmm?

"Churchgoing?"

"Not really."

"Not . . . dog . . . matic . . ." She said the words I hadn't said slowly as she typed them in.

"So, would you want to bring your child up as a Catholic?"

"No . . . ?"

"Hmm."

"I mean yes . . . ?"

"Hmm."

"I'd ask it . . . ?"

"You'd ask *it*. Yes, I think that's best. Now, what sort of food do you cook?"

On and on it went. From my Mediterranean diet—"fresh fruit and vegetables, yes . . . no, I wouldn't put garlic in everything"— to my love of horses, which was almost as bad as my Roman Catholicism.

"Would you take your children riding?"

"No . . . ?"

"That's a pity. Such a healthy sport."

"I mean yes!"

"Hmmm. It's quite dangerous, though, isn't it?"

It was literally impossible to say the right thing.

Midway through she took a break to drink her tea and scrutinize the kitchen again with her beady eyes. She looked at the line of drinks by the fridge. "Are all those wine bottles yours?"

There were two bottles of cheap red wine, both of them bought by my young cousin who had been staying with me.

"Er those, er, those are actually my cousin's. He's staying with me for a few weeks."

"I see. And where is this cousin?"

"He's out at the moment."

"I see." She typed for a long time. "Well," she said as she shut her laptop. "I think that just about covers it. If you're approved to go to the next stage you will be invited for a formal interview. And then we would have to start talking to a lot of people to get references. At this stage I can see no major reason why you wouldn't at least be considered." She looked doubtful. "But I think the main problem you'll have is your reasons for wanting a child, which are a bit emotional, a bit needy, and your lack of experience. If you're really serious about this you ought to get some voluntary work with children under your belt."

This was the catch-22 of adopting. If you wanted a child so badly that you got emotional and had female urges about it, then you were considered too needy and narcissistic. On the other hand, if you didn't want a child badly enough to go and work for free in a nursery on your only day off a week, you weren't showing enough interest and dedication.

I didn't really see that there was any way round this powerful bureaucratic double-bind. I might as well have given up.

As we stood at the door, she promised me that rigorous standards meant that I would, no matter what happened, come hell or high water, get a decision in writing or by e-mail within six weeks. There were strict rules ensuring that as a single person I would get a fair hearing. The very least I could expect was a response either way within a few weeks, and if she had anything to do with it, she would make sure I received a reply even sooner than that. Everything possible would be done to treat me, the single woman applicant, as fairly and as transparently as possible while the decision-making process went forward.

I never heard a thing.

8

Last Tango in Balham

In which I meet my Marlon Brando on the dance floor of Surbiton Assembly Rooms but thankfully do not have to do anything with a packet of Country Life butter.

"What you need is to have some fun."

The eight most terrifying words in the English language.

"Please no," I said. "I hate fun. Don't make me have fun."

But my friend Anna was determined. She had been going to a special dance class called Ceroc since her divorce and it was her rather spurious contention that it had turned her life around. Until Ceroc, she had just been like any other abandoned wife living in Surrey with a load of horses and nothing to do in the evenings. Now she was reborn. It was clearly what I needed, she said. It would put a smile on my face. Really? Did I need a smile on my face? Wasn't that a bit drastic? My face is not used to smiling. It might break, or get more creased than it needs to if I turn the corners up. I ran it past Sally. "Have you ever been to Ceroc?"

"No. But I've heard about it. It's a massive group dance class with people dancing jive and salsa in pairs. Don't do it. You'll hate it. It's a load of lecherous old men pawing younger women."

Just as I thought. All organized fun-based activities come to no good in my experience. Once you start to organize fun you are in dangerous territory. Fun is resistant to organizational efforts. What you end up with when you effect to design fun is about as far from the concept of fun as it is possible to get. This is because fun is like energy. You cannot produce it from nowhere unless you happen to have a Hadron Collider. Such were my beliefs, and I was sticking to them. Then I was sitting on my own one night feeling really sorry for myself when Anna texted, "get urself to esher civic center 7:30 P.M. x" and not one but two smilies and I thought, "Ah, what the hell."

I pulled off my slouch tracksuit and heaved myself into a pair of skinny jeans before texting back, "c u there" with not one, not two, but three smilies. I was now entering an irony-free zone. "Abandon hope all ye who enter here," I thought.

Fine, I'll go to Ceroc partner dancing. And I'll hate it. And that will show them.

I looked ridiculous in the skintight jeans—there was no doubt about it, I was developing horse-rider's bottom—but I was so far gone I didn't care. I squeezed my top half—horse rider's arms and all—into a skintight bright-red T-shirt with strappy sleeves. "Let them cop a load of these biceps," I thought defiantly.

When I got to the big, drafty hall at the civic center I realized immediately that there was no point in my even trying to compete to be the most inappropriately dressed middle-aged woman. There were some truly amazing sights. If I thought my stomach cleavage was proud, I was sadly mistaken. This lot didn't give two hoots how much flesh was hanging out. And they didn't care how much of it was jiggling about, either.

The rules were clearly different here.

I sat on a plastic chair at the side of the room and waited for Anna. When she arrived she looked nothing like the dowdy middle-aged country housewife in Hunters I knew and loved. She had a face full of bright, gaudy makeup, her hair scraped high in a raunchy ponytail and a pair of jeans that made mine look baggy.

She nodded to me, then paraded around the room flirting with men until the instructor called everyone to the floor.

I sat glued to my chair, but Anna came over and pulled me up. "Come on, you're not allowed to sit down. And if someone asks you to dance you have to say yes."

"What sort of rules are they?"

"Just keep smiling!"

She pushed me into the practice line, where about thirty women were standing opposite thirty men.

The man in front of me had greased hair and buckteeth. He was wearing lace-up black-and-white dance shoes and one brightly colored leather golf glove on his right hand. He grinned broadly.

"Good evening, I'm Bernard," he said.

I made a desperate little noise that was half giggle, half cry for help.

The instructor started explaining the moves we would be doing, but I was transfixed by Bernard. I couldn't take my eyes off his mysteriously gloved hand. After a while, the instructor counted us in and the DJ started the music.

"Offer the hand, step back, and in, and back, turn your partner, to the side, turn your partner, return . . ."

At the end of the sequence we came back to a halt. I have no idea what I did, but Bernard seemed to have reached a conclusion.

"Would you excuse me one moment. I think I'm going to need my other glove."

When he came back he did indeed have both golf gloves on. "Well," I thought, "at least he matches now."

Then I thought, "That's really not the most immediate of my worries."

The music started, the instructor counted us in, and we started again.

"Offer the hand, step back, and in, and back, turn your partner, to the side, turn your partner, reeee-turn . . ."

"Stop leading," said Bernard, crossly.

"I can't help it," I said, equally crossly. "You keep going wrong."

"It's not me going wrong; it's you not following. I lead, you follow."

"No thumbs!" the instructor kept yelling from the platform. Seriously? I know Surrey is a hotbed of good manners, but touching thumbs? Or was this a euphemism that was going over my head? Like poor Bernard's arms as I pushed him around.

Then the instructor announced we were to "move ten down." This meant I had to walk ten men to the left.

The next guy didn't have a golf glove, but he did have a really profound squint. I couldn't work out if he was looking at me or the ceiling. "Hello, I'm Malcolm," he said.

"Offer the hand, step back, and in, and back, turn your partner, to the side, turn youre partner, reee-turn . . ."

After the first run-through he, too, was begging me to stop leading. I tried to explain that I was doing it instinctively, that I was so used to having to take the initiative when it came to men that I had no reason to believe he would be able to cope, or not throw me on the floor in a heap if I didn't lead.

"Just follow my lead, please," said Malcolm with improbable self-assurance.

"Offer the hand, step back, and in, and back, turn your partner, to the side, turn your partner, reee-turn ... Five ladies down, please. Five ladies down."

Each time we swapped partners it was the same. A complaining man would tell me off for leading and I would have to get to grips with a whole new set of personal tics. I coped with several squints, a lot of sweaty palms, some terrifying nose hair, and at least one major twitch.

After about half an hour I came back to glove man.

"Hello again!" he said. Despite myself, I felt pleased to see him.

"Hello.."

"Still smiling, are we? Ha ha ha ha ha!" he said, laughing artificially like people do in lifts when they can't think of anything to say.

"Offer the hand, step back, and in, and back, turn your partner, to the side, turn your partner, reee-turn ..."

"Just try to switch off and let me do the thinking," said Bernard.

"Fine," I thought, "I'll show you. I'll stop thinking and we'll see where it gets us. We'll be on the floor in a heap in no time."

The music started, the instructor counted us in, and we began the steps. I blanked my mind, went as limp as a rag doll, and did nothing. And the routine went perfectly. Bernard swizzled me around the floor, folded me in a "basket," twirled me under his arms, and returned me to the place where I'd started with precision timing.

"What the hell just happened?" I said, feeling as though I had woken into another reality. "You let me lead," he said. "Well done. You're rather good. Ha ha ha ha ha ha ha!"

"OK, guys, you're in freestyle!" the instructor exclaimed suddenly.

"What does that mean?" I said to Bernard. But Bernard

didn't answer. He didn't say another word. A look of intense concentration had come over his face. The next thing I knew I was spinning around on one foot, then I was hurtling sideways across the floor. I screamed.

Bernard laughed.

The more I screamed, the more he threw me about and laughed. He was still laughing like he was in a lift, which was weird and kind of scary, but he was also acting a bit, well, macho. It reminded me of the time I went to Iraq as a reporter and an American top gun in a Black Hawk flew me to the Green Zone in Baghdad by repeatedly looping the loop backward until we made such a spectacle of ourselves we got shot at. The more I screamed the more he looped backward. Improbable as it may sound, something similarly testosterone-fueled was going on with Bernard as he flung me around Esher Civic Center.

After the dance had finished I looked at him with fresh eyes before staggering back to my seat by the wall. No sooner had I got there than a huge man with long silver hair, who was sweating so profusely that the sweat was actually pouring off him as if he'd just got out of a swimming pool, asked me to dance.

I said yes not because you were supposed to say yes but because he looked like he might pick me up, throw me over his shoulder, have a heart attack, and fall on top of me, crushing me to death if I said no.

Improbably, the big hairy man didn't have a heart attack. He had endless energy and threw me around even harder than Bernard. This was something else. The masochist in me was beginning to enjoy myself.

At the end of the dance, big hairy man looked at me intensely and said, "You want to know why we men come here? It's because it's the only place where we get to boss women around."

Normally, if a man said something like that to me, I would shoot back a killingly witty put-down. But to my amazement the words that came out of my mouth were, "Thank you very much."

The next man was a bit of a pro, and in his expert hands I started to spin quite nicely. I caught myself fantasizing that I was on *Dancing with the Stars*. He even did that thing where the man sticks his leg between your legs and then whirls you round and round very quickly.

The evening passed in a daze. The more I did nothing, the better I danced. The more I thought nothing, the more spectacularly I whirled around the floor. Could this be The Answer to Everything? Never mind "less is more"; when it comes to getting on with men, is doing absolutely nothing the key?

At the end of the evening I had danced with every man who asked me, which was a lot of dancing.

Anna found me looking tousled, grinning, and rosy-cheeked: "You see. I told you you'd have fun," she said.

I tried to straighten out my face. "Well, it was OK. I might come again. I don't know."

On the way out I bought a discount block-booking to the next twenty sessions.

೧൦

When I wasn't dancing I was thinking about dancing. When I slept, I dreamed about doing double spins. This was bordering on the obsessive. But it wasn't really about the dancing. I had found a way to be around men that men approved of; I had found a way to force myself to be useless. This was a sort of licensed uselessness, permissible to me if I only put it on when I entered a dance hall and left it at the door. I was hooked.

"Do you fancy a ride this evening?" said Sonia.

"I can't. I'm dancing."

"Pizza tonight?" said Lydia.

"I can't. I'm dancing."

"Come round to dinner on Thursday," said Sally.

"I can't. I'm dancing."

"Again? You must be as good as Ginger Rogers by now."

"I am pretty good."

In fact, I decided I was so good I deserved a pair of proper dancing shoes.

So I went to Capezio in Covent Garden.

It was full of little girls trying on pointe shoes For some reason this made me cry. I don't know why memories of lost youth erupt violently like that.

I stood in Capezio with my eyes so blurry with tears that I couldn't see the fancy ballroom shoes. I picked a pair at random and tried walking in them on the special dance mat.

The little girls, *en pointe*, moved over to make room for me.

"Those are absolutely gorgeous," said one of the ballet mums, eyeing my glittery ballroom dancing shoes.

I looked at myself in the mirror. I had lost a bit of weight. Also, I have good feet. They are my best feature. They looked pretty darn sexy in the glittery shoes, even if I do say so myself. "Not bad," I thought. "Not bad at all."

ৎৄ

The classes were dotted about the more suburban areas of Surrey and Southwest London. The next one was at a church hall in Surbiton. I arrived early wearing leg warmers. Yes, leg warmers. I unpacked my professional dancing shoes from their little velvet drawstring bag, glancing furtively around the room to see if anyone had noticed how accomplished I looked.

Laugh if you want to, but the shoes paid off because the first man who asked me to dance after the class was one of the instructors. "You're great to dance with," he said.

"Really?" I said, beaming with pride.

"Yes," he said. "You're an instinctive follower."

Who would have thought it?

The next person to ask me was one of the really good young dancers, who was quite good looking if you half shut your eyes. He slid me across the dance floor in some complicated moves that were so raunchy they bordered on obscene. He wasn't exactly handsome, unless you like lithe, bendy little men who remind you of Fred Astaire. But after three dances I was developing a crush on him. After a while I realized I was waiting all night for him to ask me to dance. He did this really sexy move where he bent me backward and then flopped me back upright. I started to conclude that electricity was running between us.

The next time I went I danced with him three times in one evening. The time after that, five. In the end we were meeting three nights a week on the commuter-belt Ceroc circuit.

We met in dance halls in Surbiton, Esher, Dorking, Hammersmith, and Clapham Junction.

I didn't even know his name. I didn't want to know it. We knew nothing about each other and that was just fine. We just came together, two strangers, in this anonymous space and set the world alight. As our dancing became more and more risqué, people started eyeing us with suspicion. I started to wonder how much more explicit our moves could get before someone made an official complaint.

Then one day he disappeared. I didn't see him for weeks. I

turned up and sat on the chairs at the sides of the room brooding, and did the unforgivable thing of telling men who asked me to dance that I was tired. I searched for him everywhere. Dorking, Guildford, Epsom, Ewell. I wandered the dormitory towns of the Southeast. I couldn't believe he had left without a trace. I didn't know his name so I couldn't even Facebook him.

I pined. I became angry. I wondered why he had abandoned me, abandoned us.

Then he reappeared one night suddenly at Surbiton. I was already dancing with One-Glove, but he eyed me as soon as he strode into the room.

When I was finished, he walked up to me, grabbed me, and we started to dance. I asked where he had been. He told me he'd been away on business.

At the end of the night, he said, "So, do you fancy going for a drink?"

We arranged to meet near my home in Balham the next night.

"Are you sure you want to do this?" said Sally over chicken-and-apricot salad. "You do know what happens in *Last Tango in Paris*, don't you?"

"I always forget. Is that the one where he drips ice cubes over her or the one where he does something horrible with a packet of margarine?"

"The last one. And it's butter, actually. But the point is, after he does the thing with the butter they make the mistake of telling each other who they are and the sexual tension evaporates; they have a huge row and she ends up shooting him."

"I think you're being a little negative. I know I've a poor record with men but I think I can manage not to shoot my Ceroc dance partner."

I was breathless with excitement as I got myself ready. It felt weird not to be meeting him in my dancing shoes. I put on a pair of extra high boots over my skintight jeans and sat waiting on the bed. He was coming to my house at 9 p.m. to pick me up.

At exactly 9 p.m., not a second earlier, not a second later, he knocked very quietly at the door. My heart sank. The preciseness of the arrival was somehow depressing. Had he been standing outside looking at a stopwatch before knocking as the second hand hit the hour? Also, a quiet knock was not what I had been expecting. I had been expecting a big, thumping, Marlon Brando–type knock. The sort of knock that presages something raunchy happening within seconds of me opening the door.

I sat on the bed contemplating not opening the door. I wondered how long I would have to sit there to make him go away. "If I don't make a noise he might leave."

The problem was, he didn't make a noise either. Possibly, he was standing on the other side of the door thinking, "If I keep really quiet maybe she won't hear me and I can go away . . ."

This was silly. I got up and answered. He was standing there grinning nervously. He looked different in real shoes.

We walked a little way down my street until he said, "This is my car." He had come in a large white van. He was a furniture mover.

We went to a local bar where he ordered fruit cocktails and we perched on high stools. Immediately after we had placed our order we stopped having anything to talk about. The cocky Australian bartender tried to cheer us up by asking us excitedly where we were from, as if we'd come in from a sandstorm and might have some intrepid stories to tell him about our trek across the outback.

"Down the road? Oh yeah! I used to live down the road. It's good down there, isn't it?" Nothing doused his enthusiasm.

But the second he stopped yapping on about how many cocktails he could make and how quickly and how much cheaper they
were in this bar than in any other bar in the Western Hemisphere,
neither of us could think of a single thing to say. When the bartender went off to serve other customers we fell into a stupefying
silence. "So," I said, "what's your name?"

His name was Tim, which was just silly, for some reason. I
told him my name and a few things about myself, what I did for a
living and so on, and he seemed to think that I was silly, in reality, too.

We sat in silence, turning our noses up at every bit of information we gleaned from each other until a tune came on the jukebox
that we were used to dancing to.

"I love this song. This song's brilliant to dance to."

"Yeah," I said. "I love this song. It's brilliant to dance to."

For a second we smiled and the mood lightened. If only we
could have got off our stools and done a turn on the bar dance floor
we would have been all right, but we couldn't. We were stuck on
our stools, talking to each other.

We fell back into silence.

The look on his face said, "I could be watching Fulham versus
Newcastle." The look on my face said, "I could be scrubbing the
floor tiles with a really small toothbrush."

In the end, the silence became so horrifying that I had to break
it by telling him how much I wished I was married, how much I
wanted children, and how badly wrong all my relationships had
gone. I couldn't think of anything else to say. And a précis of the
troubles in my private life at least filled up a good twenty minutes.

He listened without interjecting a word and then said, "Maybe
you should just chill out."

"Yes, maybe I should," I said, with venom. It was clear he

hated me and I really hated him. What a damned cheek he had, telling me I should chill out when he was the most boring person in the universe. If he chilled out any more he'd be on a mortician's slab.

I fantasized about pulling a gun out of my jeans and shooting him. Would he stick his chewing gum under the bar before he fell down dead like Marlon? "He was just a stranger who tried to dance with me," was the alibi I would give the police.

"Right, I've got to be up early in the morning," I said.

"Me, too. Got a big removals job."

He drove me home in silence in his white van and I never went dancing again.

❧

I collapsed into my chair at Pizza Express.

"I've tried having fun. It doesn't work. I don't want to have any more fun, ever."

"You've tried it for a few weeks. You didn't really persevere," said Lydia, who was wearing a particularly fabulous Jackie O–style pink Chanel jacket, which her husband had bought her in a fit of guilt. Lydia was all for perseverance. She herself had been persevering heroically for many years at staying with her cheating husband who lavished on her jewelry and Chanel. She was a kept woman, and she was keeping it that way.

"Let me ask you a question?" I asked confrontationally. "When you get home from work do you have the energy to go out and have fun?"

"God, no. I'm exhausted."

"Thank you. Precisely my point. So am I. Just because I'm single doesn't mean I have more energy than you, that I've got special, energy-efficient DNA or something. I'm just like you. Why is it automatically assumed that single women want to have fun? Just because you haven't got a man doesn't mean you necessarily want to go out to bars all the time. I like going for walks and cooking and having friends round so I can relax and not have to bother, just like you. I like sitting in front of an open fire in the evenings, just like you. I like going to bed early, just like you. I like long baths and scented candles and all the other stuff women like when they get old, just like you. I'd quite like to kick back and have a cheating guilty husband buy me Jackie O jackets from Chanel, if you want to know the truth. Just for a few years, for a break, at least. It would make a nice change for me. Instead of having to do everything on my own and be interesting and dynamic . . ."

"Fine, I get it. You're knackered and middle-aged."

"Exactly. I don't want to have fun. Just because I'm single does not mean I want to wear lots of makeup and grow old disgracefully, and have people remark on what a character I am.

"I haven't got that much emotional energy. I only have a few ambitions left. I want a dog. I want to ride with my dog running alongside my horse. Then I want to come home and light a fire and go to bed early. Just because I don't have a husband, or children, doesn't mean I don't want all the cozy things I might have by now if I did have a husband. Why can't I grow old gracefully? Why can't I get slightly fat and cut my hair and go for horse rides with my dog like a boring married woman. Is it too much to ask?"

Lydia took a deep breath in and surveyed me very seriously. "I . . . think . . . you . . ." she said very slowly and dramatically, in that way she has of announcing things that are apparently earth-shatteringly wise and of near psychic quality, but are actually just her skilfully telling me what she thinks I want to hear before I go totally mad, "should get yourself a dog and move to the country. I've got a very strong feeling suddenly. I think a new phase in your life is about to begin."

Then she popped her glasses on the end of her nose and squinted at the menu. "I don't know why we look at the menu, do you? We always order the same thing."

9

A Modest Proposal

In which I navigate my way through a series of unsuitable romantic denouements.

At last. This was what I had always wanted. I was about to begin an exciting new chapter of my life in which I would get a dog, stop wearing makeup, move to the country, and set about the important business of getting boring and old. But before then Simon invited me to spend a week at his villa in Marbella.

Going to stay with your gay best friend in Marbella is not the obvious way to eschew glamor and become a fat unkempt spinster, so I decided to put that project off until I came back from Spain with a fabulous suntan. However, I made some preparations for my new life of austerity in readiness for my return.

I had a word with the gamekeeper: "How are those cocker spaniel puppies coming on?"

"Nearly ready," he said. "You want one? I need to tell Long John if you're interested because they're selling like hotcakes."

Long John was a very tall cocker spaniel expert who ran a

spaniel training camp from the back garden of his house just outside the village where I kept my horses and supplied the local shoot
with their gundogs. It was hard core. If Al-Qaeda trained spaniels
they wouldn't come out as dedicated and willing to die for their
masters as Long John's spaniels.

He wasn't my first port of call, mind you. I had tried to give a
stray a home by applying to Battersea Dogs Home, but this
turned out to be more of a bureaucratic nightmare than trying to
adopt a child. Interviews, form-filling, home visits. Criminal rec-
ords bureau checks on my existing pets. There was particular
suspicion about my house rabbits. If they had the temerity to get
themselves eaten by the new dog, you see, there was a chance I
might sue. It didn't matter that I was prepared to sign a waiver
forgoing all my pet bunny–preserving rights under the EU con-
vention. They had to cover themselves for all eventualities. After
three weeks of battling canine-authority red tape I was starting
to think, fine, I'll just have to abandon the idea of helping an un-
wanted animal. Fine, you win, I give up. I'll buy a puppy. This
was a shame because I really identified with the little mutts behind the bars at Battersea. "I know how you feel, poppet," I said
to a particularly scrappy looking Chihuahua called Jingles, who
according to the blurb on his cage had been looking for someone
to love him longer than any of the other dogs.

"Don't worry, Jingles," I told him, "all the best people get rejected." He yapped pathetically and hurled himself at the bars. I
don't think he was reassured by me identifying with him at all.

I offered to take Jingles immediately. Of course I did. But the
dog wardens with clipboards were not convinced of my suitabil-
ity as a prospective Chihuahua adopter. Jingles was difficult, they
explained sternly. He was a problem dog. I don't think they were

impressed by my response: "How big a problem can he be? If he plays up you can just zip him in your handbag."

They asked all the same questions as the social workers. Was I going to be at home twenty-four hours a day, and if not why not?

When they demanded a signed letter from a dog-walking service to demonstrate that I had thought about what I would do with Jingles when I went on holiday—again, "Put him in my bag" didn't go down well—I decided enough was enough.

I felt pretty bitter about this. As I left the interrogation room, I looked at a family of hugely fat people in the waiting area, walking in and out to chain-smoke. I fancied that they were going to get a dog no questions asked, because they were never going to leave the house. And neither was their dog. Except when they set him on their neighbors during boundary disputes.

I realized I was becoming twisted, and far too right-wing. If I suffered any more rejection I was going to end up like Jingles, hurling myself at people and biting their ankles. So I told the gamekeeper to tell Long John that when they were ready, whatever that meant, I would have one of the spaniels.

"Please, I beg of you, don't get a dog," said Sally as I sat at her breakfast bar eating pistachios.

"I'm not getting it for a while yet," I explained. "I'm going on holiday with Simon first."

"Please, I beg of you, don't go on a holiday," said Sally.

"Is there anything you consider me capable of doing?"

"Not really. Not in the space you're in. You shouldn't make any major decisions until . . ."

"Until what? Until I'm eighty?"

"Yes. At least."

〇〇

Packing to go on holiday with a gay man is so much easier than
packing to go away with a boyfriend—or girlfriend, for that matter. I couldn't get over how easy it was. I just filled a huge case
with loads of really nice clothes and shoes and all the face creams
and cosmetics I felt like taking and didn't worry about turning
up with too much stuff. I just knew Simon wouldn't make snide
comments. And I was right.

When I got there, he didn't even remark on the weight of the
case, nor the amount of clothes I had hanging all over my room
after I'd unpacked. When I came down to breakfast in a tiny little
bright-red bikini he said, "Nice boobs!" When I put a huge pink
kaftan dress on to have dinner he said, "Darling, you look wonderful."

"Gay men get me," I thought.

I knew we were going to see eye to eye when I came down
to the pool on the first morning and he had laid our towels out
on the sun loungers. When I made a huge fuss about getting my
suntan lotion on right, he made a huge fuss, too. "You don't mess
with UV rays," said Simon.

"Exactly!" I said.

We spent ages reading the blurb on a bottle of melanin enhancer. Then we spent a blissful half hour reminiscing about the
suntan lotions of our youth, concluding that Bergasol factor-two
tanning oil was the all-time classic eighties nostalgia item, remi-
niscent of a simpler time when people hadn't heard of skin cancer
and were, in their blissful ignorance, having a fine time cultivat-
ing the life-threatening problem for later.

We mutually decided within seconds of dipping our toes into
the pool that it wasn't quite body temperature and Simon disap-

peared off to turn the pool heater up. We both got in like sissies, swam one width, and got straight back out again.

"It's just to get wet," said Simon, diving into a big fluffy towel and handing me mine. "Exactly," I said. We agreed about everything.

"Fucking Olympics," he said, reading the news on his iPad. "They won't be able to move for traffic. When it came to London, you couldn't park anywhere, not even in South Kensington."

"Thank you," I said, vindicated at last.

When we played backgammon, he set the board out on a little side table between our sunbeds. When he made me a drink of fizzy water he put a twist of lime in it that made it delicious. He had little bowls of salted almonds about the house that he replenished as soon as a handful was taken out. Everything had a ring of old-fashioned glamor to it. I was in heaven.

He was always, always immaculately groomed, even when we were lying on our sunbeds. His dark hair was cut classically, he was always clean-shaven, he wore dark aviator shades, he was evenly tanned. He was slim, with a neat, unobtrusive six-pack and not an ounce of extraneous fat. When he got out of the pool his designer trunks sagged slightly with the weight of the water to reveal a tantalizing glimpse of perfectly sculpted buttock. He looked exactly like the fantasy man I had told myself I would marry when I was a little girl.

But the best thing of all was that he didn't bat an eyelid when I got in a mess. He barely flinched as I faffed about trying to log on to my e-mail, cursing the fact that my laptop wouldn't work. When I dropped my BlackBerry and flew into a blind panic because I thought I'd broken it, he simply reached out from his sunbed while not even sitting up or taking off his shades and said, "Give it to me," fixed it by rebooting it, and then handed it back.

He gave every impression that he did not in any way disapprove of my prima donna dramatics.

"Of course he doesn't," I thought suddenly. "He understands the urge to dramatize. He's gay. Gay men get me. Straight men have never got me. I'm not made for straight men. I'm made for gay men!" I lay on my sunbed dwelling long and hard on this epiphany. Maybe humankind is evolving to allow straight women to get together with gay men because there aren't enough straight men to go round. I read once that because of a massive boom in female births in the seventies there was now a desperate shortage of men. Maybe mother nature in her wisdom had come up with a neat pragmatic solution: make use of the gay men to breed with for a while until the numbers even out.

I texted Sally a précis of my idea. She texted back, "are you still there? fck me are you actually gonna see out a whole holiday?"

"I think so this is a record for me three days and I haven't had any kind of row or crisis we r blissfully happy had huge panic yesterday he didn't mind at all"

"hmm maybe you should marry him"

Sitting by the pool we talked about our dreams. "I suppose I should go on one of those dating sites and look for a serious relationship," said Simon. "If I don't find someone soon I'm going to be even more saggy than I am now"—he pointed to his taut, flawless six-pack of a stomach—"and then no one will want me."

I sighed. I felt I was past that. I was at the next stage. The nuclear moment. "I suppose I should look for a gay man to co-parent with," I said, not even thinking.

After a few moments of silence I looked over at him. He had a strange expression on his face. "What's the matter? Is it something I said?"

"I like how you don't even consider me," he said rather tartly, "for your co-parenting lark."

"I do nothing but consider you, but I never dreamed you'd be interested," I cried.

"No, no, I'm not," he said nonchalantly, shutting his eyes.

"I'm just saying."

In the late afternoon we went into town and strolled around the streets in the mellow end-of-the-day heat. In the pharmacy, we were like kids in a candy store looking at all the different face creams we couldn't get in England. Simon bought another melanin enhancer and I bought some conditioner made from seaweed. Outside the shop he suddenly said, "Stop right there, I want to take a picture of you." He snapped me in front of a pretty courtyard with his iPhone. I caught him admiring the picture as we walked on. Intellectually, I had no word for what this was, although I knew what it felt like.

At a pavement restaurant, we ordered octopus salad and calamari (no garlic, for him) then sea bass and fries and I fell deeper into whatever it was.

The first platter of calamari arrived strewn with oil and garlic. "I'm sorry, but I ordered no garlic."

"*Si signor,* garlic."

"No, I don't want garlic."

"*Si.* Garlic."

"No. No garlic."

"No garlic?"

The waiter stood staring at the plate. "But . . ."

"Just fry the calamari in oil, but don't put any garlic in."

"No garlic?"

"No garlic."

"No garlic?"

"No garlic."

"No garlic ?"

"You do realize this could go on all evening," I said, mindful of the time. If we didn't get to our main course by 9 p.m. Simon would start to worry about his digestion overworking in order to cope with the late hour. You see, I was already starting to finish his sentences before he even said them.

Simon made a very elegant go-away sign with his hands. The waiter walked off holding the plate mournfully as if it contained a relic from the cross of Our Lord. Ten minutes later he appeared with another plate, which he set down brusquely as if he couldn't care less about it.

"Are you sure you didn't just scrape the garlic off?" Simon asked the waiter, narrowing his eyes as he surveyed the plate.

"No garlic."

"Yes, but is it a new one?"

"Is no garlic."

"It can't just be the old one with the garlic scraped off. Or rinsed under the tap."

I scooped up a squid and licked it. "Really, there's no garlic on there."

Simon picked suspiciously at his food as I wolfed down my octopus. As I ate, and he pushed squid pieces around the plate, he told me the story of his ex and how he'd left him because he picked his clothes up from the floor, folded them, and put them on a chair after sex.

"He said I was a control freak. But I was just being . . ."

"Caring," I said, finishing his sentence, my mouth full of octopus.

"Exactly!" he said, beaming his smile of gorgeous white teeth and chiseled jaw. "Caring. That's what I said." Our eyes met and something passed between us. Embarrassed, we looked in opposite directions. In the end, I broke the silence. "How's the squid?"

"Full of garlic."

"I thought so," I said, before adding, "Oh God, you're too perfect."

"I know," he sighed with huge sadness.

"You're wasted on men," I told him.

"I know," he said, sighing again.

"If you were my boyfriend I would let you tidy my clothes after sex. I would love it."

He sighed and shrugged. We were perfect for each other. It was all too tragic.

We sat in silence for a while. Then I told him the story of my gay friend Marcus who, despite having multitudes of affairs with men, had only ever loved one person in his life, a woman called Honoria Bertwhistle. He hadn't been able to marry her, on account of being gay and wanting to have sex with boys all the time, which would have been a bit of a fly in the ointment, so she married another man. But they never stopped loving each other and after many years of marriage, and two children, she came back to him and asked him to give it another go, at which point he really did give it some serious thought, being alone, single, and in his late forties, but unfortunately the project was scuppered again because he had his eye on a young popsy called Ryan who worked behind the counter at Tommy Hilfiger. Even so, I felt I was onto something.

"Isn't it possible that human beings might find their soul mate in the wrong gender? I mean, if soulmates are about souls then surely your soul mate might be in any body?"

"I suppose it's possible," said Simon, looking doubtful.

"But hopefully I won't find a soul mate with as stupid a name as Honoria Bertwhistle. Your name's not too bad, I suppose."

On our last day together, we sat by the pool playing backgammon and sipping water with twists of lime. "Look at this," I said, handing him my BlackBerry. A guy I had been on a few dates with had sent me a message informing me that he had been to see something called an exhaustion doctor. Simon peered at the message over his designer sunglasses.

"What a wuss," was his verdict.

"Gay men really are the only real men left," I thought, as I lay next to my unreconstructed male-chauvinist gay hero in the sun, the palm trees rustling over our heads, our glasses of gently fizzing water with a twist of lime glinting on the equidistantly placed side table.

"Gay men are strong, decisive, dynamic, and tidy," I thought, as I drifted off to sleep to the buzz of cicadas. "Gay men," I mused as I entered my happy dreams, "are the apex of evolutionary achievement on earth."

When I was getting ready to leave, Simon was preparing for a new boyfriend to arrive to stay for a week. "Have a lovely time with your loverrrrrr!" I said in a silly French accent.

"Oh whatever," he said, brushing me away.

"Well, the taxi's here so I'm going now."

"Fine," he said, looking lost suddenly.

"Hell, I'm just going to hug him," I thought. The problem was that once I started hugging I didn't want to let go. I couldn't peel myself away from the rare, comforting sensation of taut abs coupled with the delicious smell of fastidious cleanliness and expensive soap. "Why can't straight men ever get grooming this right?" I thought. He bore it manfully for a while, before peeling me off and putting me into my taxi.

Then as I turned away he landed a huge smacker of a kiss on my cheek. "Bye, doll face," he said, winking.

◌ೖ

As soon as I got home it was back down to earth. "I suppose I had better make an effort with a heterosexual," I thought, as I answered a text from MF asking whether I was back.

For our little reunion, we went to an Italian restaurant where he told me all about his latest business deal and I sat checking my phone that was on my lap in case Simon had texted.

Afterward, he walked me to the station. "I missed you while you were away," he said when we reached the ticket barrier. He looked like he might be about to declare his undying love and tell me he was leaving his wife. But he didn't.

In real life people don't make huge romantic leaps in the dark. We stood in front of the train announcement board and when my train was called I started to walk away. He grabbed me and we kissed. I pulled away. He pulled me back. "It's not *Brief Encounter*," I said. "I'm only going to Balham."

◌ೖ

"You sure you want this puppy?" said the gamekeeper. "Because when we get to Long John's you won't be able to say no."

I assured him that I did, that I had thought about it and that I was ready to take on whatever responsibilities came with it, which apparently, according to most people I asked, included sacrificing my entire life to devote myself to it twenty-four hours a day. I would never have a boyfriend now; I would never have time to get married or have children; I would never go out; I would never get

my highlights done again; I would in all likelihood not have time
to get any work done or earn money. I would probably end my days
in poverty, alone, covered in mud and poo, just me and the puppy.
And I was happy with that.

"Right, get in then," said the gamekeeper, opening the passenger door to his battered Defender. We drove the short journey to
Long John's, over fields, down tracks, and through woods, the
gamekeeper pointing out places of interest along the way: "There's
my pheasant pens," and so on.

"See that cottage," he said, pointing to a pretty house down a
dirt track on the land of a larger farmhouse. "It's about to go on
the market for four hundred grand. It's worth at least six hundred. Owner's desperate to sell."

"Maybe . . ." I said, staring through the muddy window at the
little red-bricked house with its semi-wild cottage garden and
picture-postcard picket fence. Long John answered the door and
led us to the back of the house where he kept his spaniel training
camp. The new pups were in the first run. All I could see was a
wriggling mass of furry black cuteness. There were at least eight
of them, although it was impossible to count because none of
them stayed still long enough and they all looked identical. Apart
from one, which had a yellow collar on.

"C'mere Cinnamon," said Long John as he reached down into
the run and pulled out the pup. "Last one left," he said, holding
her in his big arms and letting her lick his face. Last one left. Last
one left. "We'll get along just fine," I thought.

Long John held the wriggling little body out to me. It couldn't
have been more moving if he had been a midwife and I had just
given birth to the furry little critter myself. "Oh she's beautiful,"
I said as I took the writhing black piglet of a dog and tried to

hold her with limited success. Her head flopped about and she whimpered a lot. "See, it's just the same," I thought.

"Six hundred quid," said Long John. "Bring her back if you can't cope. There's always a home for her here." OK, so maybe that part is a bit different.

If babies are anything like puppies it's probably a good thing I never had one—a baby I mean. As billed, the puppy ruled my life and I soon realized that not only had I not had my highlights done for months, I had not brushed my hair for months. I was permanently wearing yesterday's clothes. For the first few weeks I seemed to do little else but chase around the house after it shouting, "No, no, no, no, drop it, drop it, no, no, please!" Then we would both flake out on the sofa and sleep. When she slept, I slept. I couldn't go anywhere because I had to give her so many feeds. She ate rice pudding for her midmorning snack and late supper. My clothes were covered in globs of it, as well as holes where her little teeth had nibbled me. My arms and legs were covered in bites and bruises. I looked a mess.

I should probably not have attempted to go to a film premiere. My hair was now almost completely brown, with blond bits on the ends, but there was no question of a visit to the hairdresser beforehand. When I tried to brush it I realized there was a chunk missing at the back. I had been sleeping with the pup and, as well as eating the wax earplugs out of my ears, she had chewed a patch of hair at the back of my head in the night. I got out a dress I doubted I would fit into, dug out a pair of snakeskin Manolos Scott had bought me, and laid them out.

I ran a bath and sank into the warm water while surveying the damage. My entire body was covered in tiny little puncture marks surrounded by black-and-green bruises. I looked like a heroin addict in the final stages. I closed my eyes. Everything would be all right when I moved to the cottage in the country . . .

I don't know what came first, the whoosh or the yelp. For a second I couldn't work out what was happening, but suddenly, in a tremendous cacophony of splashing and barking I was water wrestling with a spaniel puppy. There were arms and legs everywhere, some of them hers, some of them mine. She was lapping the water and licking my face and slapping me with her paws and barking and yelping and having a fantastic time.

I was an hour late when I got to Sally and Bobby's and they were waiting on the doorstep. Neither said anything as we sat in the black cab; they were too busy checking their phones to look at me. When we got to the red carpet, the usual photographer made a beeline for Bobby shouting, "Robert! Sir Robert! This way!"

As the three of us stopped and posed the snapper did the thing where he sighed and pointed his camera in the air and clicked it at nothing, but for some reason I decided to confront him this time. "I can tell you didn't take that picture, you know," I said, marching up to him.

He looked me up and down. "I don't do battered wife photos, love. No market for them in celebrity magazines."

"You have puppy scratches all over your face," said Sally through her teeth as she smiled for the banks of cameras.

They say that when you are tired of London you are tired of life, and I was happy to throw in the towel at this point. The next day I took the puppy to the country to see the horses and maybe go and have a look at that cottage with the picket fence. I called in at the sandwich shop at the truck stop where I was in the habit of buying tuna baguettes from a guy called Steve who was covered in tattoos and piercings.

"Where have you been? I haven't seen you in ages," he said,

starting to butter a baguette as soon as I strode up. "You've got scratches all over your face."

"Puppy," I said, gesturing to the car where she was sleeping in her travel cage.

"I wanted to ask you something," said Steve, eyeing me carefully. "Would you consider modeling for me?"

"Modeling?"

"Yeah. It sounds strange, but I'd like to put you in a plaster cast and make a model of you. It's all perfectly hygienic. I've been doing it for a while." His partner, who was flipping burgers, gave me a look. "I use a special hypoallergenic gel."

This is the sort of thing that can only happen to me. I nip somewhere for a tuna sandwich and end up being sucked into a fetish ring. "And where would this model making take place?" I asked.

"My house in Chertsey."

Of course it would. "Unfortunately, I'm claustrophobic," I said, before taking my baguette.

"There will be a lot more of this sort of stuff when I move to the sticks," I thought. Lord knows what they get up to in Surrey to while away the long dark winter months. Still, it's better than making a fool of myself at film premieres.

∽

The puppy settled down nicely and we got into a routine. Every night we would go for a walk, then we would retire to bed together, she curling up at the end of the bed and chewing the blankets. It was better than having a man because the chaos was, on balance, more manageable. Or so I thought.

"Come on then, bedtime," I said one night, getting up from

the sofa at the end of a movie, ready to turn in. The living room was in darkness and I picked up the remote to switch off the TV. I pressed the button I thought was the on/off switch, and then disaster struck.

"Smart Mode!" the TV screen announced.

"NO!" I screamed. This was precisely what had happened before when I'd ended up having to call out the cable repair man for £80.

I pressed the button again, but it didn't take it off Smart Mode—that would be too simple. I pressed another button, and another. "No Channels Stored!" the screen said.

"NO!" I screeched hysterically. "NO! DON'T DO THIS TO ME!"

I switched the TV on and off and it still came up on Smart Mode, which wasn't smart at all; it was just a blank screen.

"OH GOD NO, I BEG YOU, PLEASE DON'T DO THIS!"

At which point the puppy raced excitedly into the room and joined in. She leaped on to the coffee table, knocked over a glass of water, slid back off, ran around the room, jumped back on to the coffee table, and knocked the glass on to the floor.

"NO!" I'm afraid to say I shouted at the puppy. "PLEASE DON'T! NOT NOW! PLEASE STOP IT! OH GOD NO!"

It only took five minutes for a squad car to turn up outside my house, which I suppose is impressive. The first two officers banged on the door as I sat like a startled rabbit on my sofa, frozen to the spot in terror. So they shone torches through the window and around my living room.

"Answer the door, madam!" they shouted.

I ran to the front door and the puppy shot past me, so I flew down on to the floor to grab her. When I got the door open, the police found me on my knees, tears streaming down my face, clutching the puppy for dear life.

"Oh God," I said, "this isn't what you think."

"Where is he?" the first officer shouted, barging into the hall-way. "Where is he? Tell me now!"

"Who?" I wailed pathetically.

"The man who assaulted you. Quickly. You need to tell me where he is."

"Oh dear, there is no man, honestly."

"Madam, we've had three separate reports from neighbors of an assault taking place at this address. I am going to have to search the house. Stand aside, please."

The two officers checked the living room was secure, like they do in the movies, then ushered me inside and told me to stay there. "Mind the puppy doesn't get out, Dean," said one to the other, which, even in my compromised state, I thought was a nice touch.

They searched every room of the house, then sat me down. "If you're hiding something, you should tell us."

"I'm not hiding anything."

"Then what happened."

"I pressed the wrong button on the TV remote and it went on to Smart Mode. It's happened before. I have to get the cable guy out and they charge me £80."

"Has he done this to you before?"

"There is no he, honestly. It's the cable thing. It drives me crazy . . ."

"Madam, you need to tell us the truth."

"I am telling you the truth. I think I need to get it on to AV2, but I can never work out how."

"Madam, there's no point in you covering up for him."

On and on it went, until they made me sign a statement saying I was happy for them to leave me and that I didn't request further assistance.

"We're leaving you now, madam," said the first officer as they closed the front door slowly, as if expecting me to relent and invite them back.

"Yes, yes, that's fine, thank you," I said, before flopping down on to the sofa and clutching the puppy to me as she leaped on to my lap.

A few minutes later there was another knock at the door. There were six officers standing there this time. "Oh God, this is worse than the time the firemen came round," I thought.

"Madam, we've had reports that a man is fleeing through your back garden."

"What?"

"We need to search your garden, madam."

"What, all six of you?"

"Stand aside please, madam."

"Be my guest," I said wearily, leading them through to the kitchen.

While two officers searched my tiny little garden for an unfeasibly long time, four officers stood in my hallway in single file, talking into their police radios. "I was just shouting at the TV," I said as we all stood there waiting.

The officers came back in from the garden. "Nothing," they said to the others. They all started to file back out.

"You know," I said, walking behind them, "this reminds me of that scene in Monty Python's *Life of Brian*, where an entire battalion of Roman centurions files into Brian's one-room hut and comes out having found a suspicious-looking spoon."

The last officer out turned around on the doorstep and stared back at me. At last, I had their attention. "And another thing," I said, warming to my theme. "I've lived in this neighborhood for ten years and I've never seen a policeman. I've been burgled, had my bag snatched, had a thief come over the garden fence into my kitchen and steal my laptop from the table while I was in the house, I've had raiders trying to batter the front door down in the night, but I've never, ever been able to get a policeman to come round."

"Well," said the copper, "you've got six now." He had a point. It seemed such a shame to waste them.

"I don't suppose you could fix the telly?"

෨෨

When Simon got back from Spain, another doomed love affair with a younger man under his belt, we got together for dinner at our favorite brasserie. As if on autopilot, the camp fair trade waiter appeared.

He gave Simon the eye and slammed down our bottle of fizzy mineral water. Simon eyed him back as he walked away.

"How's your love life?" he said, turning the glow of his tanned face on me.

"I've bought a puppy."

"Oh dear. That good."

"Well, I don't need a love life now. I've got the best and most loyal companion a girl could ever have. And it's a working dog."

"Does that mean it loads the dishwasher?"

"No. It means it works a scent. You should see it retrieving a dead pheasant from a bramble patch."

"Sounds great. I must get one of those. The Filipino almost never clears the dead pheasants out of the bramble patches properly."

"Fine, you're not interested in my puppy."

"Is that mud on your neck or have you got a birthmark?"

I rubbed the spot he was pointing at. It was indeed mud. I'd been so busy with the puppy and the horses I hadn't had time to have a bath.

"Good God. I don't think I've ever seen mud. It really is brown, isn't it? It's disgusting."

The steaks arrived, both with beurre blanc. Simon sighed. "Waiter, I think I ordered mine without garlic, thank you."

"Oh that's right sir, yes. I just brought it with garlic to annoy you. Your actual steak will be along in ten minutes, when your friend has finished eating hers. Just the way you like it."

"He's getting a bit too bold now," said Simon, eyeing the waiter malevolently. "I might have to give him one."

Simon turned back to me and watched as I ate my steak. Usually he regaled me with all sorts of stories about his various conquests while I ate my dinner and he waited for his, but this time he just sat in silence, staring intently. Then he said, "I've been thinking. What does a wealthy Jewish gay man with low self-esteem because his father never took him to the football and who's desperately looking for someone to love, cherish, and nurture really need?"

"I don't know. Another TV heartthrob who isn't very nice to him in public because he's pretending to be straight so he can get a part in the next teen vampire movie? A waiter who brings him a steak with beurre blanc, turns him on by being catty, then gives him a blow job round the back of the kitchen?"

"No. Although well done, those are both good." He stared intently at me as I tucked into my steak ravenously.

"A child."

"I beg your pardon?"

"Well, don't sound so surprised. I do have a responsible, masculine side."

"I know you do," I said, my mouth full of steak, "but I never thought you'd go for it. We discussed co-parenting in Marbella and you said you weren't interested."

"I don't want to just co-parent. I want us to live together. I want to do this properly."

"You don't mean you want to have sex, do you?"

"Don't be silly, of course not."

"Oh," the disappointment on my face was enough to cast a shadow over the entire restaurant. "But won't that make us just like every other married couple?"

"I suppose so."

"Think about it. We both love low-factor tanning oils. We both like folding clothes."

"You're right. I suppose it could work...."

"Of course it could. You do realize you're still piling steak into your mouth, don't you?"

"I'm stressed," I said, shoveling in another forkful, cheeks bulging. "I have to eat when I'm stressed. All this is a shock. I mean, no man has proposed any kind of major commitment to me."

"Well, I am," he said, sipping from his mineral water and then straightening his place setting purposefully. "Isn't this a beautiful moment? Can I just say, with your mouth half open and full of rare meat like that, you've never looked more ravishing."

Could it be? Could the only man to make this big a romantic leap in my direction since eighteen-year-old David on the campsite in France be gay? Did it really matter that he was gay? Weren't gay men the new straight men, after all?

The waiter arrived with the new steak and plonked it down with sexually charged venom, but Simon didn't even notice. "Come

on, hurry up. I'm not some airy-fairy heterosexual, you know. I'm
going to need your answer. Will you?"

൭

The luxury I would choose on the cult British radio show *Desert
Island Discs*—in which a celebrity has to choose their favorite music and some essential items with which to be marooned on a
desert island—is a duvet. (I would also take a bottle of Coco Chanel and some strong antihistamines, in case anyone's really interested.) I couldn't live without a duvet. I dove under one for three
days after Simon "proposed." Things make more sense under a
duvet. Or they make no more sense but cease to matter. Of course,
like a whale, I came up at intervals for air. And southern fried
chicken. Also, the phone was bleeping incessantly and had to be
answered eventually. All the texts were from MF demanding to
see me.

I told him if he wanted to see me he would have to come over
because I was busy. This wasn't true and it may have sent him a
message that was entirely too provocative. We sat in the garden
and drank coffee. He looked desperate.

"I've left my wife."

"You've got to be kidding."

"I'm not kidding."

After he'd gone I was so distraught I overcame my techno-
phobia to Skype Sally, who was in Seville reviewing a spa for a
travel supplement. "I thought you wanted him to leave his wife,"
she said, bending beneath the screen as she painted her toenails.

"I did, while he was with her. What's the point of this if I can't
see you? I'm staring at a hotel bedroom wall with a painting that
looks like it's by Salvador Dalí."

"It is Dalí. Horrible isn't it?"

"I need face time. This is a major crisis."

Sally flopped back into view, hair over her face. "You've got exactly what you want. I don't know what you're complaining about."

"There is only one thing worse than not getting what you want, and that's getting what you want, as you well know."

"True. I've got to go. They're taking me to a Michelin-starred restaurant for squid-ink risotto. I just want to eat french fries in bed and watch the pay-per-view movies."

Because God has a sense of humor, the guy who walks his cats chose this moment to ask me out. He was walking a new Siamese past my house. I wasn't coming out of my house with the puppy, which would have been cute. I was kneeling on the pavement scooping up great, putrid lumps of rotting food, which had been ejected from the food waste recycling caddy in the night by the foxes my local council considers a protected minority group.

"I can't think what to call it," he said, gesturing at the aloof-looking kitty as I scooped up a heap of rotting rice, banana skins, spaghetti, and egg shells. "What goes with Bismarck and Napoleon?"

"Why don't you call it Meow Tse-tung?" I said, feeling bitter about the upset food caddy and the injustice of the lack of pest control in left-wing jurisdictions, where vermin seemed to be treated with more respect than people.

For some reason he thought this was genius. "You're very appealing when you want to be," he said.

"Thanks," I said, scooping up a heap of potato peelings.

I Skyped Sally. When she answered I was staring at the Dalí again. "I can't believe you're still painting your toenails. Is that all you've been doing since I last called?"

"Seville is really boring."

"How was the squid-ink risotto?"

"Vile. I got food poisoning. Although that may have been the three bottles of white wine. I'm having french fries in bed tonight."

"Sometimes I think it's best to keep things simple."

"Totally."

"OK, you have to help me. I'm trying to choose between a married man, a guy who walks cats, and my gay best friend."

"At least you have options."

"Yes, all of them mad. You'd think there would be something in the middle. It's all too complicated. What's the answer?"

"It's in there somewhere. You just need to tease it out."

"You choose. Quick."

"I'm not choosing."

"Fine, I'll do eenie, meenie, minie, mo."

"You can't do that. You need to choose. Who do you want?"

"I don't know. I really don't know." I thought about it. "I just want my happy ending."

"If it's a happy ending you want," said Sally, disappearing beneath the screen again, "maybe you should just go to the Shangri-La."

10

How To Build A Happy Ending

....

In which God, or whoever is up there, devises a more satis-
factory conclusion to this book than I would have managed
had I been left to my own devices.

....

I went for a Thai massage once. It was agony and when I looked
round to see what was going on this tiny woman was running up
and down my back in her bare feet shouting, "You wan' haaar'
massage!" Therefore, I was determined not to go to the Shangri-
La for my happy ending and thanks to a strange, almost mystical
series of events I didn't have to.

Here is what happened: once upon a time a man rescued a
racehorse.

(Bear with me, I need to go back a bit.) It was a steeplechaser
which, at the height of its career, had been bought by an Arab
prince for £150,000.

But the poor creature was now all broken down, and scarcely
middle-aged, it had been sent to a dealer's yard that was the last-
chance saloon. One day a kind man came to this yard with a friend

who was looking to buy a horse and he saw the demented creature pacing around its box and paid £1,000 for it. "You'll never
ride it," said the dealer. "It won't let anyone on its back."

But the man said he had seen something in the horse's eye. He
didn't care that it was so wildly disillusioned with life it couldn't
even return his generosity and be nice to him. In any case, he
couldn't really ride. He was a builder by trade. He just felt sorry
for the horse, and wanted to help it, so he set about looking for a
place where it could retire.

He found a nice stable yard in the countryside where it could
live. He made no demands on it at all. But he nursed the hope that
one day, maybe, if the horse learned to trust, and he learned to
ride, he might be able to get up on its back and go for a gallop.
The man and the horse became firm friends. All that natural
horsemanship magic when the damaged horse and the lonely person come together and heal each other, that all happened. There
wasn't a dry eye in the house. The man even looked a little bit like
Robert Redford. It really was a lovely story. I hope you enjoyed it.
Now, for my next trick, I will show you how this poetic tale col-
lided with my car crash of a life . . .

I was driving along a busy London street when my phone
rang. I know, I know, I should not have answered it. But I put it on
speaker in my lap. I wasn't driving along like one of those yummy
mummies with a phone clamped to her right ear shouting, "Nigel! Nigel! Have you picked Talullah up from baby ballet? Damn!
That pedestrian came out of nowhere!"

"Oh thank goodness you're there! Are you there? I mean,
where are you?"

It was Sonia, sounding hysterical.

"If her micro-pigs have escaped again I'm not going down

there," I thought. Sonia, my rich divorcée friend, was becoming more eccentric as the years passed. She was seeking increasingly inventive ways of fighting off solitude as she whiled away her empty-nesting years in her enormous country house. She had given up on having dodgy lodgers like the fireman and was now sharing her mansion with an assortment of lamas, rabbits, chickens, and micro-pigs. Her menagerie free-ranged around the house and lawns and she declared them infinitely preferable to human beings. The micro-pigs weren't micro, though. They were pigs, plain and simple. They were huge and very self-opinionated and when they escaped from the grounds of the house it usually took several people to chase them down the lanes and herd them back up the driveway.

"Problem?" I said.

Sonia was shrieking. "Oh! O-o—ooooh! It's so exciting. I've found you a man. He was wandering down Cobham high street wearing jodhpurs.

"What on earth are you on about?"

"He's divine. I put him in the back of the Bentley."

"You did what?"

"Yes, he's too young for me. But I thought he would be purrrrrfect for you! So I put him in the back of the Bentley. With my shopping. It was a bit of a squeeze."

"You can't just kidnap men off the street," I explained "There are laws against it."

"Oh no, he liked it," said Sonia. "He and I were queuing for coffee in Cobham. Well, you know, I'd taken the Bentley out for a run—it's so long since I've been out in it and the engine needed an airing. Also, I found the pigs under the hood the other day, lord knows how they got in there . . ."

This was an anecdote that could run wildly off course, I sensed. Sonia told stories that were like Russian dolls. Each one opened out to reveal another one inside it and after about six of them, and no sight of any of them concluding, one started to feel gripped by panic.

"Where is the man now?"

"Oh, he's just moving his horse. He won't be long."

"Horse?"

"Yes, can you believe it? He has a horse, just like you! So I told him the stable yard where he was keeping his horse was really not the place to be at all—monstrous place, I heard that the woman who runs it . . . Karen, I think she's called, or is it Annabelle? Oh, now, let me think, it might be Jennifer . . ."

"Sonia! Finish the bit about the man you've found!"

"Oh, yes, well, I told him he should move his horse immediately to where your horse is, where his horse would be much better looked after."

"You persuaded him to go and put his horse in a lorry and drive it to where my horse is, right now, this afternoon?"

"Yes! And he'll be arriving at your stable yard any time now, so I thought, if you go down there in, you know, your best riding getup, beige jodphurs and whatnot, then when he arrives with his horse . . ."

"I've got to go. The cops are behind me."

⟣

But once I put the phone down and started complying with the law my driving didn't improve at all. In fact, it got worse. I nearly ran over a cyclist thinking about the man who was any minute going to walk into my life down the ramp of a horse transporter, if only I did what my friend told me, and cooperated with this twist of fate . . . *

⁊

The man just wanted the best for his horse. So when a strange woman told him the horse would be much better off in another stable yard he didn't hesitate to move him.

The man was tall, blond, and handsome, and he had dressed for the occasion of bringing his new horse to its new home in white breeches and tall boots. As he led his horse down the ramp, he was mobbed by all the teenage girls who kept their ponies there.

He also noticed a moody-looking woman cursing as she watched the gamekeeper heave a sack of logs into her car.

You would think the man would be happy talking to the sixteen-year-old girls, but you have to remember he was the sort of person who was drawn to awkward things.

He overheard the moody woman complaining about how impossible it was going to be to get the logs out of her car when she got to the other end and he offered to do it for her.

When he got to her house that evening he put the logs in her hallway, then listened to her moan about how her TV was stuck on Smart Mode.

Then she told him the bedroom needed new wardrobes built because the old ones were too small, or possibly she had too

* when are they going to make driving while under the influence of daydreaming an offense? It's a scandal that motorists are allowed to cause accidents because they are thinking about something else. Why oh why do we not fit every car with remote brain sensors to set off alarms in police stations when drivers' minds wander? How many more people have to die before we take this simple safety precaution?

many clothes, but either way, she needed someone strong to do something macho in there.

She also showed him her boiler, which had exposed pipe work, badly fitted by a rogue plumber who charged by the hour.

She told him how she longed for someone to build her a boiler cupboard—her dream boiler cupboard, is how she put it.

That is when he told her that he was, in fact, a builder. She swooned, visibly.

After he had measured up for the cupboard, he took her for pizza.

༺༻

"I always have the same thing, four cheeses with tuna," I said briskly to The Builder as he scrutinized the menu. I confess, I was thinking "come on, come on, let's move this along."

But he was in a world of his own. Was he about to ask the waitress to describe every single pizza on the menu? If so, I really couldn't stand it.

"Please, please don't let him be remedial, or a maniac," I thought, as I motioned to the waitress to come over.

"I call it the Desperada. I named it after myself," I said, hoping to bring the conversation speedily around to the question of whether or not he could see me as a prospect, or I him.

I was toying with the idea, you see, of not dodging the curve-ball meted out to me by Sonia, and making him my new boy-friend. I had decided that I did, after all, have a vacancy. I couldn't really choose between a married man, a guy who walks his cats, and my gay best friend. I had to start again. Chapter 10 or not, I was at square one.

Fine, so I had only known him about ten minutes. Fine, so I didn't know the first thing about him.

But after Mr. Married, Mr. Maniac, Mr. Cat-Walker, Mr. Gay, Mr. Oh, and Mr. Alopecia, not to mention the Farting Man, the Gelded Firefighter, the Pot-bellied Plumber, the Lobster-Stewing Art-Thief, and the Fiancé-Who-Wanted-to-Change-My-Name, I was past caring whether a man was a good prospect. I barely had the energy to work out whether I was attracted to him or not. Let's face it, with my history, what did I know about anything anyway?

I was tired of dating. And romance. And love. And All That (yes, I mean sex). I wanted peace. I wanted a man, but I was tired of looking for The Man. The Man might not exist and if he did exist, he might exist in the Hindu Kush, or Cornwall, which was way too far to go in either case.

In the absence of The Man, I would happily settle for A Man who was suitable in three or four ways. He needn't tick all the boxes. Three boxes . . . OK fine, two big boxes would do.

This one was handsome, and he could fix things. Two major, major boxes. Oh, and he loved horses. That was three boxes ticked.

We're ticking on gas, I thought, as I totted it all up in my head. The Builder, meanwhile, was still staring down at the menu.

The Not Remedial box was definitely unticked. "Tsk. You can't have it all," I thought.

"Are you ready to order?" I prompted, as he squinted and brought the menu so close to his face he looked like he was trying to hide from someone.

With any luck he was just short-sighted.

This is what I have learned about finding a man in your late thirties.

1. Don't choose him yourself. It is better to let an eccentric girlfriend who lives with two pigs and a herd of lamas drag a man randomly off the street and forcibly shoehorn him into your life by delivering him to you in the back of her vintage Bentley, bound and gagged if needs be, than try to exercise your own powers of selection, which have been scientifically proven to be woeful in every single way.

2. Be open-minded about dating tradesmen because you need to

3. Consider your boiler. Do you want to be at the mercy of Tony the plumber all your life?

The first night I spend with The Builder—which is only the date after the pizza date—I realize how handsome he is. He has beautiful blue, soulful eyes, blond tousled hair, and ruddy, weatherbeaten skin.

He has the loudest laugh of anyone I have ever met, which is a lot of people, because I am now dangerously middle-aged.

He talks like a cockney. He is a bloke. A geezer. He wears T-shirts when it is minus 4. He's a straight-talker. He has come up the hard way. He didn't have any formal education and yes, he struggles with a menu when there are too many choices, though not because he can't read. He taught himself to read. He can't choose between a lot of different types of food because he still remembers the time when, as a child growing up in the mean streets of South London, he often didn't have enough to eat. And so despite being a man of the world now, he still panics when he see a lot of choices on a menu.

But he can build a great boiler cupboard. He is funny. He is kind. He is quick. He is clever, notwithstanding his lack of education and the fact that he left school at thirteen. He has big, calloused hands. The sides of his eyes are lined beyond his thirty-eight years from working on rooftops. His blond hair is always windswept.

His laugh really is the loudest laugh in the world. It's so loud it makes you duck. But every now and then he says something wonderful.

Before he closes his eyes that first night, he turns to me and says: "I have been looking for you all my life."

ভ৹

Sally was enraptured.

"You are going to have the most gorgeous babies!"

"Why does everything involve babies with you?"

"Because there are all these cute outfits in Baby Gap right now and I don't have a single friend with small kids I can dress up."

"Fair enough," I said, forking a heap of marinated endives, toasted fennel seeds, ricotta, and orange pieces into my mouth. "You know what the best thing is? He's funny. That night we had pizza we never stopped talking. He told me all these brilliant stories about jobs he's done and women who've thrown themselves at him as he's mended their roof and so on, and we screamed with laughter. For hours."

Bobby tap-danced into the kitchen. "Did I hear you say you've got a new man, darling?"

"It's a builder, Bobby," said Sally, proud as can be.

"How deeee . . . fucking . . . lightful!" said Bobby, executing a natty pas de deux. "I simply adore builders. I bet he's a knockout in bed." And he did a jazz-hands finish.

৩৩

Lydia was not so sure.

"You can't date a man who pays for everything in cash and doesn't have a passport," she pronounced.

"It's not that he's never been anywhere. He's just let his passport run out."

"You can't date a man who just lets his passport run out."

"The cash thing is how tradesmen are. He may well have a bank card; he just doesn't use it."

Lydia raised her eyes to heaven and gasped. "Dear god."

"He earns good money. It's just not as much as what I earn."

"It will never work."

"He's incredibly artistic. He could have been an architect if his mother hadn't abandoned him as a baby and his father had to bring him up. They didn't have much and although his father wanted him to go to school, he couldn't because back in those days men weren't just left alone to bring up kids; social services would have got involved and might have taken him into care, so his dad took him out of school as a child and they went on the run . . ."

"Stop!" said Lydia, with her hands over her ears. "I can't listen for another second! You're dating a poor person! UGH! I feel all itchy! I'm breaking out in hives!"

৩৩

Simon was philosophical.

"How's The Builder?" he would ask, whenever we met for steak and erroneous beurre blanc with a dollop of waiter sarcasm.

"He's quite hard up," I would say. "The other day, for example, he only had ten pounds left in the world until he next got paid for a roofing job. Apparently, it's how a lot of people live."

"Well, what do you need money for anyway?"

"To pay the bills. You know, gas, electricity?"

"What do you need gas and electricity for? You can huddle together for warmth, can't you?"

"We'll never be able to eat out together at places like this. Unless I pay."

"But places like this are horrible. What would you want to come here for?"

And the waiter would arrive with a steak, lavishly garnished in garlic and chives and all the other substances Simon had expressly told him he could not eat for fear of dying from his allium allergy and I would think, "you're right. We shall lead a simple life, unfettered by the vain trappings of wealth and all its empty promises."

☙

The only trouble was, once we tried to settle down and practically work out the logistics of two people living the simple life, unfettered by the vain trappings of wealth and all its empty promises it all got very complicated.

I didn't want another man moving into my flat, and The Builder was renting a house nearby in the region of London known to locals as "the arse-end of Wimbledon, not the posh bit where the tennis is."

I didn't want to live in "the arse-end of Wimbledon, not the posh bit where the tennis is" and he didn't want to upset me by living in my space. So we carried on living in our separate homes.

But that wasn't the biggest problem. The biggest problem was that when he stayed over at my place I kept finding little pieces of evidence that pointed toward us being totally incompatible.

For example, one day, I found a bag of money in the refrigerator.

"And?" he asked, after I demanded he explain himself.

"It's a plastic shopping bag full of fifty-pound notes," I gasped.

"And?"

"It's in the salad crisper!"

"I'm sorry. You're point is?"

"What if I had thrown it out, thinking it was some moldy old lettuce?"

"Have you?"

"No."

"Well then."

Reader, I panicked. It felt like I was nearing my happy ending and it had to be an oversight on God's part that it involved a man who kept all his worldly possessions next to my vine-ripened tomatoes.

"And another thing," I told Simon, as he looked disgustedly at his beurre blanc, although you would have thought he would be used to it by now, "he has lunch every day at a place called The Chinese Caff. I mean, it's a café, but it's not pronounced *caffay*. It's pronounced *caff*. They stir-fry everything, even the English breakfasts. I can smell the stir-fry oil coming out of his pores. I try to neutralize it by serving him salad for dinner but the fried food is too strong for me. I can't fight it.When he comes home in the evening he smells of brick dust and bacon."

"Oy vey!" said Simon, who was most Jewish when things really disgusted him. "But it needn't be a problem. You just need to put a digestive cleanse through his system. I can give you a terrific detox smoothie recipe."

"You have an answer for everything, don't you?"

☙

I was losing my nerve. Was this it? Was this my happy ending?

If I stayed with The Builder, it would involve me turning into a bad version of Gwyneth Paltrow, making quinoa, blueberry, and nutmeg smoothies every morning and possibly liquidizing the money we were due to pay the mortgage with if I picked up the wrong bag in the refrigerator. One panic sparked another panic.

I soon realized that if I was going to forge my happy ending with a guy who kept his life savings in a supermarket bag I would have to guard my financial independence from him. I would have to keep all my assets separate in case he turned out to be one of those men who wanted to marry me and then divorce me and take my worldy goods from me in the divorce settlement on the basis that he had been a "kept man." Well, you never know. I couldn't let that happen. I would have to live in my house while he kept his house. This also solved the problem of me worrying about losing my single persons council tax discount.

A big part of me was quite willing to get rid of a relationship that looked like it was going somewhere in order not to jeopardize it, especially if the person involved was not wealthy enough to make me sanguine about losing the discount. The Builder, therefore, could not be allowed to move in permanently.

He would just have to go on living with his ex-girlfriend. Yes, I know, this is all sounding more and more complicated. You are starting to doubt that this builder fellow has anything to do with a happy ending. You are not the only one.

"What do you mean, your builder boyfriend is still living with his ex-girlfriend?" said Sally, screwing up her face, although that could have had more to do with the huge heap of watercress, goat cheese, and smoked chicken salad she had just put into her mouth. "Hmm, this is experimental. I'm not sure about it."

"Do you mean the salad, or my living arrangements with The Builder."

"Both."

"How long have you been married? You have no idea what singletons have to cope with in this godless age, do you? The last time you were single, women used to be courted then get marriage proposals."

"You're right. I'm ancient. I remember heavy petting."

"Please. Nowadays the whole dating thing is a war zone, a hideous, wretched, desolate no-man's-land strewn with bruised, bleeding, brokenhearted people half dead from the effort of crossing moral boundaries they swore they never would."

"Didn't I tell you to avoid the new David Hare play, darling?" said Bobby, skidding into the kitchen on a new pair of black-and-white tap shoes. "It's worse than the one where Bill Nighy recites the phone book."

"Hmm," said Sally, nauseously, although this could have had more to do with the second mouthful of cheesy-smoked chicken salad.

"What do you mean hmm?"

"I mean hmm."

"No, you don't mean hmm, you mean hmm I'm an idiot. You mean: hmm who goes out with a man who's living with his ex-girlfriend? I know your hmms. That was definitely a judgmental hmm, not a nonchalant hmm or an I-don't-like-this-salad hmm."

"I don't like this salad."

"It's the smoked with the goat."

"Should have used ricotta."

"Personally, I don't think you can put any kind of cheese with chicken."*

"But they were together a long time. When they split up, it made sense to go on sharing a house. It's the modern way. Virtually all couples who break up carry on living together now. There's an acronym for it."

"Really? What is it then?"

Unfortunately, I couldn't think. After some frenzied Googling on my iPad, I found some people called Living Apart Togethers, or LATs.

LATs are together, romantically speaking, but live at separate addresses, for practical, financial, and/or spiritual reasons ("I just so need my space," and so on).

Couples who have split up but continue to live, claustrophobically enough, under the same roof because they can't afford to divide things down the middle, or, as in the case of The Builder and his ex, because they can't be bothered to, are called Separated But Living Togethers, or SBLTs. Not a very satisfying acronym. Not an acronym at all, really.

So, in the interests of providing others like me with a respectable epithet for use in tabloid stories about their kind, I invented the term DAMWISLE (Dating a Man Who Is Still Living with

---

* I am prepared to concede the important exception of chicken Caesar salad. But I think we can all agree that that is where any kind of decent marriage between chicken and cheese begins and ends and let us hear no more said about it.

His Ex) while Sally invented SWAMTAH (Silly Woman Allow-
ing a Man to Take Advantage of Her).

∾

The Builder's ex was called Jenny. So things were not helped
when an old girlfriend of mine called Jenny arrived unannounced
from Ireland, having decided on the spur of the moment to emi-
grate to London and took up residence in my spare room while
she found herself an apartment.

"Your Jenny or my Jenny?" became a question we asked each
other endlessly until we got the hang of things.

My Jenny was always getting drunk and leaving the oven on.

His Jenny was a compulsive tidier and would leave him shitty
little notes about the state of the house.

"Jenny's got to go," The Builder would say.

"Your Jenny or my Jenny?" I would ask.

"Well, both, I suppose, ideally. Or maybe neither." In truth, he
didn't know. He had as many doubts as I did.

The thing was, if we both got rid of our Jennys, and moved in
together like normal people we wouldn't have any way back.

Besides, much as we sometimes resented our Jennys, they were
the ideal living partners. My Jenny was hardly ever there, on account of being a workaholic alcoholic, either at the office or the bar
next door to the office. She barely ever made it home, and when she
did, I soon got used to intercepting her efforts to cook a ready-meal
by leaving it in a blazing-hot oven for three hours with the door
open. She would be in bed sleeping off the wine by the time I found
it burned black. What's more, she was still registered to an address
in Ireland so my 25 percent tax discount was safe and sound.

The Builder's Jenny was also the perfect tenant because she

was there all the time, tidying and organizing him, and he liked this because he got lonely. Plus, she knew all his bad habits and had well-rehearsed techniques for coping with them, mostly by leaving him shitty little notes.

Maybe she could be his weekly housewife, I could be his weekend wife, and my Jenny could be my weekly companion. And then maybe one day His Jenny and My Jenny could come together, inspired by their common hatred and annoyance at us, and live happily ever after.

"Do you think our Jennys should meet?" was a question we often asked each other, and debated long into the dark winter evenings.

In the meantime, there was something very comforting about sending my boyfriend home to his ex-girlfriend when I had had enough of him. And then settling down to a quiet night in with a girl who was paralytic in her bed after failing to cook a ready-meal.

"If this is the only way I can do a relationship," I thought, "then so be it."

∽

To confuse matters further, MF called and said he wanted to take me out to lunch. Suddenly the relief of being taken to an expensive restaurant by a man who had an office, a PA, a passport, and didn't carry a mishmash of fifty-pound notes around in a plastic bag, was, I am ashamed to say, as overwhelming as the smell of bacon and brick dust.

"You're right," I told Lydia as we ordered pizza. "I can't go out with a man who pays cash for everything. I'm not looking for the chairman of HSBC but a debit card is the least I can hope for, surely?"

Lydia bristled with vindicatory satisfaction, ordered a side salad and garlic bread to mark the occasion, and urged me to accept the Medium Fromage's invitation, which surely meant he wanted to rekindle our affair immediately, and probably marry me. "A helicopter is a helicopter," she reminded me with a grave look on her perfectly made-up face.

Simon was very upset. "I don't see why you can't earn the money and look after The Builder. What's the matter with you? Pull yourself together. Man up. Grow a pair."

Sally, meanwhile, was distraught about the sale at Jojo Maman Bebe. "I am literally never going to have another friend's baby to dress, ever. I can feel it. Time is running out. I'm watching all my girlfriends become old maids and there is literally nothing I can do about it. Oh God, this is worse than the menopause."

"It's the friendopause," I said, chewing a mouthful of pea shoots, walnuts, blue cheese, and beef jerky.

Given that she had introduced us, Sonia had the greatest right to be upset but she was strangely sanguine about it.

Only months later did I discover that she had been continuing a friendship with The Builder and keeping him together as he all but fell apart. As I sat in Sally's kitchen, being fed strangely delicious salads, The Builder was being comforted by Sonia, who had her own unique style of therapy.

As they slugged back her favorite vodka shots at her kitchen table, he told her how much he loved me and she tried to counsel him in the best ways to win me back:

"Not a credit card, you understand. Just a current account. Down the hatch!"

☙

Newly single, I wandered around on a pink cloud enjoying my freedom. "I can do this," I exulted. "I am strong, I am invincible, I am WOMAN!"

And when I tired of Helen Reddy, I played Bonnie Tyler's "Total Eclipse of the Heart," usually when I was getting maudlin in the bath.

And I played Tom Petty's "Free Fallin" as I drove along in my little convertible with the roof down. I whooped and banged the steering wheel like Tom Cruise in *Jerry Maguire*.

I even tried to change a fuse in a plug and paint a bit of scuffed baseboard. I went for a lovely lunch at an expensive new restaurant with MF and he told me he had missed me, although he was very busy and could only do hors d'oeuvres as he had to be back in the office for a conference call with the prime minister of Pakistan.

Then, possibly because of all the above activities, though probably not, I quite literally bust a gut and ended up in an NHS hospital in South London where my bravado evaporated entirely.

There is only one phrase to sum up the godforsaken place that is my local South London hospital: *Lasciate ogne speranza, voi ch'entrate.**

I would never go there voluntarily. But I didn't really have any choice. I remember sitting on the sofa watching *Catch-22*. I remember falling off the sofa onto my knees on the floor. I remember dialing the emergency services with my BlackBerry. I remember the ambulance arriving. I remember draining the gas and air tank inside the ambulance. I remember the world looking very nice indeed for the few seconds that the gas and air were working. And then I just remember pain, like a lead blanket.

* Well, then, you should have listened during Italian class, shouldn't you?

Three doses of morphine and I lost count. I lay on a trolley for hours. Then I was pushed into a side room.

People everywhere screamed. I thought feverishly of the character from *Catch-22*, wrapped from head to foot in bandages so that no one even noticed when he died. Time slowed down until I was watching everything in slow motion. This must be hell, I thought, slipping quietly into unconsciousness. This must be because I took the Lord's name in vain, or didn't eat my greens, or something.

A nurse came in and as she was changing the drip in my arm, asked me if there was someone they could call. Someone? Some . . . one?

I slipped into a deep, morphine-induced sleep.

༉

When I opened one eye, The Builder was sleeping at the side of the bed. He hadn't moved all night. I had a vague memory of him arriving, shouting at the doctors. I remember him staring at the ultrasound scans they had done of my stomach and yelling: "Even I can see that's a burst cyst you *&^%ing *&^! Now pull your finger out of your *&%$ you *&%$ and *&%^ing do something!"

He might not have a chequing account. He might be a bit rough around the edges. He might eat at a café pronounced *caff* where an angry Chinese lady filled him with bacon fried in peanut oil. He might do all these things, and he might always do them. But he might also really love me.

While I was convalescing, The Builder filled the refrigerator with ready-meals; walked the dog, who was very pleased with the turn of events that had brought him back to us; and looked after me like I was a fragile little swallow. And I balled and screamed and complained 24/7. But he didn't seem to mind.

As soon as I was well enough we talked about trying to give it another go, for real this time. But when I tried to persuade The Builder to stop living with his ex-girlfriend he fretted about money and said he didn't ever want me to feel he was taking advantage of me.

And we argued on and on until in the end it was easier for me to say, "I can't see a way that it is going to work" than it was to find a solution to our living arrangements.

∞

Then Sonia rang me in a tizz.

"You are never going to guess what's happened?"

"The micro-pigs have escaped and eaten the starter motor of the Bentley?"

"No, or I don't think they have. Oh dear, maybe I had better look . . ."

"What was the thing you were ringing about?"

"Oh yes, well, you see, it was about the Bentley . . ."

It turned out that the night before, over countless vodka shots, and an episode during which they had managed to get one of the micro-pigs inebriated, The Builder had revealed to Sonia that he had driven past a classic car dealer and found a 1928 Vanden Plas Bentley for sale that matched exactly the description she had once given him of the beautiful old car her mother had once owned but had sold a few years before she died and which she, Sonia, now desperately wanted to buy back to honor her mother's memory. Upon further investigation it turned out to indeed be the car. And the matter of The Builder being the one to find it was doubly poignant when you consider that she had met The Builder while out driving her existing vintage Bentley, which had been her father's car.

"So you see, my father's car has found my mother's car!"

"So, an omen, you mean? It makes it fate, right? The Builder and me?"

"Totally," said Sally, "and just in time for the Harvey Nicks winter childrenswear sale!"

"I suppose I had better contact him."

"You'll be lucky if he'll still have you," said Simon. "You're a disgrace, running out on him like that when you're obviously destined to be together."

"But if this is fate, why doesn't it feel better?"

Sonia became serious, which was rare. "Because you're scared," she said.

༄

It might all have been a bit of a moot point because at that very moment I got the opportunity to take out a lease on a small rental in the country. The gamekeeper found it for me. It was a converted barn on the estate where I kept my horses. It was idyllic, and wouldn't break the bank. I could keep my flat in London and have a weekend place. I would be living the dream.

But after a few nights luxuriating in rural solitude, I sat alone in the barn with the spaniel, watching reruns of *Dallas* as the owls and the bats hullaballooed outside and moths and daddy longlegs fell from the ceiling onto my face every few seconds and thought "I don't know if I can do this for the rest of my life."

And then, as if by magic, my phone pinged and a text came in from The Builder: "I miss you and the dog," it said. I think it was his missing the hound that did it.

Without thinking, I started typing a reply. "If you're passing," I told him, "pop in." He wasn't passing. He couldn't have been. It was nearly 11 P.M. But fifteen minutes later, his pickup truck was making its way up the dusty track that led to my barn.

∽

The next morning, as I made my way down the track in my little car, the gamekeeper stopped his Land Rover on the tracks and wound his window down.

"Never go back," said the gamekeeper.

"What are you saying?"

"If something doesn't work the first time, it won't work the next time neither."

"Do you know about everything that is happening? I mean, he came up this track in the dark last night. And he left before dawn this morning. No one could possibly have seen him."

"No one but me," said the keeper, staring philosophically into the middle distance, as was his way. "I see everything. It's a gift I sometimes wish I didn't have . . ."

It was deeply unnerving that the gamekeeper had declared my relationship with The Builder doomed. The gamekeeper couldn't possibly be wrong, could he?

Either the keeper was wrong and my entire value system was about to crumble, or the keeper was right, as usual, and my love affair with The Builder was pointless.

"And another thing," said the keeper, looking down at my tiny wheels, one of which had yet another puncture, "you're gonna need a bigger car."

It was true. I had gone down so many potholes and ripped up so many tires since I moved to the country I should have bought shares in Kwik-Fit tire-fitters. I definitely needed a big four-wheel drive to go with my new lifestyle.

"Volvo XC90. 100k miles. One owner. Never towed." When I got to the showroom the only space to pull in was at the car wash where some Eastern Europeans allowed me to put my battered and bruised little Fiat beneath a jet-washing machine.

"You sure you don't want wash?" said one of them, a lean, muscular chap with his overalls pulled down to reveal his tanned, bare chest. The spaniel sat on the front seat panting at him.

"No, it's fine, thank you."

"We wash good."

"Yes, I'm sure."

I was starting to feel this was a bad idea. Here I was, a single woman, about to test-drive a four-by-four. I was going to be taken for a ride, in many more ways than one.

I then realized the Eastern Europeans were washing the XC90. It was gunmetal gray, with a rusty old bike rack on the back. I peered through the windows and there were candy wrappers all over the seats. Oh, and the mark from an auction sticker was still visible in the windscreen.

A salesman showed me inside. I pressed something on the dash and a CD of *James and the Giant Peach* popped out. I opened the arm rest and a Haribo wrapper fluttered into the air. I felt a pang. What would I put in the seven seats? Once Cydney was installed in the boot, it would be so empty back there where the kids had once clambered about, giggling at the start of a trip, as dad checked the diesel level and mum put on everyone's favorite Roald Dahl CD and . . .

"You gonna start it?" said the salesman.

I tried to make the car move but an alarm went off.

"Handbrake," he said, looking the other way out of the passenger window.

"Ah ha ha," I said, trying to keep up the pretense a bit longer. Then I had to give in.

"Actually, I don't know how to drive an automatic. The last time I drove one I drove it over the sea wall in Saint-Tropez harbor."

"Just forget your left foot," he said, still staring out the window.

I lurched dangerously around the block like a learner driver and when we got back he said: "You wan' it?"

Oh god. Oh god.

And then, The Builder's pickup truck appeared and everything went into slow motion. He didn't so much park his truck as hurl it through the entrance and screech to a halt in the most outrageous way in the middle of the forecourt. He leaped out, leaving the van door flung open, like Mr. Darcy getting off a horse and throwing aside the reins. He ran toward me in slow motion. Really, he did. His hair was looking its most blond and windswept. My jaw dropped open and I stood there openmouthed.

"You can't park there!" yelled one of the jet-washers.

But The Builder started to speak a special language called "tradesman." All I heard was "Five minutes mate . . . sort you out mate . . . down the road on a job mate . . . yeah, that's right, Fat Dave! Yeah, he is! Ha ha! Yeah go on then, two sugars . . ."

He turned to the salesman: "Ha ha! You were gonna brave her

driving then, were you? Ha ha! Oh you know Fat Dave? Yeah, he is! Where you from? Sri Lanka? Vanakkam!"

I left him to it in the end. I went to sit in the little car with Cydney and watched as he lifted the hood of the Volvo and started pulling the engine to pieces as it ran. Smoke everywhere, he was shouting about when the cam belt had been done and whether they knew Spikey from West London Automatics.

When he'd finished he came and sat with us. Cydney went wild.

"How did you know where to find me?"

"I'm doing a job roofing down the road. I saw you pulled up on the forecourt. Didn't I, Cydney? Yes! And I thought, oh dear, mummy's about to get ripped off buying a big Volvo! Yes! I did!"

Then he announced that a car I had expected to pay £9,000 for was £6,700, taxed.

"Tight bastards," he said, staring down at the sales invoice and shaking his head at the bottom line. "I reckon I can get him down a bit more if I go back in there and tell him Spikey will . . ."

"Please," I said, taking my wallet out, "I'm happy. I'm really, really happy."

෴

During my "invincible" phase, I had decided to properly renovate my London flat, just in case I wanted to sell it and up sticks once and for all to the country. Stefano the Albanian had been helping me. He was, of course, delighted to get the call. He got to work with gusto, sawing up wood and sanding everything he could get his hands on. After three days I walked into the room to find him standing proudly next to an elaborate four-door cupboard, which went right up to the window frame, leaving no room to hang curtains. He refused point-blank to dismantle it.

Even when I cried he refused. Even when I made the special howling sound he said there was no way he was going to change it. It was my fault, apparently, because I should have specified that I wanted a window frame with space to hang curtains, and that as things were I would just have to content myself with a roller blind.

"A roller blind?" I said, much as Lady Bracknell said, "A handbag?"

॰॰

The Builder turned up that evening in his battered pickup truck, the back of which had a new and impressively butch dent. His hair was looking particularly dust-filled and tousled.

He strode into the main bedroom and surveyed the wardrobe. "Don't worry. We can sort this . . ."

I don't think God could have been any clearer. The curtain tiebacks were the clincher. A man who will fly to the rescue at a moment's notice to resolve your curtain-hanging problems is obviously a keeper.

But before I wind things up completely, I would like to take this opportunity to pay a brief tribute to Stefano, and all the other pseudo-husbands I have ever had.

People think single women don't have menfolk but that's not true. I have been privileged to call many men my stand-in-husband, from Tony the plumber to the gamekeeper who manfully hauls logs into my car whenever I feel weak and pathetic.

To my many, many stand-in-husbands I say this: you know who you are. And I thank you.

But I want to streamline things now. I want to rationalize all my "husbands" into one. It is time to choose the one man who out of everyone reaches more of the places than the others reach.

It is time to put my faith in just one Mr. Fix-It, a man who specializes not only in fixing my wardrobes, but in fixing me as well.

The Builder and I settle on a plan whereby we rent out my place in town, let his place go, and rent my country place together.

He promises not to eat fry-ups at The Chinese Caff. Well, no more than once a week. He will put the money he used to store in the refrigerator into a joint account.

"I can't think why we made such hard work of this," I say, as we sit across from each other at our country kitchen table eating roast chicken with the spaniel at our feet making yowling noises and occasionally leaping up to try to snatch meat off our plates.

"Down!" says The Builder, shielding his roast chicken like a child, then relenting and giving her a piece.

I feel blessed. He makes me feel like my failings don't matter.

౷

He arrives on the doorstep every night calling, "Daddy's home!" The spaniel throws herself at the door, hysterical with love for him.

I rush to open it, and he throws his arms around me and the dog leaps up and squeezes herself into the middle of our embrace as we are kissing. We all get mixed up into a bundle of hugging and wiggling dog. He always has a huge smile on his face, like I am the best thing he has ever seen. Even though I am wearing my old sweat pants, he says "Come here you!" and when he has stopped kissing me and asking me about my day he grabs the spaniel and the pair of them fall to the floor and throw themselves around playing spaniel games. It is a chaotic mess, but a wonderful one.

Whatever our difficulties, we have somehow, against all the odds, become a family.

Our friends are delighted. We are not the most conventional family, for sure. But I tell Sally that if she is desperate enough she can always take the spaniel to Baby Gap.

ᥫᩍ

Over dinner, I tell him my troubles and he responds to all of them by saying "Don't worry about it, we'll sort it."

It turns out that he can pretty much fix everything. He can "just stick the cable in the back" of almost anything.

When I start stressing about how I can't do relationships, he looks across the kitchen philosophically and says, "Have you thought about opening that chimney up? You could put a range in."

"You do know you're a total genius don't you?" I ask him as he clears the back garden one day of the overflowing recycling sacks I've been unable to get the council to collect because they've got minuscule bits of cellophane in them.

I'm keen for him to know how utterly he has nailed the technique of being my boyfriend.

It's perfectly simple, really. All I ever wanted was for a man to be handsome, resilient, dependable, patient, kind, and capable of fixing everything.

I'm worried about Stefano, though. He has worked out that something is definitely up. He was due to start painting some scuffed skirting.

"The thing is," I say, "I've got a load of stuff piled up and . . ."

"I come and start job? You need me soon?" asks Stefano, sounding desperate.

I don't know how to break it to him that with any luck, I'll never need him again.

Epilogue

Oops, I nearly forgot. My mother's recipe for best-ever spaghetti bolognese:

Crush and fry four cloves of garlic in olive oil and add four diced rashers of bacon. Add a chopped onion and two sticks of chopped celery and set aside. Now brown some lean ground beef. Stir in half a tube of tomato puree. Add a half cup of beef stock. Stir in the bacon bits, onion, and celery. Add some grated carrot, a can of tomatoes, and season. Transfer to a large casserole dish ready to put in the oven on a low heat for two hours. Lastly, and this is the really clever bit, stir in a tablespoon of sugar. You wouldn't think something as obvious as sweetness was the magic ingredient, but it really is.